THE CHURCH GUIDE TO COPYRIGHT LAW

Third Edition

*Complete coverage of all
important copyright issues
for churches and clergy*

Richard R. Hammar. J.D., LL.M., CPA

THE CHURCH GUIDE TO COPYRIGHT LAW
Third Edition

This publication is designed to provide accurate and authoritative information in regard to the subject matter covered. It is sold with the understanding that the publisher is not engaged in rendering legal, accounting, or other professional service. If legal advice or other expert assistance is required, the services of a competent professional person should be sought. "From a Declaration of Principles jointly adopted by a Committee of the American Bar Association and a Committee of Publishers and Associations."

ISBN 1-880562-49-9

Published by
Christian Ministry Resources
PO Box 1098
Matthews, NC 28106
704-821-3845
704-821-3872 (fax)
www.iclonline.com

Printed in the U.S.A.

Table of Contents

HOW TO USE THIS BOOK

For a quick summary of most issues, turn to the topical summaries (arranged in alphabetical order) in chapter 9. Each topical summary concludes with references to sections in the text where the particular issue is considered in greater detail. Or, simply use the index or table of contents to direct you to pertinent sections in the text. As time permits, it will be most helpful to read the book through cover to cover.

INTRODUCTION

This book was written to provide ministers, lay church leaders, musicians, choir directors, publishers, and attorneys with a nontechnical explanation of copyright law and its application to the kinds of common church practices described above. Mark Twain once remarked that "only one thing is impossible for God—to find any sense in any copyright law on this planet." This formidable task is the purpose of this book. It is an important task, since few areas of law affect church practices more pervasively than copyright law. Copying of choral music or church school literature, insertion of hymn or chorus lyrics in church bulletins, compilation of "chorus booklets," use of overhead projectors and transparencies in religious services and in teaching, making of audio and video tapes of church services, copying computer programs, web sites, the broadcast of religious services over radio or television, use of copyrighted translations of the Bible, performance of copyrighted music in the course of religious services, and the use of videotapes in church youth services—these are but some common church practices that are directly affected by copyright law. Further, copyright law involves the application of special rules that are not clearly understood by church staff members, church leaders, musicians, and even some publishers and attorneys. As a result, there is considerable confusion regarding the application of copyright law to churches. This confusion has contributed to widespread misinformation and noncompliance with the law. Such noncompliance, even if unintentional, can result in substantial damages.

Before proceeding with an explanation of copyright law, there are a few preliminary comments that must be considered.

First, churches cannot afford to persist in acts of copyright infringement because they know of "several other churches that are doing it." It is time for church leaders to apprise themselves of their obligations under copyright law, and to act responsibly. Many ministers and lay church leaders, when apprised of the relevant provisions of the copyright law, may disagree vigorously with some of those provisions. They will not be the first to do so. However, disagreement with a provision of the law is no justification for violating it. Expressing disagreement with the law through willful violation can have disastrous consequences, since damages for copyright infringement are substantially higher when the infringement is willful.

Second, this book was not written to justify copyright law or defend the position of publishers and authors. Rather, it was written to explain the pertinent issues of copyright law in an objective and intelligible manner.

Third, this book was not written to dictate any particular course of conduct. Again, the purpose is educating church leaders so they can make informed decisions concerning their response to the issues addressed.

Finally, this is the third edition of this text. The first edition was published in 1988, and the second edition was published in 1990. It is time to address the application of copyright law to church use of computers and electronic media including CDs and the internet. In addition, much of the text has been rewritten in light of changes in the law. The purpose of the text, however, remains the same as stated in the introduction to the first edition, "to provide churches, church leaders, clergy, choir directors, musicians, publishers, and attorneys with a nontechnical explanation of those provisions of the copyright law of greatest significance to churches."

Richard R. Hammar, J.D., LL.M., CPA

July 2001

1

Copyright Basics

1.1 What Copyright Is

historical background

What is copyright? How long have we had a "copyright law"? Where does copyright law come from? Answering these questions is an excellent way for us to begin our study of copyright law and the church. Article I, Section 8, of the United States Constitution gives Congress the authority "to promote the progress of . . . the useful arts, by securing for limited times to authors . . . the exclusive right to their respective writings." This clause not only helps to define the concept of copyright, but it also expresses the purpose underlying copyright law. According to this clause, a copyright is an exclusive right of an author in his or her writings that is secured for a limited time by federal law. Pursuant to this authority, Congress has enacted a number of copyright laws, the most recent being the Copyright Act of 1976 (which took effect on January 1, 1978).

purposes

Why did the drafters of the Constitution give Congress authority to bestow upon authors the "exclusive right to their respective writings"? Was it to make authors and publishers wealthy at the expense of the public? While this is a common conception, the Constitution itself clearly indicates otherwise. Copyright law exists to "promote the progress of the useful arts." The theory is simply this—unless authors are given exclusive rights in their works, they will have little if any incentive to produce artistic works, and the public itself will be the loser. The United States Supreme Court stated the rationale as follows:

> The economic philosophy behind the clause empowering Congress to grant . . . copyrights is the conviction that encouragement of individual effort by personal gain is the best way to advance public welfare through the talents of authors . . . in the useful arts. Sacrificial days devoted to such creative activities deserve rewards, commensurate with the services rendered. *Mazer v. Stein, 347 U.S. 201 (1954).*

effect of copyright infringement

Let's illustrate this concept further. Bob is the music pastor at First Church. He wants to save the church money, and so several times during the year he purchases a single octavo that he duplicates 30 times for each member of the church choir. The senior pastor is advised that this practice infringes upon the copyright of various music publishers and composers. He reacts with indignation: "The publishers are only concerned about money! I cannot believe that they would not let a church copy music for worship services. As a matter of principle, I refuse to acknowledge that I am doing anything wrong." The senior pastor tells Bob to continue making copies of music for the choir. The pastor's actions may save the church some money in the short run, but consider the effect they will have on the publisher and composer. If enough churches engage in similar practices to "save money," the publisher will soon discover that it is not profitable to publish sacred music. Two alternatives then exist. First, it can charge much higher prices for its music in an effort to remain profitable (this obviously will induce even more churches to duplicate the music). Second, it can refrain from publishing sacred music.

Similarly, composers receive less compensation for their labors when churches duplicate music for members of the church choir. If enough churches engage in this practice, then many composers will conclude that the remuneration from composing music is not worth the hours and days of labor. After all, not many persons can afford to work for free.

The result, from the perspective of either the publisher or the composer, may be a reduction in the quantity of available music. And, the ultimate loser in such a case will be the churches themselves, which are deprived of music that otherwise would have been available. One more point—it is entirely possible that the music pastor in the example above is mistaken in his assumption that he is "saving the church some money" by making unauthorized copies on church duplicating equipment. Many accountants would argue that the "true cost" of making the unauthorized copies (including electricity, supplies, depreciation, labor, overhead, etc.) is in fact higher than the cost of purchasing legal copies.

> *Example. A religious radio station that broadcasts copyrighted religious music without permission was found guilty of "willful infringement" and was assessed statutory damages of $52,500. The station manager admitted that he played copyrighted songs on the radio, and that he had no license or permission to do so. He defended his actions by noting that "the artists have publicly stated their intent to minister through their Christian music" and that "their intent to minister is further accomplished by radio stations broadcasting their music to a listening audience." The court rejected this reasoning and assessed statutory damages of $52,500 against the station for willful copyright infringement.[1]*

property right It is important to recognize that a copyright in a particular work is a property right created by law. Like any other property right, a copyright can be sold, donated, leased, inherited, and divided into parts. It is also protected by law against wrongful use. Section 201 of the Copyright Act makes it clear that "the ownership of a copyright may be transferred in whole or in part by any means of conveyance or by operation of law, and may be bequeathed by will . . . ." Like certain kinds of property, a copyright exists only for a limited term. The rules defining copyright duration are fully considered later in this book.

> *Example. Janet owns both a copyright in a book and an acre of land. The copyright and land represent property rights, created by law, that can be transferred, donated, pledged, leased, or distributed to heirs upon the owner's death. Such rights also are protected by law against most forms of conduct inconsistent with the owner's interests. As a result, the law protects against trespass to the land, or infringement upon the copyright.*

Recognizing that a copyright is a property right helps to explain why the music pastor in the example above cannot copy, without authorization, music for his choir. Such copying amounts to a wrongful infringement upon the property rights of the copyright holders. Consider the following analogy. Assume that you purchase a Maytag washing machine. You now own the property and have the legal right to use it, sell it, or otherwise dispose of it. However, you do *not* have the legal right to make duplicate Maytag washing machines. Only Maytag can do that. Similarly, if you purchase a copy of sheet music, you own that piece of paper. You can sell it, donate it, bequeath it to your heirs, or do anything else with it that is consistent with your ownership interest. But like the Maytag washing machine, you ordinarily do *not* have the legal right to make copies of it. The important principle is this: a copyright is legally distinct from a material work in which the copyright is embodied. The owner of the copyright in a sacred song has a legal right to the copyright that can be sold, donated, leased, bequeathed, or otherwise disposed of. Likewise, a purchaser of a piece of sheet music containing the copyrighted song has a legal right to that piece of paper, and can dispose of it in any manner he or she chooses. But, the copyright owner does not necessarily have any legal rights in the published copies of the music, and the purchaser of a copy of the music does not have any legal claim to the copyright in the work.

This distinction between copyright and "a material object in which the copyright is embodied" is clarified in section 202 of the Copyright Act (see Appendix). Understanding this important principle is essential to an appreciation of the law of copyright and the rights of the copyright owner and a purchaser of a copy of the copyrighted work.

exclusive rights

You will recall that the Constitution (quoted above) empowers Congress to "secure for limited times to authors . . . the exclusive right to their respective writings." Section 106 of the Copyright Act provides that a copyright owner has the exclusive right to do or authorize any of the following (subject to certain limitations discussed later):

(1) to reproduce the copyrighted work in copies or phonorecords;

(2) to prepare derivative works based upon the copyrighted work (such as a translation or revised edition of a literary work or an arrangement of a musical work);

(3) to distribute copies or phonorecords of the copyrighted work to the public by sale or other transfer of ownership, or by rental, lease, or lending;

(4) in the case of literary, musical, dramatic and choreographic works, pantomimes, and motion pictures and other audiovisual works, to perform the copyrighted work publicly; and

(5) in the case of literary, musical, dramatic and choreographic works, pantomimes, and pictorial, graphic, or sculptural works, including the individual images of a motion picture or other audiovisual work, to display the copyrighted work publicly.

All of these exclusive rights will be explained in further detail later in this book.

Copyright law, since 1978, has been exclusively federal. Prior to 1978, unpublished works were protected under state law. The Copyright Act of 1976, which took effect in 1978, makes both unpublished and published works subject to protection under federal law.

1.2 Subject Matter of Copyright

What can be copyrighted? Section 102 of the Copyright Act specifies that copyright protection "subsists . . . in original works of authorship fixed in any tangible medium of expression." It defines "works of authorship" to include

works of authorship

(1) literary works, such as books, periodicals, manuscripts, phonorecords, film, tapes, disks, or cards;

(2) musical works, including any accompanying words;

(3) dramatic works, including any accompanying music;

(4) pantomimes and choreographic works;

(5) pictorial, graphic, and sculptural works, which include both two and three-dimensional works of fine, graphic, and applied art, photographs, prints and art reproductions, maps, globes, charts, drawings, diagrams, and models;

(6) motion pictures and other audiovisual works;

(7) sound recordings; and

(8) architectural works.

compilations and collective works

Section 103 provides that "works of authorship" include "compilations," which are defined as any work "formed by the collection or assembling of preexisting materials . . . that are selected, coordinated, or arranged in such a way that the resulting work as a whole constitutes an original work of authorship." Compilations include "collective works," which are defined as any work "such as a periodical issue . . . or encyclopedia, in which a number of contributions, constituting separate and independent works in themselves, are assembled into a collective whole." To illustrate, most hymnals are collective works since they consist of a number of separate and independent works. The key point is this—if a hymnal is a collective work, then it is eligible for copyright protection. Note, however, that the copyright protection only applies to the material contributed by the compiler of the collective work, such as a foreword, any editing, and the arrangement or order of the separate works comprising the collective work.

hymnals

Section 103(b) emphasizes that "the copyright in such a work is independent of, and does not affect or enlarge the scope, duration, ownership, or subsistence of, any copyright protection in the preexisting material." This is a significant clarification. Assume that a publisher assembles a hymnal consisting of 200 copyrighted hymns and 100 "public domain" hymns having no copyright protection. The publisher arranges the hymns in a topical manner, and then obtains copyright protection in the hymnal as a whole in the year of first publication. What is the significance of copyrighting the hymnal? Does it extend the copyright term of any of the copyrighted hymns? Does it resurrect copyright protection in the public domain hymns? The answer to both questions, according to section 103(b), is an unqualified no. What the copyright does is to protect against anyone else making a compilation of the same hymns in exactly or substantially the same order, and to protect any original materials contributed by the compiler. Public domain hymns remain in the public domain, and the term of copyrighted hymns is not affected. Of course, the compiler cannot legally include any copyrighted hymn in the hymnal compilation without the express authorization of the copyright owner. Including copyrighted hymns without authorization would violate the copyright owners' exclusive right of reproduction.

Speaking of hymn compilations, is it necessary for the hymnal to list a copyright notice for each copyrighted hymn in the compilation? Often, you will see such notices accompanying each copyrighted hymn in a hymnal. And, while many copyright owners condition their consent to the inclusion of their work in a compilation upon the printing of a copyright notice, the Copyright Act indicates that this is not technically required. Prior to March 1, 1989, section 404 of the Copyright Act specified that

> a separate contribution to a collective work may bear its own notice of copyright . . . .
> However, a single notice applicable to the collective work as a whole is sufficient to
> satisfy the requirements [of copyright notice] with respect to the separate contributions
> it contains . . . regardless of the ownership of copyright in the contributions and
> whether or not they have been previously published.

Similarly, section 401(b)(2) provides that "in the case of compilations . . . incorporating previously published material, the year date of first publication of the compilation . . . is sufficient."

These provisions continue to govern works published prior to March 1, 1989.

Berne Convention

Works published on or after March 1, 1989, are governed by the copyright law as amended by the Berne Convention. Since copyright notice is no longer required for such works, there technically is no need for a hymnal to contain any copyright notice to protect either itself or any individual hymn that it reproduces (and that was first published on or after March 1, 1989). Of course, few if any hymnals will contain only hymns published on or after March 1, 1989. Hymnals published on or after March 1, 1989, containing hymns first published prior to March 1, 1989, should print an appropriate copyright notice (defined later) either with respect to each individual hymn (published prior to March 1, 1989) or the hymnal as a whole. Copyright Office Circular 3 states,

> [A] separate contribution to a collective work may bear its own notice of copyright, and in some cases, it may be advantageous to utilize the separate notice. As a practical matter, a separate notice will inform the public of the identity of the owner of the contribution. For works first published before March 1, 1989, there may be additional reasons to use a separate notice. If the owner of the collective work is not the same as the owner of an individual contribution that does not bear its own notice, the contribution is considered to bear an erroneous notice.

While copyright notices are no longer required to obtain copyright protection in works published on or after March 1, 1989, the Copyright Office notes that such notices are "often beneficial." One of the benefits of such notices is that infringers will not be able to claim that they "innocently infringed" a copyrighted work.

In summary, while in some cases a copyright notice may no longer be technically required, it nevertheless should always be used. These considerations are discussed more fully in section 1.3.

works not eligible for copyright protection

Some works generally are not eligible for copyright protection. These include

(1) works that have not been fixed in a tangible form of expression, such as musical compositions that have not yet been reduced to writing;

(2) titles, names, short phrases, and slogans; familiar symbols and designs; ornamentation, lettering, and coloring; lists of ingredients or contents;

(3) ideas, procedures, methods, systems, processes, concepts, principles, discoveries, or devices;

(4) works consisting entirely of information that is common property and containing no original authorship, such as standard calendars, rulers, and lists or tables taken from public documents or other common sources.

> *Example.* Pastor Smith prepares his sermons in writing before delivering them to his congregation. The written sermons prepared by Pastor Smith are eligible for copyright protection.

> *Example.* Anne composes the music and lyrics to a sacred song. According to section 102 of the Copyright Act, both the music and the lyrics are eligible for copyright protection. If Anne obtains copyright protection in both the music and lyrics, then it constitutes copyright infringement for anyone else to reproduce the music and lyrics as an integrated whole, or to reproduce either the music or lyrics individually. Therefore, it is no defense to infringement to argue that you have copied "only the lyrics" of a copyrighted song.

> ***Example.*** *Howard has written a financial guide for churches entitled "The Law and the Profits." Thinking this title to be creative, he seeks to copyright it. Copyright protection is not available for titles. The book of course is eligible for copyright protection.*

> ***Example.*** *Handel is said to have composed much of Messiah in his head before committing it to writing. A musical composition that exists only "in one's head" is not eligible for copyright protection, even if the composer hums or whistles the music or plays it on a piano. One who overhears such a composition is legally free to reduce it to writing and publish it without violating any copyright interest of the original composer.*

Titles, names, and marks may be entitled to protection under federal trademark law, if certain conditions are satisfied. For example, a religious organization that produces a daily radio program cannot "copyright" its program name. But the name may be eligible for trademark or tradename protection if it is used to identify particular goods or services and the name is not confusingly similar to the preexisting name of another organization that offers similar goods or services. Trademark and tradename protection may be pursued by filing an application with the Commissioner of Patents and Trademarks in Washington, DC.

> ***Resource.*** *For additional information on the protection of names, see section 6-05 in Richard Hammar's book,* Pastor, Church & Law *(3rd ed. 2000). The protection of names under state nonprofit corporation law, tradenames, and the law of "unfair competition" are all addressed.*

1.3 Securing Copyright Protection

As we have seen, copyright is a valuable property right. How, then, does one acquire copyright protection in a work? Answering this important question not only will help church staff members recognize those persons or organizations that have acquired copyright protection in a given work, but also will help pastors, musicians, and other writers and composers of religious materials understand how they can protect their creative works.

Under the current copyright law, copyright is secured automatically in any "original work of authorship" the moment it is "fixed in a tangible medium of expression." No registration with the Copyright Office is required. This "initial" copyright protection exists up until the time the work is "published," at which time other rules come into play that are discussed later.

pre-publication protection

Initial, *pre-publication* copyright protection is available to any "work of authorship" that is original and fixed in a tangible medium of expression. The term "work of authorship" was defined in section 1.2. "Originality" is not defined by the Copyright Act, but has been interpreted often enough by the courts that its meaning is clear. Basically, a work is original if an author created it by his or her own skill, labor, and judgment, and not by directly copying or evasively imitating the work of another.

originality

One court has stated that "originality means that the work owes its creation to the author and thus in turn means that the work must not consist of actual copying."[2] The key point is this—originality means independent creation, not novelty. If one independently creates a poem or work of literature, not knowing that an identical work had previously been created by another writer, the new work is certainly not novel, but it is original in the sense that it was the independent creation of the author. A federal court expressed this concept as follows: "[I]f by some magic a man who had never known it were to compose anew Keats' 'Ode On a Grecian Urn,' he would be an author, and, if he copyrighted it, others might not copy that poem, though they might of course copy Keats's."[3] Obviously, such an author would have a difficult time convincing a jury that he or she independently created the work.

The courts have held that the test of originality is much stricter when a particular work is based on a pre-existing work than if it is not. This certainly makes sense. If one writes a song or a poem that is unlike anything ever written before, it will almost automatically satisfy the test of originality. However, if the song or poem is based on or is substantially similar to a pre-existing work, then the requirement of originality will be much more difficult to establish. This is so whether or not the pre-existing work is copyrighted (of course, if the pre-existing work is copyrighted, then the new work not only risks failing the test of originality, but also risks liability for copyright infringement). As a result, the courts have required that new works based on, or similar to, pre-existing works must contain some "substantial, not merely trivial, originality."[4]

To illustrate, a composer who merely makes slight rhythmic changes in a public domain song, or who adds an alto part to a public domain song that did not have one, has not satisfied the requirement of originality and accordingly cannot obtain copyright protection for the variation.[5] However, the Copyright Office has stated that "a revision consisting of a change in fingering of two measures, added dynamics in four measures, and three measures of additional music could, in the aggregate" be copyrighted. In any of these cases it must be emphasized that the pre-existing work no longer has copyright protection. If it did, then the issue would not be originality but rather copyright infringement since the right to make derivative works is one of the exclusive rights of the copyright owner. Note also that the requirement of originality is relevant in deciding whether a "derivative work" prepared by a copyright owner (or one having permission from the copyright owner) is eligible for copyright protection separate from the pre-existing copyrighted work upon which it is based.

> ***Example.*** *Joan composes a musical arrangement to a hymn that contains substantial variations in the musical score (the lyrics are not changed). If the underlying hymn is in the public domain (i.e., no longer subject to copyright protection), then Joan's arrangement probably has met the test of originality, and is eligible for copyright protection. However, if the underlying work is still subject to copyright protection, then Joan cannot make a derivative work based on that pre-existing work (such as a musical arrangement) without the consent of the copyright owner. As a result, her new arrangement not only is not copyrightable, but it is an infringement on the exclusive rights of the copyright owner.*

fixation

The next requirement for initial, pre-publication copyright protection is that the work be "fixed in any tangible medium of expression, now known or later developed, from which they can be perceived, reproduced, or otherwise communicated . . . .[6] This requirement is intended to restrict copyright protection to only those works that are reduced to some tangible form. A song or book conceived in one's mind is not protected until it is reduced to a tangible form.

In summary, initial copyright protection automatically arises in the author of a "work of authorship" that satisfies the requirements of originality and tangible form. The duration of this protection is explained in Chapter 3.

post-publication protection

Once an author *publishes* a work, he or she may have to comply with certain other requirements to perpetuate the initial copyright protection.

A. Works First Published Before March 1, 1989

For works published prior to March 1, 1989, section 401(a) of the Copyright Act specified the following:

> Whenever a work . . . is published in the United States or elsewhere by authority of the copyright owner, a notice of copyright as provided by this section shall be placed on all publicly distributed copies from which the work can be visually perceived, either directly or with the aid of a machine or device.

notice requirement This requirement is known as the "notice" requirement, and compliance with it was essential to the continuation of copyright protection following the publication of a work first published prior to March 1, 1989. No registration was necessary to perfect copyright protection in a work first published before March 1, 1989.

> ***Key point.*** *The Uruguay Round Agreements Act of 1994 modified the effect of publication without notice for certain foreign works. Under this Act, copyright is automatically restored, effective January 1, 1996, for certain foreign works placed into the public domain because of lack of proper notice or noncompliance with other legal requirements. Although restoration is automatic, if the copyright owner wishes to enforce rights against those who, relying on the public domain status of a work, were already using the work before the Act was enacted, he or she must either file with the Copyright Office a Notice of Intent to Enforce the restored copyright or serve such a notice on those who are relying on the public domain status of the work.*

B. Works First Published on or after March 1, 1989

Berne Convention On March 1, 1989, the United States became a party to the "Berne Convention"—an international copyright convention established in 1888 and endorsed by most nations. Participation by the United States in this significant convention has increased the international protections available to American authors.

To become a party to the convention, Congress had to make various changes in our copyright law (unwillingness to make the required changes was one of the major reasons that it took the United States a century to join the convention). Perhaps the most important change related to copyright notice. Mandatory notice of copyright has been abolished for works published for the first time on or after March 1, 1989. Failure to place a copyright notice on copies of works that are publicly distributed can no longer result in the loss of copyright. Obviously, this was a significant change in our copyright law, since prior to March 1, 1989 the failure to affix a valid copyright notice to a publicly distributed work could have resulted in loss of copyright protection. While copyright notices are not required to obtain copyright protection in works first published on or after March 1, 1989, the Copyright Office maintains that copyright notices are "often beneficial." One of the benefits of such notices is that infringers will not be able to claim that they "innocently infringed" a work. In summary, while in some cases a copyright notice no longer may be technically required, it should still be used.

The Berne Convention is not retroactive. As a result, the notice requirements for works first published prior to March 1, 1989 remain unchanged. To illustrate, works first published between January 1, 1978 and February 28, 1989 without a valid copyright notice (as defined below) generally lost their copyright protection unless they were registered with the Copyright Office within five years of first publication (and a valid notice added to all copies distributed after discovery of the omission). Works first published before January 1, 1978 without a valid copyright notice generally lost all copyright protection immediately, with some exceptions.

The elimination of the notice requirement has caused much confusion among church staff regarding the copyright status of literary or musical works. For example, suppose that a church would like to make copies of a piece of sheet music. The fact that the music does not bear a copyright notice does not mean that the work is not copyrighted. Clearly, with the elimination of the notice requirement in 1989, it has become more difficult for church staff to determine whether or not they are free to make copies of some works. Church employees cannot safely assume that a work is "in the public domain" merely because it does not contain a valid copyright notice.

copyright notices In summary, while copyright notices are no longer technically required for most works first published on or after March 1, 1989, they should still be used. What, then, is a valid copyright notice? And, how does the copyright law define "publication"? Let us now turn our attention to these important questions.

The contents and placement of a valid copyright notice are described in section 401(b) and (c) of the Copyright Act. A valid notice consists of three elements: (1) the "C in a circle" symbol (©), the word "Copyright," or the abbreviation "Copr."; and (2) the year of first publication of the work (in the case of compilations and derivative works incorporating previously published material, the year date of first publication of the compilation or derivative work is sufficient); and (3) the name of the owner of copyright in the work, or an abbreviation by which the name can be recognized, or a generally known alternative designation of the owner.

> **Example.** *Randy Roe writes and publishes a book in 2001. A valid copyright notice would be "Copyright 2001 Randy Roe."*

phonorecords

A special notice provision applies to "phonorecords." The copyright law defines "phonorecords" as "material objects in which sounds, other than those accompanying motion pictures or other audiovisual work, are fixed by any method . . . and from which the sounds can be perceived, reproduced, or otherwise communicated, either directly or with the aid of a machine or device." The term includes records, audio tapes, cassettes, and CDs. Phonorecords are not copyrightable, since they are merely a physical object embodying a sound recording of a literary or musical work, but that does not mean that the recording is unprotected. Section 101 of the Copyright Act excludes phonorecords from the definition of "copies." As a result, there is no requirement under section 401 that a copyright notice be affixed in order to protect the underlying literary or musical work embodied in a phonorecord, since the section 401 notice requirement extends only to "publicly distributed copies" from which the underlying work can be "visually perceived." However, the copyright law does specify that "sound recordings" are eligible for copyright protection (see section 1.2). Sound recordings are defined by the Copyright Office as "a series of sounds . . . produced on a final master recording that is later reproduced in published copies." This original master recording must be distinguished from phonorecords (which represent publicly distributed copies embodying the sound recording). Since the sound recording embodied in a phonorecord is copyrightable, as is the underlying musical or literary work upon which it is based, Congress was concerned that use of the section 401 notice requirement for both phonorecords of sound recordings and the underlying literary or musical works themselves would result in public confusion. As a result, the copyright law prescribes a different notice for phonorecords of sound recordings. Section 402 specifies that the notice appearing on phonorecords of sound recordings shall consist of (1) a "P in a circle" symbol (℗); and (2) the year of first publication of the underlying sound recording; and (3) the name of the owner of the copyright in the sound recording. Section 402 clarifies that "if the producer of the sound recording is named on the phonorecord labels or containers, and if no other name appears in conjunction with the notice, the producer's name shall be considered a part of the notice." A phonorecord notice clearly distinguishes a claim of copyright in the sound recording from copyright in the underlying literary or musical work.

> **Example.** *Pastor White delivers a sermon. If the church records the sermon on a phonorecord (tape or record), the work is thereby reduced to a tangible form and receives initial or pre-publication copyright protection if it is original. The phonorecords containing the sermon need not bear any copyright notice to preserve copyright in the sermon, since phonorecords are not "copies" and therefore the section 401 notice requirements (discussed above) do not apply. However, if copyright in the sound recording of the sermon is to be preserved, then all tapes publicly distributed for the first time before March 1, 1989, should bear the copyright notice applicable to phonorecords of sound recordings, discussed above. This notice is not required, but is strongly recommended, for tapes first published on or after March 1, 1989.*

placement of copyright notices

Section 401(c) provides that the notice shall be affixed to copies of the work "in such manner and location as to give reasonable notice of the claim of copyright." To illustrate, Copyright Office regulations specify that a copyright notice for a work published in book form may be affixed on the title page, the page immediately following the title page, either side of the front or back cover, the first page of the main body of the work, the last page of the main body of the work, or any page between the front page and first page of the main body of the work if there are no more than ten pages between the front page and the first page of the main body of the work and the notice is prominently displayed and set apart. Similar rules apply to musical works. Other rules apply to single-leaf works, audiovisual works, machine-readable works, and pictorial works. The Copyright Office regulations themselves provide that they merely illustrate acceptable notice placements. They are not exhaustive, and acceptable alternatives probably exist. Of course, it is prudent to follow the Copyright Office guidelines since compliance with them is conclusive evidence that you have affixed your copyright notice in an appropriate position.

> ***Example.*** *James Smith writes a book in 2001 that is published in 2002. The published book contains the following notice on the title page: "Copyright 2002 James Smith." This is a valid copyright notice.*

> ***Example.*** *A copyright notice reads "Copyright Two Thousand and Two." Spelling out the year of publication rather than using numerals is acceptable.*

> ***Example.*** *A copyright notice reads "Copyright MMII by James Smith." Stating the year of first publication in Roman numerals has been upheld by the courts, and is a common practice of some publishers. The idea is this—since most readers cannot read Roman numerals, the copyright term of a particular work can be "extended" by reciting the date in Roman numerals. Most persons will be unaware of the actual age (or remaining copyright term) of the work, and will assume that the copyright term has not expired.*

> ***Example.*** *James Smith's name appears as the author of a book on the title page, and several inches below, at the bottom of the page, is the following notice: "Copyright 2001." If Smith is in fact the copyright owner, is this notice sufficient? Section 406(c) of the Copyright Act provides that "where copies . . . distributed by authority of the copyright owner contain no name or no date that could reasonably be considered a part of the notice, the work is considered to have been published without any notice . . . ." As a result, it is imperative that each of the three elements of the copyright notice form a recognizable entity.*

defective or omitted notices

What is the effect of a work that is published with a defective or omitted notice? Works first published on or after March 1, 1989, require no copyright notice, so an omitted or defective notice has no legal effect. However, section 401(d) of the Copyright Act specifies that if a work first published on or after March 1, 1989 contains a valid copyright notice, "then no weight shall be given" to an "innocent infringement" defense. That is, infringers cannot argue that they "innocently" infringed on another's work if that work contained a valid copyright notice. If the notice does not satisfy the requirements of sections 401(b) and 401(c), the implication is that an infringer can assert an innocent infringement defense. The same concept applies to phonorecords under section 402(d).

What about works first published prior to March 1, 1989? Section 405(a) of the Copyright Act specifies: "With respect to copies and phonorecords publicly distributed by authority of the copyright owner before [March 1, 1989], the omission of the copyright notice described in sections 401 through 403 from copies or phonorecords publicly distributed by authority of the copyright owner does not invalidate the copyright in a work if"

> (1) the notice has been omitted from no more than a relatively small number of copies . . . distributed to the public; or

(2) registration for the work has been made before or is made within five years after the publication without notice, and a reasonable effort is made to add notice to all copies . . . that are distributed to the public in the United States after the omission has been discovered; or

(3) the notice has been omitted in violation of an express requirement in writing that, as a condition of the copyright owner's authorization of the public distribution of copies . . . they bear the prescribed notice.

Also, note that if someone distributes copies of a copyrighted work without authorization from the copyright owner, and no copyright notice appears on such copies, the copyright in the work is not affected since the copies were made and distributed without authorization.

"innocent infringement"

Can one be guilty of copyright infringement for innocently infringing on a copyrighted work from which the copyright notice had been omitted? For works first published on or after March 1, 1989, the answer is yes—since copyright notices are no longer required to ensure copyright protection. However, the Copyright Act indicates that an infringer can assert the defense of "innocent infringement" to avoid or reduce damages if the infringed work either had no copyright notice or had a defective notice (not meeting the requirements of sections 401(b) and 401(c)). What if the work was first published prior to March 1, 1989? Assuming that the omission of the copyright notice did not invalidate the copyright (i.e., one of the three exceptions mentioned above applies), the innocent infringer incurs no liability for any infringing acts "committed before receiving actual notice that registration for the work has been made . . . if such person proves that he or she was misled by the omission of notice."[7] Omission of copyright notice ordinarily will result in loss of copyright protection (in works first published before March 1, 1989) if none of the three exceptions described above applies.

errors in copyright notices

A related question is the effect of an error in the copyright notice. For example, what if a notice has an error in the name of the copyright owner, or in the date of first publication, or either the name or date is omitted? The copyright law specifies that if the name listed in a copyright notice is not the name of the copyright owner, the copyright in the work is not affected. In some cases, innocent infringers are protected if they were misled by the recital of the wrong person in the copyright notice.[8] If a copyright notice recites a year of first publication that is more than one year later than the year in which publication in fact first occurred, the work is considered to have been published without any notice. If the notice recites a year of first publication that is earlier than the actual year of first publication, the copyright in the work is not affected, but any period of time computed from the year of publication for purposes of any provision in the copyright law is computed from the erroneous date.[9] Finally, if a copyright notice contains either no name or no date, the work is considered to have been published without any notice.[10]

"publication"

Next, we must define the term *publication* since this term dictates when the copyright notice should be affixed to copies of the work, and it is relevant for other reasons that will be addressed later. Section 101 of the Copyright Act defines publication as

> the distribution of copies or phonorecords of a work to the public by sale or other transfer of ownership, or by rental, lease, or lending. The offering to distribute copies or phonorecords to a group of persons for purposes of further distribution, public performance, or public display, constitutes publication. A public performance or display of a work does not of itself constitute publication.

The courts have held that publication may occur upon public distribution of a single copy of a work,[11] but it does not occur upon the mere printing of a work prior to public distribution[12] or the delivery of a manuscript to a publisher.[13]

Example. Mark composed a song in 1988, reduced it to writing, but never publicly distributed copies (i.e., there has been no publication). Mark performs the song in church services on several occasions. Since section 101 of the Copyright Act defines "publication" to exclude public performances, Mark's public performances do not constitute a publication. This result ordinarily will not be affected by the recording of the service in which the performance occurred, since the resulting phonorecord (tape or record) will not constitute a copy of the work.

Example. Same facts as the preceding example, except that Mark makes a slide of his song and displays it publicly during a church service to assist the congregation in singing it. This is a public display of the work, and a public display does not constitute a publication.

Example. Assume that Mark, instead of performing or displaying the song, copies it on pieces of paper that are inserted in church bulletins for use during a morning worship service. The inserts contain no copyright notice. This practice unquestionably constitutes a publication that is not in compliance with the section 401 notice requirements, and therefore Mark's copyright in the work is nullified unless he can qualify for one of the three exceptions described in section 405(a) of the Copyright Act (mentioned above).

Example. Same facts as the previous example except that Mark composed the song in 2001. His copyright in the song is not affected, since no notice is required for works published on or after March 1, 1989.

Example. First Church obtains permission from a copyright owner to make a transparency of a published song (first published before March 1, 1989) for use during morning worship services. The transparency need not contain a section 401 copyright notice since the public display of the copy through overhead projection does not constitute public distribution of the copy (the notice must appear only on publicly distributed copies).[14] Publishers sometimes condition the fabrication of transparencies and other copies upon the insertion of a valid copyright notice in an appropriate location, even though this is not legally necessary. The same result would apply to works first published on or after March 1, 1989.

Example. Jean writes an article and submits her manuscript to a publisher for review. The submission of a manuscript to a publisher does not amount to a publication of the work. It is appropriate and desirable for an author to note on the title page of a manuscript submitted to a publisher that the manuscript is unpublished, that the author claims copyright protection in the manuscript, and that it is submitted with the understanding and upon the express condition that it not be circulated or in any manner distributed publicly by the publisher without the author's written authorization. This puts the publisher (and any potential infringers) "on notice" of the owner's copyright, and probably eliminates the availability of any "innocent infringement" defense. In the event the publisher elects to publish the work, then it will enter into a contractual agreement with the author by which the author either retains the copyright and grants the publisher a license to distribute the published work publicly, or transfers the copyright in the work to the publisher in exchange for royalty payments.

1.4 Copyright Ownership

Who owns the copyright in a work, and what difference does it make? This section will address both of these questions. Section 201(a) of the Copyright Act states simply that "[c]opyright in a work . . . vests initially in the author or authors of the work." There is very little difficulty in understanding this provision. The copyright law goes on to state that "the authors of a joint work are co-owners of copyright in the work." Again, this is straightforward and needs no explanation. There are a few aspects of copyright ownership that are more difficult to understand, including the following:

- works made for hire

- contributions to collective works

- assignments

- the so-called "divisibility" of copyright ownership

- the distinction between copyright ownership and the material object in which the copyrighted work is embodied

The last of these issues was considered previously (section 1.4). Works made for hire and contributions to collective works will be considered in turn. The related topics of divisibility and assignment or transfer of copyright are considered separately in another chapter.

A. Works Made for Hire

In general

works made for hire

It is common for church employees to compose music or write books or articles in their church office during office hours. What often is not understood is that such persons do not necessarily own the copyright in the works they create. While the one who creates a work generally is its author and the initial owner of the copyright in the work, section 201(b) of the Copyright Act specifies that "[i]n the case of a work made for hire, the employer or other person for whom the work was prepared is considered the author . . . and, unless the parties have expressly agreed otherwise in a written instrument signed by them, owns all of the rights comprised in the copyright."

The copyright law defines "work made for hire" as "a work prepared by an employee within the scope of his or her employment." There are two requirements that must be met: (1) the person creating the work is an employee, and (2) the employee created the work within the scope of his or her employment. Whether or not one is an employee will depend on the same factors used in determining whether one is an employee or self-employed for federal income tax reporting purposes.[15] However, the courts have been very liberal in finding employee status in this context, so it is possible that a court would conclude that a work is a work made for hire even though the author reports his or her federal income taxes as a self-employed person.

scope of employment

The second requirement is that the work must have been created within the scope of employment. This requirement generally means that the work was created during regular working hours, on the employer's premises, using the employer's staff and equipment. This is often a difficult standard to apply. As a result, it is desirable for church employees to discuss this issue with the church leadership to avoid any potential misunderstandings. Section 201(a), quoted above, allows an employer and employee to agree in writing that copyright ownership in works created by the employee within the scope of employment belongs to the employee. This should be a matter for consideration by any church having a minister or other staff member who creates literary or musical works during office hours, on church premises, using church staff and church equipment (e.g., computers, printers, paper, library, secretaries, dictation equipment).

> *Example. Pastor B is senior minister of his church. He is in the process of writing a devotional book. Most of the writing is done during regular church office hours, in his office in the church, using church equipment and a church secretary. Pastor B's contract of employment does not address the issue of copyright ownership in the book, and no written agreement has ever been executed by the church that addresses the matter. Under these facts, it is likely that the book is a "work made for hire." The result is that the church is the "author" of the book, it is the copyright owner, and it has the sole legal right to assign or transfer the copyright in the book.*

> *Example. Pastor T is minister of music at her church. She has composed several songs and choruses, all of which were written during regular office hours at the church, using church equipment (piano, paper, etc.). The church has never addressed the issue of copyright ownership in a signed writing. It is likely that the songs and choruses are "works made for hire." The result is that the church is the "author" of these materials, it is the copyright owner, and it has the sole legal right to assign or transfer the copyright in these works.*

> *Example. Same facts as the preceding example, except that Pastor T composes the music in the evening and on weekends in her home. While she is an employee, she did not compose the music "within the scope of her employment," and therefore the music cannot be characterized as "works made for hire." The legal effect of this conclusion is that Pastor T owns the copyright in the music, and is free to sell or transfer such works in any manner she chooses without church approval.*

> *Example. Same facts as the previous example, except that Pastor T composes many of her works both at home and at the church office. Whether or not a particular work is a work made for hire is a difficult question under these circumstances. The answer will depend upon the following factors: (1) the portion of the work that is composed at the church office, compared to the portion composed at home; (2) the portion of the work created with church equipment, compared to the portion created with Pastor T's personal equipment; (3) the portion of the work created during regular office hours, compared to the portion created after hours; and (4) the adequacy of Pastor T's personal records to document each of these factors. Unfortunately, a staff member's records may be inadequate. In such a case, work made for hire status will depend upon the staff member's own testimony, and the testimony of other witnesses (such as other staff members).*

> *Example. A federal court in New Jersey ruled that an innovative educational program created by a police officer was not a work made for hire because it had not been created in the course of his employment.[16] When the city with whom the officer was employed learned that he was marketing the program to other cities, it sued him. The city claimed that the program was a work made for hire, and as such the city owned the copyright in the program. The court disagreed. It conceded that the officer was an employee of the city, but concluded that he had not prepared the educational program "within the scope of his employment." The court defined "scope of employment" to include all three of the following elements: (1) the employee's work is the kind he was employed to perform; (2) it occurs substantially within authorized work hours; and (3) it is prompted, at least in part, by a desire to serve the employer.*

The court concluded that the officer's program failed the first test, for the following reasons: (a) The courts rely heavily on an employee's job description in deciding whether a particular project is the "kind of work" the employee was hired to perform. In this case, the officer's job description said nothing about creating educational programs. (b) The court also noted that the degree of control an employer exercises over an employee's project is relevant in determining whether or not the project is the "kind of work" the employee was hired to perform. In this case, the city exercised no control whatever over the officer's creation of the program. Indeed, the city was not even aware he was working on the project. (c) Courts also consider whether the employee relied on knowledge gained within the scope of his or her employment in deciding whether or not a project was the "kind of work" the employee was hired to perform. The officer in this case gained nothing from his present employment that was useful to him in creating his program. (d) The court quoted from a century-old case: "We do not think . . . that if the defendant in spare moments wrote a book or taught a night school or sang in a church the fruits of his extra toil on his own behalf should be swept into the tills of the bank."[17] The court also concluded that the officer's program failed the second test, since there was no evidence that he produced any portion of the program during authorized work hours. The officer testified that he created the program at home during off-duty hours, and that he did not use any city facilities or resources. Finally, the court concluded that the officer's program failed the third test, since the officer was not motivated by a desire to serve his employer when he created the program. Rather, the officer was motivated by a desire to make the program available to many cities, including his own.

Example. A federal appeals court addressed the application of the work made for hire doctrine to works created by a religious leader prior to the January 1, 1978 effective date of the Copyright Act of 1976.[18] Under the Copyright Act of 1909, which governed copyright law until 1978, a work made for hire was described as follows: "[W]hen one person engages another, whether as employee or as an independent contractor, to produce a work of an artistic nature, . . . in the absence of an express contractual reservation of the copyright in the artist, the presumption arises that the mutual intent of the parties is that the title to the copyright shall be in the person at whose instance and expense the work is done." In short, for an employer to own the copyright in a work made for hire, the work must have been created by the employee at the employer's "instance and expense." The court then summarized the "instance and expense" test by noting that "the motivating factor in producing the work was the employer who induced the creation." The court concluded that the religious order had introduced no evidence "that would demonstrate that it was at [its] 'instance' that [its leader] decided to write, teach, and lecture. Works motivated by [his] own desire for self-expression or religious instruction of the public are not works for hire. Furthermore . . . throughout much of the life of the 1909 Act, courts applied the work for hire doctrine only to traditional, hierarchical relationships in which the employee created the work as part of 'the regular course of business' of the employer. In the last decade that the Act was effective, courts expanded the concept to include less traditional relationships, as long as the hiring party had 'the right to control or supervise the artist's work.' We have described the rationale for the doctrine as a presumption that 'the parties expected the employer to own the copyright and that the artist set his price accordingly.'"

The church's tax-exempt status

If a church transfers the copyright in a work made for hire to an employee, this may be viewed by the IRS as "private inurement" of the church's resources to an individual. If so, this could jeopardize the church's tax-exempt status. Neither the IRS nor any court has addressed the tax consequences of such an arrangement to a church. Here are some options:

1. *The church transfers copyright ownership to the staff member.* This may constitute private inurement. The IRS construes this requirement as follows:

> An organization's trustees, officers, members, founders, or contributors may not, by reason of their position, acquire any of its funds. They may, of course, receive reasonable compensation for goods or services or other expenditures in furtherance of exempt purposes. If funds are diverted from exempt purposes to private purposes, however, exemption is in jeopardy. The Code specifically forbids the inurement of earnings to the benefit of private shareholders or individuals. . . . The prohibition of inurement, in its simplest terms, means that a private shareholder or individual cannot pocket the organization's funds except as reasonable payment for goods or services.

When a church employee writes a book during office hours at the church, using church equipment, supplies, and personnel, the copyright in the work belongs to the church. If the church chooses to renounce its legal rights in the book, and transfers the copyright back to the employee, then it is relinquishing a potentially valuable asset that may produce royalty income for several years. Few if any churches would attempt to "value" the copyright and report it as additional taxable compensation to the employee, and as a result it is hard to avoid the conclusion that such arrangements result in inurement of the church's assets to a private individual. The legal effect is to jeopardize the church's tax-exempt status. This risk must not be overstated, since only a few churches have had their exempt status revoked by the IRS in the last fifty years, and none because of a transfer of copyright to an employee who created a work made for hire. But the consequences would be so undesirable that the risk should be taken seriously.

2. *The church retains the copyright.* The risk of inurement can be minimized if not avoided if the church retains the copyright in works made for hire, and pays a "bonus" or some other form of compensation to the author.

> **Example.** *Pastor G is senior pastor of his church. He writes a devotional book in his office at the church during office hours and using church equipment. He reads an article about works made for hire, and is concerned about the legal implications. He discusses the matter with the church board. In order to eliminate any risk to the church's tax-exempt status, the church board decides that the church will retain the copyright in Pastor G's book. The publisher is contacted, and agrees to list the church as the copyright owner on the title page and to pay royalties from sales of the book directly to the church. The church board agrees to pay Pastor G a "bonus" in consideration of his additional services in writing the book. The bonus is added to Pastor G's W-2 at the end of the year. This arrangement will not jeopardize the church's tax-exempt status.*

3. *The church urges employees to do "outside work" at home.* Do you have a writer or composer on staff at your church? If so, it is possible that this person is doing some writing or composing on church premises, using church equipment, during office hours. One way to avoid the problems associated with work made for hire status is to encourage staff members to do all their writing and composing at home. Tell staff members that (1) if they do any writing or composing at church during office hours, their works may be works made for hire; (2) the church owns the copyright in such works; and (3) the church can transfer copyright to the

writer or composer, but this may constitute "inurement" of the church's assets to a private individual, jeopardizing the church's tax-exempt status. By urging staff members to do all their personal writing and composing at home, the church also will avoid the difficult question of whether works that are written partly at home and partly at the office are works made for hire.

4. *Sermons*. Are a minister's sermons "works made for hire" that are owned by the employing church? To the extent that sermons are written in a church office, during regular church hours, using church secretaries and equipment, it is possible that sermons would be considered works made for hire since they are created by an employee within the scope of employment. However, this issue has never been addressed directly by any court, so it is difficult to predict how a court would rule.

lecture notes A professor's lecture notes provide a comparable example. College professors often prepare their lecture notes in their office on campus, using campus equipment. Are these notes, and the lectures themselves, works made for hire? If so, the college owns the copyright in the notes and lectures, unless it has transferred the copyright back to the professor in a signed writing. Prior to the enactment of the Copyright Act of 1976, it was generally assumed that professors' lectures were an exception to the work for hire doctrine.[19] Perhaps the best example of this view is a decision by a California appeals court in 1969.[20] The court addressed directly the question of whether a professor (Admiral Rickover) or his employing university owned the copyright in his lectures. In ruling that Admiral Rickover owned the copyright, the court observed the following:

> Indeed the undesirable consequences which would follow from a holding that a university owns the copyright to the lectures of its professors are such as to compel a holding that it does not. Professors are a peripatetic lot, moving from campus to campus. The courses they teach begin to take shape at one institution and are developed and embellished at other. That, as a matter of fact, was the case here. Admiral Rickover testified that the notes on which his lectures were based were derived from a similar course which he had given at another university. If [this] is correct, there must be some rights of that school which were infringed at [the professor's current university]. Further, should [he] leave [his current university] and give a substantially similar course at his next post, [the university] would be able to enjoin him from using the material, which according to [the university], it owns.

The court referred to a federal appeals court decision addressing the copyright ownership in Admiral Rickover's speeches.[21] The speeches in question were prepared by the admiral after normal working hours or while traveling. The California court noted that

> a person in Admiral Rickover's position . . . has no normal working hours any more than a university professor. Whatever distinctions between "on" and "off-duty" hours might be appropriate in the case of an hourly employee who punches a clock, they are quite out of place in cases such as Rickover and the one at bar. . . . It is thus apparent that no authority supports the argument that the copyright to [professor's] notes is in the university. The indications from the authorities are the other way and so is common sense.

It is important to note that any special exemption professors' notes enjoyed from the work made for hire doctrine was seriously undermined if not abolished by the Copyright Act of 1976. As noted above, the section 201(b) of the Act specifies that "in the case of a work made for hire, the employer . . . is considered the author . . . and, unless the parties have expressly agreed otherwise in a written instrument signed by them, owns all of the rights comprised in the copyright." As a result, cases decided before 1978 (when the Act took effect) are of limited relevance, since prior copyright law contained no provision comparable to section 201. Copyright ownership in a minister's sermons likely will be determined solely by focusing on whether or not the minister created the sermons within the scope of his or her employment.

Excessive compensation

Staff members who retain ownership of a work made for hire because of a written transfer signed by the church may be subject to intermediate sanctions. Intermediate sanctions are excise taxes the IRS can assess against persons who receive excessive compensation from a church or other charity. The point is this—since the church is the legal owner of the copyright in a work made for hire, it is legally entitled to any income generated from sales of the work. By letting the writer or composer retain the copyright, and all rights to royalties, the church in effect is paying compensation to him or her in this amount. If the work generates substantial income, then this may trigger intermediate sanctions. This would expose the writer or composer to an initial excise tax of 25 percent of the amount of taxable compensation that exceeds what the IRS deems to be reasonable. There is an additional 200 percent tax that can be assessed against the writer or composer if he or she does not return the excess amount to the church. Board members who authorized a transfer of the copyright to the writer or composer may be collectively assessed a tax of 10 percent of the excessive compensation up to a maximum of $10,000.

> **Resource.** *The subject of intermediate sanctions is addressed fully in chapter 4 of Richard Hammar's* Church and Clergy Tax Guide *(published annually by the publisher of this text).*

> **Key point.** *Intermediate sanctions can be imposed only against "disqualified persons" and "managers." IRS regulations define a disqualified person as any person who was in a position to exercise substantial influence over the affairs of the organization at any time during the five-year period ending on the date of the transaction. While a senior pastor ordinarily will meet this definition, other staff members may not. As a result, in many churches the risk of intermediate sanctions will be limited to senior pastors who create works made for hire and are allowed by their church to retain the copyright.*

Table 1-1
Works Made for Hire—A Checklist of Important Points

- A "work made for hire" is any book, article, or piece of music created by an employee in the course of employment.

- Factors to consider in deciding whether or not a work was created in the course of employment include the following: (1) Was the work written or composed during office hours? (2) Was the work created on church property? (3) Was the work created using church equipment? (4) Was the work created using church personnel?

- The employer owns the copyright in a work made for hire.

- An employer, by a signed writing, can transfer copyright in a work made for hire to the employee who created it.

- A church that transfers the copyright in a work made for hire to the employee who created it is jeopardizing its tax-exempt status, since this may constitute "inurement" of its assets to a private individual.

- A church that transfers the copyright in a work made for hire to the employee who created it may be exposing the employee to intermediate sanctions.

Key point. Church board members are exposed to an excise tax if they authorize a transfer of copyright in a work made for hire to the employee who created it, if the work generates substantial income.

Specially commissioned works made for hire

specially commissioned works

There is a second kind of work made for hire. The copyright law defines "work made for hire" to include "a work specially ordered or commissioned for use as a contribution to a collective work, as part of an . . . audiovisual work, as a translation, as a supplementary work, as a compilation, as an instructional text, as a test, as answer material for a test, or as an atlas, if the parties expressly agree in a written instrument signed by them that the work shall be considered a work made for hire."

The second type of work made for hire, as noted above, is "a work specially ordered or commissioned for use as a contribution to a collective work, as part of an . . . audiovisual work, as a translation, as a supplementary work, as a compilation, as an instructional text, as a test, as answer material for a test, or as an atlas, if the parties expressly agree in a written instrument signed by them that the work shall be considered a work made for hire." Most of these terms are defined in section 101 of the Copyright Act (see appendix). Note that for a commissioned work to be a work for hire, the following three requirements must be satisfied:

(1) the work must be one of the specific types of works listed (audiovisual work, translation, etc.),

(2) the work must have been commissioned by another party, and

(3) the parties must have both signed a written instrument characterizing the work as a work made for hire. A work generally is "commissioned" if one party requests another to prepare it.

Example. A publisher asks Pastor Judy, a seminary professor, to write a commentary on the Psalms for use as an instructional text. Pastor Judy is not an employee of the publisher. A written contract is signed, but no mention is made regarding the status of the work as a work made for hire. The commentary is a specially commissioned work (an instructional text), but it is not a work made for hire since the parties did not agree in a signed writing that it would be a work made for hire. The result is that Pastor Judy is the author and retains the copyright ownership in the work, unless such ownership is otherwise transferred to the publisher or another party.

Example. A publisher asks Pastor Steve, a minister of music, to prepare a musical arrangement of a public domain hymn. Pastor Steve is not an employee of the publisher. A contract is signed by both parties, in which the arrangement is characterized as a work made for hire. A musical arrangement is one of the types of works that may qualify as a specially commissioned work made for hire (the definition of "supplementary works" in section 101 of the Act includes "musical arrangements"). Since the arrangement was commissioned, and the parties both signed a written agreement characterizing the work as a work made for hire, the requirements for a specially commissioned work made for hire are satisfied. The result is that the publisher is deemed the author of the arrangement, and therefore is the copyright owner.

Example. Same facts as the preceding example, except that the written contract did not characterize the arrangement as a work made for hire. Under these circumstances, the work cannot qualify as a specially commissioned work made for hire, and accordingly Pastor Steve remains the author and copyright owner unless ownership is otherwise transferred.

> ***Example.*** *A religious periodical asks Pastor Larry to write an article on a selected issue. A contract is signed that merely recites a deadline and the amount of compensation. Pastor Larry is not an employee of the publisher. This cannot be a specially commissioned work made for hire (contribution to a collective work) since the parties did not sign an agreement characterizing the article as a work made for hire. As a result, Pastor Larry is the author and copyright owner unless ownership is otherwise transferred.*

B. Contributions to Collective Works

Section 201(c) of the Copyright Act specifies that "[c]opyright in each separate contribution to a collective work is distinct from copyright in the collective work as a whole, and vests initially in the author of the contribution. In the absence of an express transfer of the copyright or of any rights under it, the owner of copyright in the collective work is presumed to have acquired only the privilege of reproducing and distributing the contributions as part of that particular collective work, any revision of that collective work, and any later collective work in the same series." This provision certainly makes sense. At the time a contribution to a collective work is created, the collective work is not yet in existence. As a result, the basic rule of section 201(a), that "copyright . . . vests initially in the author or authors of the work," applies.

Let's see how this provision works in the context of a hypothetical situation. Assume that ABC Press is the publisher of a monthly devotional magazine that consists of articles submitted to it by various authors. The magazine meets the definition of a collective work. John is a minister who prepares an article and submits it to ABC Press for possible publication in the magazine. The article, first written by John in April of 2001, is accepted for publication in the December 2001 issue. ABC Press and John sign a simple contract under which John is to receive $100 for his article, and John gives permission to ABC Press to publish it in the December 2001 issue. Under these circumstances, section 201(c) prescribes the following consequences: (1) John is the copyright owner of the article (assuming that it is not a work made for hire); (2) John has not "expressly transferred" the copyright in the article to ABC Press according to the terms of the simple contract that was signed; (3) ABC Press has acquired only the "privilege of reproducing and distributing the contributions as part of that particular collective work, any revision of that collective work, and any later collective work in the same series." If, five years later, ABC Press decides to reprint John's article in the same devotional magazine, it has the right, according to section 201(c), to do so even without John's authorization.

If, however, another publisher sees the article in the December 2001 issue and writes ABC Press to request permission to republish the article in its publication, such a request must be forwarded to John since only he has the authority (being the copyright owner) to grant such permission. Of course, the result in this example would be entirely different had John "expressly transferred" the copyright in the article to ABC Press. In such a case, ABC Press would become the copyright owner, and could use the article in any manner it chose. In addition, it would have the sole right to authorize subsequent publication of the article by other publishers.

One thing is clear—authors and publishers must be careful to clarify plainly, and in writing, the nature of the rights being transferred. Misunderstandings are all too common.

Endnotes

[1] Meadowgreen Music Company v. Voice in the Wilderness Broadcasting, Inc., 789 F. Supp. 823 (E.D. Tex. 1992).

[2] L. Batlin & Son, Inc. v. Snyder, 536 F.2d 486, 490 (2nd Cir. 1976), *cert. denied,* 429 U.S. 857 (1976).

[3] Sheldon v. Metro-Goldwyn Pictures Corp., 81 F.2d 49, 54 (2nd Cir. 1936) (Judge Learned Hand).

[4] See note 1, *supra.*

[5] Norden v. Oliver Ditson Co., 13 F. Supp. 415 (D. Mass. 1936); Cooper v. James, 213 Fed. 871 (N.D. Ga. 1914).

[6] Copyright Act section 102(a).

[7] Copyright Act section 405(b).

[8] Copyright Act section 406(a).

[9] Copyright Act section 406(b).

[10] Copyright Act section 406(c).

[11] Burke v. National Broadcasting Co., 598 F.2d 688 (1st Cir. 1979).

[12] Nimmer on Copyright section 4.04 (1999).

[13] *Id.*

[14] *Id.* at section 7.06[A].

[15] *See* R. Hammar, *Church and Clergy Tax Guide* chapter 2 (published annually by the publisher of this text).

[16] City of Newark v. Beasley, 883 F. Supp. 3 (D.N.J. 1995).

[17] Hillsboro National Bank v. Hyde, 75 N.W. 781 (1898).

[18] Self-Realization Fellowship Church v. Ananda Church of Self-Realization, 206 F.3d 1322 (9th Cir. 2000).

[19] *See,* e.g., R. Dreyfuss, *The Creative Employee and the Copyright Act of 1976,* 54 Univ. Chi. L. Pastor 590 (1987).

[20] Williams v. Weisser, 78 Cal. Rptr. 542 (Cal. App. 1969).

[21] Public Affairs Associates, Inc. v. Rickover, 284 F.2d 262 (D.C. Cir. 1960).

2

Copyright Registration and the Deposit Requirements

2.1 Advantages of Registration

As we have seen in chapter 1, copyright protection arises automatically as soon as an original work is embodied in a tangible form. At no time does the work or the claim of copyright have to be "registered" with the Copyright Office in Washington, D.C. Section 408(a) of the Copyright Act specifically states that "registration is not a condition of copyright protection."

Nevertheless, section 408 permits the copyright owner of any published or unpublished work to register the copyright claim by filing an application and fee with the copyright office. Why would a copyright owner ever want to register a copyright claim in a work if it is not required? What advantages and disadvantages are there to registration? What procedure is used to register a copyright claim in a work? These questions will be addressed in this chapter.

First of all, why would a copyright owner ever wish to register a copyright claim? Consider the following advantages associated with registration:

(1) precondition to bringing infringement suits

infringement suits Section 411 of the Copyright Act provides that "no action for infringement of the copyright in any work shall be instituted until registration of the copyright claim has been made . . . ." This is a significant advantage of registration. Unless you have registered your copyright claim in a work, you cannot seek redress in the civil courts for acts of infringement. A number of courts have held, however, that a copyright owner of an unregistered work can sue an infringer by simply registering the claim of copyright even though the infringement occurred prior to registration.[1] This rule would not apply if the infringement suit were brought after the limitations period (generally 3 years) following the initial act of infringement. Works whose "country of origin" is not the United States need not be registered prior to filing suit for infringement. Congress carefully considered eliminating the requirement of registering works published in the United States as a precondition to bringing infringement suits on the ground that this constituted a copyright "formality" generally prohibited by the Berne Convention (which took effect March 1, 1989). This position ultimately was rejected.

(2) statutory damages

statutory damages   Section 504(c) of the Copyright Act allows a copyright owner to collect "statutory damages" from an infringer in lieu of proving actual damages. Statutory damages ordinarily range from $750 to $30,000 per violation, and they often comprise the only meaningful measure of damages since actual damages are difficult to prove.[2] Statutory damages are available only for infringements that occur after a work is registered, with one important exception. Section 412 specifies that "no award of statutory damages . . . shall be made for (1) any infringement of copyright in an unpublished work commenced before the effective date of its registration, or (2) any infringement of copyright commenced after first publication of the work and before the effective date of its registration, unless such registration is made within three months after the first publication of the work."

Key point. Statutory damages are available for any infringements occurring after registration of a work, or for infringements occurring prior to registration if the work is registered within three months following first publication. Otherwise, only an award of actual damages and profits is available to the copyright owner.

Example. In January of 2002 Ruth composes an original song that she reduces to writing. She does not publish or register the work. In October of 2002 James obtains an unauthorized copy of the song and publishes it. Since Ruth had not registered the unpublished work as of the date of the infringement, she is not eligible for statutory damages. She cannot register the work and then sue for statutory damages, although, as noted above, she can register the work and then sue for infringement and recover any actual damages that she can prove (assuming the infringement suit is brought within the three-year limitations period following the initial act of infringement). Since actual damages are often difficult to prove, the loss of statutory damages is a serious matter. Ruth could have preserved her right to sue for statutory damages by registering her unpublished work as soon as she reduced it to a tangible form (prior to the infringement).

Example. Same facts as the preceding example, except that Ruth published the song on August 1, 2002. Under these circumstances, Ruth can sue James for statutory damages only if she registers the work within three months after August 1, 2002 (the date of first publication). Section 412 specifies that "no award of statutory damages . . . shall be made for . . . any infringement of copyright commenced after first publication of the work and before the effective date of its registration, unless such registration is made within three months after the first publication of the work." So, for Ruth to be entitled to statutory damages for "post-publication, pre-registration" infringements, she must register the work within three months of first publication. As a result, if she fails to register the work by November 1, 2002 then she cannot sue James for statutory damages, although, as noted above, she can register the work and then sue for infringement and recover any actual damages that she can prove (assuming the infringement suit is brought within the three-year limitations period following the initial act of infringement).

Example. Same facts as the previous examples, except that Ruth composes and publishes the song in August of 2002, registers the copyright in March of 2003, and James' infringement does not occur until 2004. Since James' infringement occurs after Ruth registered the copyright in her work, she is entitled to statutory damages. It doesn't matter that she did not register the work within three months of publication. That rule only applies to "post-publication, pre-registration" infringements.

(3) "prima facie" evidence of copyright validity

evidence of validity   Section 410(c) provides that "[i]n any judicial proceedings the certificate of a registration made before or within five years after first publication of the work shall constitute prima facie evidence of the validity of the copyright and of the facts stated in the certificate." What is the significance of this rule? Simply this—a copyright claimant who has registered a claim of copyright in a work within five years before or after first publication does not have the burden of proving the validity of the copyright claim in an infringement suit.

To illustrate, assume that Gail writes and publishes an article in 2001, and registers it in the same year. If Andrew later infringes on Gail's copyright claim, then Gail can sue Andrew for infringement, and the court must presume that Gail's copyright claim is in fact valid. The burden of proof is on Andrew to prove that Gail's copyright claim is defective. It may surprise you to learn that the Copyright Office ordinarily does not examine a copyright registration application for basic validity before a certificate of registration is issued.[3] In this sense, a copyright claim differs from a patent application. As a result, a certificate of registration is of little value apart from the "prima facie" validity conferred by section 410(c).

(4) "constructive notice" of recordation

notice of copyright   Section 205(c) of the Copyright Act provides that "[r]ecordation of a document in the Copyright Office gives all persons constructive notice of the facts stated in the recorded document, but only if . . . registration has been made for the work." This provision means that the public is "on notice" of any transfers, licenses, mortgages, and other documents pertaining to copyrights if such documents are recorded in the Copyright Office and the underlying works are registered.

To illustrate, assume that Mark is the owner of a copyright in a book, and that he assigns his copyright in the book to John, who records and registers the transfer in January of 2002. Assume further that Mark tries to assign the copyright in the same book to Esther in May of 2002. According to section 205(c), Esther has constructive notice of the earlier transfer to John, and cannot use her ignorance of the previous transfer as a legal justification for her position.

(5) "curing" the effect of an omitted copyright notice

"curing" omitted notice   Generally, omission of a valid copyright notice from a work first published before March 1, 1989 invalidates the copyright in the work. However, section 405(a)(2) of the Copyright Act provides that omission of the notice on such a work will not invalidate the copyright if "registration for the work has been made before or is made within five years after the publication without notice, and a reasonable effort is made to add notice to all copies or phonorecords that are distributed to the public in the United States after the omission has been discovered."

> **Example.** *Samuel writes a book and decides to publish it himself with the aid of a local printer. Samuel has 10,000 copies printed, and sales to the public begin in January of 1998. Samuel discovers in July of 2002 that none of the books contained a copyright notice. As of July of 2002, 3,000 of the books had been sold to the public, 2,000 were in the hands of a number of bookstores, and the remaining 5,000 were in Samuel's garage. By registering the work before the end of 2002, and using reasonable efforts to add a valid copyright notice to the 2,000 copies in the bookstores and the 5,000 copies in his garage, Samuel may prevent the loss of his copyright interest in the book. Reasonable efforts to correct the omission of notice would include printing labels containing a valid copyright notice, and providing them to the bookstores with a request that they be affixed to the title page of each book, and affixing the same labels to the books still stored in the garage.*

(6) detection of errors

detection of errors The Copyright Office reviews every application for registration to ensure that the legal formalities needed to ensure protection are satisfied. Often, the Copyright Office will call to the attention of a copyright owner an error in the registration application or in the copyright notice that can ensure that copyright protection is preserved. Note, however, that this review is limited to the applicant's compliance with technical requirements. The merits of a particular claim of copyright ordinarily are not evaluated.

(7) marketability

marketability Registration of a copyright in some cases may enhance the marketability of an author's or composer's work. For example, a person checking Copyright Office records on a particular subject may inadvertently find your work, and contact you regarding a publishing opportunity.

(8) compulsory licenses

compulsory licenses As we will learn later, registration of a musical work may entitle you to "compulsory royalty payments" in the event that someone else makes a recording of the work. This provision has special relevance in the context of audio recording of church worship services in which copyrighted music is performed.

2.2 When to Register a Work

Let's assume that you are convinced that the benefits associated with registration are worth the effort. When should you pursue registration of the copyright in your work, and what is the procedure? First, let's look at the question of timing—when should a work be registered? Section 408(a) of the Copyright Act states that "[a]t any time during the subsistence of the first term of copyright in any published or unpublished work in which the copyright was secured before January 1, 1978, and during the subsistence of any copyright secured on or after that date, the owner of copyright or of any exclusive right in the work may obtain registration of the copyright claim . . . ." Authors or composers can wait for many years following the publication of a work to seek registration, or they can seek registration as soon as a work is embodied in a tangible form (prior to publication). In general, registering your work between completion and within three months of publication is the best course to follow. While it is possible to register each chapter or section of a work as it is completed, such a procedure is costly and time-consuming, and ordinarily is not warranted. On the other hand, if you have decided to register a work, there is nothing to be gained by delaying registration once the work is completed.

It is possible to register an unpublished work. Whether registration prior to publication is desirable or not depends upon the circumstances. Generally, it can be said that registration prior to publication is justified if the work is going to have exposure to the public prior to publication. For example, if Anne writes a song and sends it to several music publishers to review for possible publication, and also sends it to several of her friends for their comments, it would be well for her to consider registration prior to publication because of the widespread pre-publication exposure the song has had. Registration of the unpublished work can help prevent loss of control over the work. On the other hand, if Anne plans to publish and distribute the work herself, and does not send any copies to anyone else (for review or any other purposes) prior to publication, there is little reason to register the work prior to publication.

> *Key point. Authors and composers who send their unpublished works to publishers for review should be sure to insert a notice on their works (on the title page) stating that the work is an unpublished manuscript that is being submitted solely for review purposes, and that no publication or public distribution is authorized without the express written permission of the author or composer.*

If your work will have significant public exposure prior to publication, and you have decided to register it before it is published, you may also "re-register" the work after it is published. Section 408(e) of the Copyright Act specifies that "[r]egistration for the first published edition of a work previously registered in unpublished form may be made even though the work as published is substantially the same as the unpublished version."

published works   Let's say that you have decided to register your work, but that your work will not have any public exposure prior to publication. Under these facts, it ordinarily is best to register the work within three months following publication since this will preserve your right to statutory damages (and attorneys' fees) in the event someone infringes upon your work at any time following publication but before registration. That is, if you register your work within three months following publication, you are entitled to statutory damages for infringing acts that occur after publication but before registration. This is an important exception to the general rule that statutory damages are available only for infringing acts that occur after registration.

Often, an author or composer is not aware of the advantages of registration until long after a work is published. As noted above, registration can be pursued at any time during the term of copyright. Obviously, it is helpful if registration occurs within five years from the date of publication, since in some cases this can prevent loss of copyright in a work (first published before March 1, 1989) on account of an omitted or defective copyright notice. Further, section 410(c) of the Copyright Act provides that "[i]n any judicial proceedings the certificate of a registration made before or within five years after first publication of the work shall constitute prima facie evidence of the validity of the copyright and of the facts stated in the certificate." This is further reason to register a work within five years of publication. But if registration is not accomplished within five years of publication, this is no reason to dispense with it if you have determined that the benefits to be gained are worthwhile and desirable.

2.3 How to Register a Copyright Claim

A. In General

Let's assume you have decided to register your work. How do you proceed? Happily, copyright registration is a fairly simple procedure in most cases. To register a work, send the following three items in the same envelope or package to the Register of Copyrights, Copyright Office, Library of Congress, Washington, D.C. 20559:

(1) *A properly completed application form.* Be sure to complete the application using black ink or a typewriter or printer, and either an original Copyright Office form or a clear photocopy made on a good grade of white paper. Applications not meeting these requirements will be returned. There are several registration forms. Use the following table to determine which one is appropriate for you:

form	when used
TX	for published and unpublished nondramatic literary works
SE	for serials, works issued or intended to be issued in successive parts bearing numerical or chronological designations and intended to be continued indefinitely (periodicals, newspapers, magazines, newsletters, annuals, journals, etc.)
PA	for published and unpublished works of the performing arts (musical and dramatic works, pantomimes and choreographic works, motion pictures and other audiovisual works)
VA	for published and unpublished works of the visual arts (pictorial, graphic, and sculptural works, including architectural works)
SR	for published and unpublished sound recordings

short form TX, PA, VA	short versions of applications for original registration (see Copyright Office Publication SL-7 for further information)
RE	for claims to renew copyright in works copyrighted under the law in effect through December 31, 1977 (1909 Copyright Act) and registered during the initial 28-year copyright term

Note. *All of the forms listed in the table can be obtained from the Copyright Office, free of charge, by contacting the Copyright Office forms hotline at 1-202-707-3000. For informational purposes, Forms TX, PA, and SR are reproduced in an Appendix at the end of this book. You can also request forms by regular mail by writing Library of Congress, Copyright Office, Publications Section LM-455, 101 Independence Avenue S.E., Washington, D.C. 20559-6000.*

Tip. *All Copyright Office forms are available on the Copyright Office Website in fill-in version. Go to www.loc.gov/copyright/forms/ and follow the instructions. The fill-in forms allow you to enter information while the form is displayed on the screen by an Adobe Acrobat Reader product. You may then print the completed form and mail it to the Copyright Office. Fill-in forms provide a clean, sharp printout for your records and for filing with the Copyright Office.*

(2) *A nonrefundable filing fee of $30 (effective through June 30, 2002) per application.* The $30 fee applies to all of the forms described in the table, except for Form RE for which a $45 fee applies.

(3) *A nonrefundable deposit of the work being registered.* The deposit requirements vary in particular situations. The general requirements are as follows:

(a) If the work is unpublished, one complete copy or phonorecord.

(b) If the work was first published in the United States on or after January 1, 1978, two complete copies or phonorecords of the best edition.

(c) If the work was first published in the United States before January 1, 1978, two complete copies or phonorecords of the work as first published.

(d) If the work was first published outside the United States, whenever published, one complete copy or phonorecord of the work as first published.

(e) If the work is a contribution to a collective work, and published after January 1, 1978, one complete copy or phonorecord of the best edition of the collective work.

There are a number of special registration rules. Consider the following:

renewal registrations

Renewal registrations. Consider the following rules:

(1) works copyrighted before January 1, 1978

The copyright law provides a first term of copyright protection lasting 28 years followed by a second term of protection known as the renewal term. However, these works were required to be renewed within strict time limits to obtain a second term of copyright protection. If copyright was originally secured before January 1, 1964, and was not renewed at the proper time, copyright protection expired permanently at the end of the 28th year of the first term and could not be renewed. Congress enacted legislation in 1992 that amended the copyright law with respect to works copyrighted between January 1, 1964, and December 31, 1977, to secure *automatically* the second term of copyright and to make renewal registration optional. The renewal term automatically vests in the party entitled to claim renewal on December 31 of the 28th year of the first term. Congress enacted legislation in 1998 that extended the renewal term an additional 20 years for all works still under copyright, whether in their first term or renewal term at the time the law became effective. The 1992 and 1998 laws do not retroactively restore copyright to U.S. works that are in the public domain.

In summary, a work is eligible for renewal registration at the beginning of the 28th year of the first term of copyright, but there is no requirement to make a renewal filing in order to extend the original 28-year copyright term to the full term of 95 years. However, there are benefits from making a renewal registration during the 28th year of the original term.

The copyright law provides that, in order to register a renewal copyright, the renewal application and fee must be received in the Copyright Office within the last (28th) calendar year before the expiration of the original term of copyright or at any time during the renewed and extended term of 67 years. To renew a copyright during the original copyright term, the renewal application and fee must be received in the Copyright Office within 1 year prior to the expiration of the original copyright. All terms of the original copyright run through the end of the 28th calendar year, making the period for renewal registration during the original term from December 31st of the 27th year of the copyright through December 31st of the following year.

Form RE is the renewal application. The filing fee that must accompany this form is currently $45.

(2) works copyrighted on or after January 1, 1978

The copyright law has eliminated all renewal requirements and established a single copyright term and different methods for computing the duration of a copyright.

corrections

Corrections and amplifications. To deal with cases in which information in the basic registration later turns out to be incorrect or incomplete, the law provides for "the filing of an application for supplementary registration, to correct an error in a copyright registration or to amplify the information given in a registration." The information in a supplementary registration augments but does not supersede that contained in the earlier registration. Note also that a supplementary registration is not a substitute for an original registration or for a renewal registration. Form CA is used for supplementary registrations, and it is available from the Copyright Office.

group of contributions to periodicals

Group of contributions to periodicals. Section 408(c)(2) of the Copyright Act permits "a single registration for a group of works by the same individual author, all first published as contributions to periodicals . . . within a twelve-month period, on the basis of a single deposit, application, and registration fee . . . (A) if the deposit consists of one copy of the entire issue of the periodical . . . in which each contribution was first published, and (B) if the application identifies each work separately, including the periodical containing it and its date of first publication." Copyright Office Form GR/CP is used for this kind of registration. Note that the Form GR/CP is an "adjunct application" that is used in addition to Forms TX, PA, or VA. To illustrate, if an author writes 10 articles in 2002 and all of them are published in a variety of periodicals, the author can register all 10 works simultaneously by using Form GR/CP. But, the author must also complete and submit with the Form GR/CP a Form TX registration application for each article. Prior to March 1, 1989 this group registration procedure was not available unless each individual work bore a separate copyright notice. While a separate copyright notice was technically not necessary to preserve the copyright in a contribution to a periodical or other compilation if the periodical or compilation itself bore a valid copyright notice,[4] it was a precondition to a group registration by the author of the article and therefore was a desirable practice for periodicals to follow. Thanks to the Berne Convention, this requirement no longer exists.

effective date

There are just a few more issues to summarize regarding copyright registration. First, what is the effective date of registration, and second, who may file an application form. A copyright registration is effective on the date of receipt in the Copyright Office of all the required elements (discussed above) in acceptable form, regardless of the length of time it takes thereafter to process the application and mail the certificates of registration. The length of time required by the Copyright Office to process an application varies. You will not receive an acknowledgement that your application has been received, but you can expect within 120 days a letter or telephone call from the copyright examiner if additional information is needed, and a certificate of registration to indicate that the work has been registered (or, if the application cannot be accepted, a letter explaining why). If you want to know when the Copyright Office receives your material, you should send it certified mail and request a return receipt from the post office.

who may submit an application

Any of the following persons are legally entitled to submit a copyright registration application:

(1) *The author.* This is either the person who actually created the work, or, if the work was made for hire, the employer or other person for whom the work was prepared.

(2) *The copyright claimant.* The copyright claimant is either the author of the work or a person or organization that has obtained ownership of all the rights under the copyright initially belonging to the author.

(3) *The owner of exclusive rights.* Under the current copyright law, any of the exclusive rights associated with a copyright can be transferred and owned separately. Any owner of an exclusive right may apply for registration of a claim in the work.

(4) *The duly authorized agent of the author, copyright claimant, or owner of exclusive rights.* Any person authorized to act on behalf of the author, other copyright claimant, or owner of exclusive rights may apply for registration.

> ***Key point.*** *There is no requirement that applications be prepared or filed by an attorney.*

B. "Informal" Registration

mailing your work to yourself

Many persons are of the opinion that by mailing a copy of their literary or musical works to themselves, by certified or registered mail, they somehow acquire legal protection (so long as the envelope remains unopened) that they would not otherwise enjoy. Is there any basis to this view? First of all, such a procedure is not a substitute for registration. Unless an author or composer registers his or her work, none of the benefits associated with registration is available. Mailing a copy of a work back to yourself in no way affects this result. Further, the mailing procedure in no way contributes toward copyright protection in the work, since copyright protection arises automatically by operation of law as soon as an original work of authorship is fixed in a tangible form of expression. What, then, does the mailing procedure accomplish? If anything, the procedure would provide evidence as to the date an author or composer actually created a work. Occasionally, this evidence can be helpful. For example, assume that Alice composes an original song and reduces it to writing in January of 2001, and that Alan composes a nearly identical song in March of 2001. If Alan accuses Alice of copyright infringement, the fact that Alice has in her possession an unopened envelope (bearing a January 2001 postmark) that had been mailed to herself and that contains a copy of her work would be very helpful to her in disproving Alan's claim. Note, however, that some courts have given very little credibility to the contents of such "unopened" envelopes, on the ground that the owner could have opened the envelope, replaced its contents, and resealed it without detection.[5] The Writers Guild of America permits authors to deposit works with it, as a means of establishing originality.

> ***Example.*** *Pastor Wilson types his sermons in advance, and would like to copyright them. He would use Form TX. If the sermons are not typed or reduced to any other type of writing, but are recorded, he would submit a Form SR.*

> **Example.** *Janet composes a sacred song (music and lyrics) that she reduces to writing. She would use Form PA to register the work. If she records the song, she could use Form SR to register both the recording and the underlying musical work, or she could submit two registrations—a Form PA for the underlying work and a Form SR for the recording.*

2.4 Deposit Requirements

Although copyright registration is not required, the Copyright Act establishes a mandatory deposit requirement for works published with notice of copyright in the United States. In general, the copyright owner, or the owner of the exclusive right of publication in a work, has a legal obligation to deposit in the Copyright Office, within three months of publication, two copies (or in the case of sound recordings, two phonorecords) for the use of the Library of Congress. Failure to make the deposit can result in fines and penalties, but does not affect copyright protection. Under section 408(b) of the Act, a single deposit can satisfy both the deposit and registration requirements. This provision requires that the single copy must be accompanied by the prescribed application and registration fee.

Copyright Office regulations exempt various kinds of works from the deposit requirements, including sermons and speeches (when published individually and not as a collection of the works of one or more authors), literary or musical works published only as embodied in phonorecords, certain "on line" computer databases available only in the United States, and works first published as individual contributions to collective works.

Endnotes

[1] *See, e.g.,* International Trade Management, Inc. v. United States, 553 F. Supp. 402 (Ct. Cl. 1982).

[2] The subject of statutory damages is considered in detail in section 5.3(D).

[3] House Report on the Copyright Act of 1976, page 157.

[4] Section 404(a) of the Copyright Act specifies that "a single notice applicable to the collective work as a whole is sufficient to satisfy the [copyright notice] requirements with respect to the separate contributions it contains . . . ."

[5] *See, e.g.,* Smith v. Berlin, 141 N.Y.S.2d 110 (1955).

3

Copyright Duration

How long does a copyright last? This is an important question not just for authors and composers who retain the copyright in their works, but also for publishers who obtain copyrights from authors and composers by a transfer or assignment. In addition, users of literary or musical materials often have an interest in knowing if the copyright in a particular work is still effective, or if it has expired.

A copyright does not last for an indefinite or unlimited time. The provision in the United States Constitution giving Congress authority to create copyright protection specifies that such protection shall be only "for limited times."[1] The "limited times" vary depending upon the circumstances.

3.1 Works Published Prior to 1978

A. In General

two 28-year terms Under the copyright law in effect before 1978, copyright was secured either on the date a work was published (with an appropriate copyright notice), or on the date of registration if the work was registered in unpublished form. In either case, the copyright lasted for a first term of 28 years from the date it was secured. During the last (28th) year of the first term, the copyright was eligible for renewal. If renewed, the copyright was extended for a second term of 28 years. If not renewed, the copyright expired at the end of the first 28-year term and the work entered the public domain, meaning that it no longer enjoyed copyright protection and could be used and copied by the public without limitation.

> **Example.** *A hymn was first published on July 1, 1930 (with a valid copyright notice). Copyright protection lasted for 28 years, expiring on June 30, 1958. The copyright owner could register the work for an additional 28-year renewal term during the 28th year of the first term.*

For some copyrights, the second term was extended beyond 28 years by special legislation. The treatment of Mary Baker Eddy's *Science and Health with Key to the Scriptures* ("Science and Health") is an interesting case in point. By 1971, all of the editions of *Science and Health* (the basic religious text of Christian Science) had lost their copyright protection except a 1906 edition whose term had been extended from year to year by special "interim" legislation. Then, in 1971, Congress enacted a statute extending until the year 2046 the copyright term of the 1906 edition of *Science and Health* (and all other editions)—a total term of 140 years! This special law was challenged by dissident church members on the grounds that it violated the first amendment's nonestablishment of religion clause. A federal appeals court agreed, noting that there was no legitimate justification for granting preferred status to a religious text.[2]

B. Effect of the 1976 Copyright Act on Existing Copyrights

Copyright Act of 1976

The old system of computing the duration of protection was carried over into the 1976 Copyright Act with one major change: the length of the second or renewal term was increased to 47 years for copyrights in existence on January 1, 1978, making such works eligible for a total term of protection of 75 years. Congress enacted legislation in 1998 further extending the second or renewal term an additional 20 years, providing for a renewal term of 67 years and a total term of protection of 95 years. In summary, the maximum total term of copyright protection for works already protected by federal law is increased from 56 years (a first term of 28 years plus a renewal term of 28 years) to 95 years (a first term of 28 years plus a renewal term of 67 years). The specific situation for works copyrighted before 1978 depends on whether the copyright had already been renewed or was still in its first term on December 31, 1977.

(1) *works originally copyrighted before 1950 and renewed before 1978*

95 years

These works have automatically been given a longer copyright term. Copyrights that had already been renewed and were in their second term at any time between December 31, 1976, and December 31, 1977 do not need to be renewed again. They have been automatically extended to last for a total term of 95 years (a first term of 28 years plus a renewal term of 67 years) from the end of the year in which they were originally secured.

> **Key point.** *If copyright protection could persist for a maximum of 56 years prior to 1978, is it not therefore necessarily true that any work bearing a copyright date before 1922 is automatically in the public domain (i.e., its copyright protection has expired)? Unfortunately, the answer is no. Here's why. Congress began considering a major revision of the copyright law as early as 1962. Since it did not know how copyright terms would be affected by the eventual legislation, it began providing for a series of "interim" extensions of existing copyrights whose second 28-year term would otherwise have expired. These extensions continued up until the effective date of the current copyright law (January 1, 1978). The result was that any work whose second 28-year copyright term would otherwise have expired between September 19, 1962 and December 31, 1977, was automatically extended for a period of 75 years from the date of the original copyright (in 1998, this 75-year term was increased to 95 years). This means that most works published before 1978 enjoy a copyright term of 95 years from the date copyright protection was originally secured. Of course, works that were not renewed prior to 1962 were not covered by this provision.*

> **Example.** *Pastor Owens, the minister of music at First Church, wants his choir to sing a hymn in a morning worship service. Pastor Owens locates the hymn in the church hymnal, and decides to duplicate a copy for each member of the choir since the hymn bears a copyright date of 1917. Pastor Owens cannot safely assume on the basis of the copyright date alone that the work is in the public domain, since the work may be protected for up to 95 years. To be safe, Pastor Owens would have to check on the copyright status of the work. This procedure is discussed later in this chapter.*

(2) *works originally copyrighted between January 1, 1950, and December 31, 1963*

67-year renewal form

Copyrights in their first 28-year term on January 1, 1978, still had to be renewed in order to be protected for the second term. If a valid renewal registration was made at the proper time, the second term will last for 67 years. However, if renewal registration for these works was not made within the statutory time limits, a copyright originally secured between 1950 and 1963 expired on December 31st of its 28th year, and protection was lost permanently.

(3) works originally copyrighted between January 1, 1964, and December 31, 1977

optional renewal term

In 1992, Congress enacted an amendment to the Copyright Act that makes renewal registration optional. The copyright is still divided between a 28-year original term and a 67-year renewal term, but a renewal registration is not required to secure the renewal copyright. The renewal vests on behalf of the appropriate renewal claimant upon registration or, if there is no renewal registration, on December 31 of the 28th year.

While owners of works that were first copyrighted between January 1, 1964 and December 31, 1977 are no longer required to secure a renewal copyright to qualify for the second term of protection of 67 years, there are several important advantages to pursuing the optional renewal registration during the 28th year of the original term of copyright. Consider the following:

advantages of renewal

1. The renewal copyright vests in the name of the renewal claimant on the effective date of the renewal registration. For example, if a renewal registration is made in the 28th year and the renewal claimant dies following the renewal registration but before the end of the year, the renewal copyright is secured on behalf of that renewal claimant, and the 67 years of renewal copyright becomes a part of that individual's estate.

2. The renewal certificate constitutes prima facie evidence as to the validity of the copyright during the renewed and extended term and of the facts stated in the certificate.

3. The right to use the derivative work in the extended term may be affected. For example, if an author dies before the 28th year of the original term and a statutory renewal claimant registers a renewal within the 28th year, that claimant can terminate an assignment made by the deceased author authorizing the exploitation of a derivative work. If a renewal is not made during the 28th year, a derivative work created during the first term of copyright under a prior grant can continue to be used according to the terms of the grant. Therefore, an author or other renewal claimant loses the right to object to the continued use of the derivative work during the second term by failing to make a timely renewal, but any terms in the prior grant concerning payment or use (such as a royalty) must continue to be honored. This exception does not apply to a new derivative work which can only be prepared with the consent of the author or other renewal claimant. A renewal registration made after the 28th year will not confer the benefits mentioned above but will confer other benefits denied to unregistered works. For example, renewal registration establishes a public record of copyright ownership in a work at the time that the renewal was registered.

4. Renewal registration is a prerequisite to statutory damages and attorney's fees for published works not registered for the original term.

Termination of Grants

For works already under statutory protection before 1978, the length of the renewal term has been increased to 67 years. This means that, in most cases, 39 years have been added to the end of a renewal copyright (previously, 28 years). The copyright law allows an author or specified heirs of the author to file a notice terminating any grant of rights made by the author and covering any part of that added period. This right to reclaim ownership of all or part of the extended term is optional; it can be exercised only by certain specified persons in accordance with prescribed conditions and within strict time limits.

In cases where no original registration or renewal registration is made before the expiration of the 28th year, important benefits can still be secured by filing a renewal registration at any time during the renewal term. These benefits would include, for example, statutory damages and attorney's fees in any infringement suit for infringements occurring after the renewal registration is made. Also, it is a requirement to get into court in certain circumstances under section 411(a), and it creates a public record both to defend against innocent infringers and to facilitate easier licensing of the work.

Form RE

Forms for renewal registration (Form RE) are available from the Library of Congress, Copyright Office, Publications Section LM-455, 101 Independence Avenue, S.E., Washington, D.C. 20559-6000, or by calling the Forms and Publications Hotline at 202-707-9100. You also may access and download Form RE and other information from the Copyright Office Website at http://www.loc.gov/copyright.

3.2 Works Originally Created on or after January 1, 1978

For works that are created and fixed in a tangible medium of expression for the first time on or after January 1, 1978, the Copyright Act of 1976 as amended in 1998 establishes a single copyright term and different methods for computing the duration of a copyright. Works of this sort fall into two categories:

A. Works Created on or after January 1, 1978

life plus 70

joint works and works made for hire

For works created after its effective date, the U.S. copyright law adopts the basic "life-plus-seventy" system already in effect in most other countries. A work that is created (fixed in tangible form for the first time) after January 1, 1978, is automatically protected from the moment of its creation and is given a term lasting for the author's life, plus an additional 70 years after the author's death. In the case of "a joint work prepared by two or more authors who did not work for hire," the term lasts for 70 years after the last surviving author's death. For works made for hire, and for anonymous and pseudonymous works (unless the author's identity is revealed in Copyright Office records), the duration of copyright will be 95 years from first publication or 120 years from creation, whichever is shorter.

B. Works in Existence but not Published or Copyrighted on January 1, 1978

Works that had been created before the current law came into effect but had neither been published nor registered for copyright before January 1, 1978, automatically are given federal copyright protection. The duration of copyright in these works will generally be computed in the same way as for new works: the life-plus-70 or 95/120-year terms will apply to them as well. However, all works in this category are guaranteed at least 25 years of statutory protection. The law specifies that in no case will copyright in a work of this sort expire before December 31, 2002, and if the work is published before that date, the term will extend another 45 years, through the end of 2047.

> **Example.** *Mary composes a religious song in January of 2002. The copyright in the song will last for Mary's life plus an additional 70 years. This is so whether Mary retains the copyright, or if she assigns the copyright to a music publisher. Thus, if Mary dies on July 1, 2003, the copyright will expire on December 31, 2073 (the last day of the year in which the 70th anniversary of the author's death occurs).*

Year-End Expiration of Copyright Terms

The copyright law provides that all terms of copyright will run through the end of the calendar year in which they would otherwise expire. This affects the duration of all copyrights, including those subsisting in either their first or second term on January 1, 1978. For works eligible for renewal, the renewal filing period begins on December 31st of the 27th year of the copyright term.

Example. Pastor Kim, an employee of First Church, composes a religious song that is properly characterized as a work made for hire. Since it is a work made for hire, the "author" of the work is deemed to be the employer (First Church). Since the employer-author of most works made for hire is a corporation or other organization, it is not realistic to use the author's "life" in the computation of the copyright term. Accordingly, the copyright in a work made for hire lasts for 95 years from first publication or 120 years from the creation of the work, whichever is shorter.

Example. A work that was first copyrighted on April 10, 1923, and renewed between April 10, 1950, and April 10, 1951, would formerly have fallen into the public domain after April 10, 1979. The current law extends this copyright through the end of 2018. These second-term copyrights cannot be renewed again. Under the law, their extension to the maximum 95-year term is automatic and requires no action in the Copyright Office.

Example. A work was first copyrighted on July 29, 1950, and a renewal registration was made on September 1, 1977. The second term of copyright was automatically extended through the end of 2045 without the need of any further renewal.

Example. A work that was first entered for copyright on October 5, 1907, and renewed in 1935, would formerly have fallen into the public domain after October 5, 1963. However, Congress enacted a series of laws extending copyright protection in such works, and the Copyright Act of 1976 established the copyright term as 75 years from the end of the year in which the copyright was originally secured. The 75-year term was later expanded to 95 years.

presumptions of death

Obviously, any reference to the author's life in the computation of a copyright term may create problems. What if it cannot be determined when an author dies? This problem will be especially acute for large publishers that will need to track the lives of hundreds or perhaps thousands of authors. Fortunately, the copyright law responds specifically to this concern by providing that "after a period of 95 years from the year of first publication of a work, or a period of 120 years from the year of its creation, whichever expires first, any person who obtains from the Copyright Office a certified report that [Copyright Office records] disclose

---

Copyright Duration in a Nutshell

- **Works Published or Copyrighted Before January 1, 1964.** Works published with notice of copyright or registered in unpublished form prior to January 1, 1964, had to be renewed during the 28th year of their first term of copyright to maintain protection for a full 95-year term.

- **Works Originally Copyrighted Between January 1, 1964, and December 31, 1977.** These works are protected by copyright for the 28-year original term and the 67-year renewal term without the need of a first term or a renewal registration.

- **Copyrights in their second term on January 1, 1978.** These works were automatically extended up to a maximum of 95 years, without the need for further renewal.

- **Works already in the public domain.** These works cannot be protected under the 1976 law or under the amendments of 1992 and 1998. The Act provides no procedure for restoring protection for works in which copyright has been lost for any reason. Note, however, that copyrights in certain foreign works whose U.S. copyright protection had been lost because of non-compliance with formalities of U.S. law were restored as of January 1, 1996, under the provisions of the Uruguay Round Agreements Act (URAA). Such works may be registered using Form GATT.

nothing to indicate that the author of the work is living, or died less than 70 years before, is entitled to the benefit of a presumption that the author has been dead for at least 70 years."[3] To help implement this provision, the Copyright Office is directed to maintain records of information relating to the death of authors based on recorded statements submitted by persons having an interest in particular copyrights.

> *Example. Apex Music Company is a publisher of religious music. In 2000 it publishes a song composed by Andrew in the same year. Assuming that Apex loses track of Andrew, and is not aware of the date of his death, the copyright in the song will expire in the year 2095 (95 years from the date of its first publication). This assumes that after a period of 95 years from the date of first publication Apex receives from the Copyright Office a certified report stating that Copyright Office records disclose nothing to indicate that the author is living, or died less than 70 years before.*

3.3 How to Check on the Copyright Status of a Particular Work

Let's assume that your church would like to duplicate a particular religious song for use by the choir. You realize that such duplication will amount to an infringement of the copyright in the work if the copyright has not expired. But if the copyright has expired, then the work is in the public domain and ordinarily can be duplicated at will. How do you know whether or not the copyright has expired? There are several ways to investigate whether a work is under copyright protection. The main ones are listed below.

(1) *examine a copy of the work for such elements as a copyright notice, place and date of publication, author and publisher*

examine the work itself

For example, the omission of a valid copyright notice from any published copy of a work first published before 1978 generally indicates that the work is not protected by copyright. However, there are a number of exceptions to this rule. The date in the copyright notice is also helpful in determining the copyright status of a work. Generally, the copyright in any work published or copyrighted more than 95 years ago (95 years from January 1st of the present year) has expired by operation of law, and the work has permanently fallen into the public domain. For example, on January 1, 2002, copyright in most works published or copyrighted before January 1, 1907 will have expired. The copyright notice (or any other information presented in the work) usually gives enough information about the publisher that you will be able to contact that person or organization to obtain information about the copyright in the work. However, note that in examining a copy, it is important to determine whether that particular version of the work is an original edition of the work or a "new version." New versions include musical arrangements, adaptations, revised or newly edited versions, translations, abridgements, compilations, and works republished with new matter added. The law provides that such "derivative works" are independently copyrightable and that the copyright in such a work does not affect or extend the protection, if any, in the underlying work.

> *Example. Bruce knows that the copyright in a particular book expired in 1987. He therefore copies significant passages from the book in a book of his own. However, Bruce was not aware that while the copyright in the original edition of the copied book expired in 1987, the author published a second edition of the work in 1960 (the copyright in which extends until the year 2055). Therefore, if the materials used by Bruce appeared in the second edition as well as in the original edition, Bruce is guilty of copyright infringement.*

(2) *make a search of the Copyright Office catalogs and other records*

search Copyright Office records yourself

If you are near Washington, D.C., you may wish to search Copyright Office records in the Library of Congress. It is open to the public, and you can search free of charge.

Copyright Office records, including registration information and recorded documents, are available through LOCIS (Library of Congress Information System) at the Copyright Office website, www.loc.gov/copyright. Two files, COHM and COHS, contain records for materials registered for copyright since January 1978. These materials include books, films, music, maps, sound recordings, software, multimedia kits, drawings, posters, sculpture, serials, etc. A third file, COHD, has references to documents that describe copyright legal transactions, such as name changes and transfers. The LOCIS Usage Guide has more information on these files.

For information on searching paper and microfiche records from 1790 through 1978, see Copyright Office Circular 22 and Circular 23.

> ***Key point.*** *LOCIS was developed in the 1970s long before the advent of Windows and other current computer technology. All commands are entered from the keyboard. The mouse is not used in this system. Many of the commands and search techniques are not "user-friendly." The Copyright Office currently is developing state-of-the-art software to replace this system.*

Please consult the LOCIS Usage Guide before conducting your search, as only limited HELP screens are available once you begin. The guide gives detailed instructions on how to search, select, and display information contained in the databases. The guide can be accessed from the Copyright Office website.

The Copyright Office does not offer LOCIS search assistance or help with software, hardware, or other computer-related problems. If you are unable to connect to LOCIS, contact your Internet service provider.

(3) *have the Copyright Office make the search for you*

have the Copyright Office perform a search

Upon request, the Copyright Office staff will search its records at the rate of $65 for each hour or fraction of an hour consumed. The Copyright Office will send you a typewritten report or, if you prefer, an oral report by telephone. Your request, and any other correspondence, should be addressed to the Library of Congress, Copyright Office, Reference and Bibliography Section LM-451, 101 Independence Avenue, S.E., Washington, D.C. 20559-6000. Or, you may call 202-707-6850.

The more detailed information you can furnish with your request, the less time-consuming and expensive the search will be. You should try to provide as much of the following information as possible: (1) the title of the work, and any possible variations; (2) the name of the author; (3) the name of the probable copyright owner (which may be the publisher); (4) the approximate year when the work was published or registered; (5) the type of work involved (book, song, sound recording, etc.). Unless your request specifies otherwise, Copyright Office searches include records pertaining to registrations, renewals, and assignments. The Copyright Office has developed a form that persons can use to submit a search request. This form is available without charge from the Copyright Office.

Searches of Copyright Office catalogs and records are useful in helping to determine the copyright status of a work, but they cannot be regarded as conclusive in all cases. The complete absence of information about a work in the office records does not mean that the work is unprotected. For example, works published on or after January 1, 1978 need never be registered to ensure copyright protection. Many authors and composers do not register their works, and accordingly no amount of searching Copyright Office materials will disclose the existence of such a work, though it in fact enjoys copyright protection.

(4) *contact the Church Music Publishers Association*

Church Music Publishers Association

Contact the Church Music Publishers Association at 615-791-0273, or the Music Publishers Association at 212-327-4044. These organizations maintain information on the copyright status of several musical compositions.

Endnotes

[1] U.S. Constitution, Article I, Section 8.

[2] United Christian Scientists v. Christian Science Board of Directors, First Church of Christ, Scientist, 829 F.2d 1152 (D.C. Cir. 1987). This special legislation was the first copyright law to be invalidated by the courts.

[3] Copyright Act section 302(e).

4

Transfers of Copyright and Publishing Contracts

4.1 Transfers

In this chapter we will address the issues of copyright transfer and publishing contracts. These two issues are being considered together because they are closely related. If you are interested in having a publishing company publish your work, you must be familiar with the subject of copyright transfers, since ordinarily you will be asked to transfer some or all of the exclusive rights which comprise your copyright.

Section 201(d) of the Copyright Act provides that "[t]he ownership of a copyright may be transferred in whole or in part by any means of conveyance or by operation of law, and may be bequeathed by will or pass as personal property by the applicable laws of intestate succession." Section 201(d) also specifies that "[a]ny of the exclusive rights comprised in a copyright . . . may be transferred . . . and owned separately. The owner of any particular exclusive right is entitled, to the extent of that right, to all of the protection and remedies accorded to the copyright owner . . . ." Section 204 provides that "a transfer of copyright ownership . . . is not valid unless an instrument of conveyance, or a note or memorandum of the transfer, is in writing and signed by the owner of the rights conveyed . . . ."

What do these provisions mean? Consider the following:

property rights

1. *Property right.* Copyright ownership is treated as a property right that can be transferred to another person by conveyance, or by will.

"exclusive rights" divisible

2. *Divisibility.* The "exclusive rights" comprising a copyright (set forth in section 106 of the Copyright Act) are "divisible," meaning that any one or more of them can be transferred to another person. To illustrate, section 106 gives a copyright owner the exclusive rights to prepare derivative works (e.g., a musical arrangement), publicly perform the work, and make duplicate copies of the work. If Ron composes an original religious song in 2000 and owns the copyright in the work, he can transfer his entire copyright to Ruth, or he can transfer any one or more of his exclusive rights to Ruth. Similarly, he can transfer exclusive rights to different persons, or transfer "any subdivision" of an exclusive right. Note, however, that unless Ron transfers his entire ownership interest in the copyright, he remains the copyright owner even though he has transferred away most of his exclusive rights. This is an important consideration, for it ordinarily means that Ron's name

will continue to appear in all copyright notices (even on works produced by the transferees of exclusive rights), and copyright registration of the work must be in Ron's name.

status of transferee   3. *Status of transferee.* A person to whom a copyright or an exclusive right is transferred by the original copyright owner "is entitled, to the extent of that right, to all of the protection and remedies accorded to the copyright owner . . . ." This means that a person to whom an exclusive right has been transferred has a legal right to proceed against an infringer of that right.

signed writing required   4. *A signed writing.* Also note that according to section 204, a transfer of copyright ownership is not valid unless "an instrument of conveyance, or a note or memorandum of the transfer, is in writing and signed by the owner of the rights conveyed . . . ." Section 101 defines a "transfer of copyright ownership" to include an assignment, exclusive license, or any other conveyance of a copyright "or of any of the exclusive rights comprised in a copyright." This means that both transfers of copyright ownership and transfers of any one or more exclusive rights must be evidenced by a writing signed by the owner of the rights conveyed. This significant rule is illustrated in the following examples.

> ***Example.*** *Brian writes a book and submits it to a publisher for consideration. The publisher agrees to publish the work, but insists that Brian convey his entire copyright ownership in the work to the publisher in return for a royalty agreement. This transfer must be evidenced by a written instrument of conveyance signed by Brian. What if it is not? Let's assume that the agreement is oral, or that a simple agreement is signed by both parties that does not refer to any transfer of copyright ownership or of any exclusive rights. In such a case, Brian will remain the copyright owner, and the agreement between the parties will define their respective rights and obligations. Being the copyright owner is important, for it means that Brian retains the exclusive rights in the book, including the right to make derivative works (e.g., a second edition or abridgement).*

> ***Example.*** *Pastor Dalton writes an article that he submits to a religious periodical for consideration. The periodical agrees to publish the work, but no written agreement is signed. Pastor Dalton remains the copyright owner. According to section 201(c) of the Copyright Act (discussed in Chapter 1), the publisher has acquired only the "privilege of reproducing and distributing the contributions as part of that particular collective work, any revision of that collective work, and any later collective work in the same series." If, five years later, it decides to reprint the article in the same periodical, it has the right, according to section 201(c), to do so even without Pastor Dalton's authorization. If, however, another publisher sees the article and writes the publisher to request permission to republish the article in its publication, such a request must be forwarded to Pastor Dalton since only he has the authority (being the copyright owner) to grant such permission. Of course, the result in this example would be entirely different had Pastor Dalton "expressly transferred" the copyright in the article to the first publisher. In such a case, the publisher would have become the copyright owner, and could have used the article in any manner it chose. In addition, it would have had the sole right to authorize subsequent publication of the article by other publishers. Authors and publishers must be careful to clarify plainly, and in writing, the nature of the rights being transferred. Misunderstandings are all too common.*

notary acknowledgements   Should a written transfer of copyright (or of one or more exclusive rights) be acknowledged by a notary public? Section 204(b) states that a notary's acknowledgment is "not required for the validity of a transfer," but that it is "prima facie evidence of the execution of a transfer." This simply means that notarization is desirable, but not necessary.

Key point. *A federal appeals court has observed, "No magic words must be included in a document to satisfy [the written agreement requirement for a transfer of copyright]. Rather, the parties' intent as evidenced by the writing must demonstrate a transfer of the copyright. . . . The requirement is not unduly burdensome. . . . The rule is really quite simple: If the copyright holder agrees to transfer ownership to another party, that party must get the copyright holder to sign a piece of paper saying so. It doesn't have to be the Magna Carta; a one-line pro forma statement will do."[1]*

Key point. *Section 101 of the Copyright Act excludes "nonexclusive licenses" from the definition of a "transfer of ownership," and therefore section 204(a)'s requirement that "transfers of copyright" be by a signed writing does not apply to transfers of nonexclusive licenses.[2]*

Example. *A federal court noted that while a "one-line statement" may satisfy the requirement of a signed writing, and need not even refer to "copyright" or "exclusive rights," it must be a clear conveyance of rights.[3]*

Example. *A court ruled that a fax did not satisfy the "signed writing" requirement for a transfer of copyright. The court pointed out that the fax contained no mention of a grant of any rights. It concluded, "Section 204(a) has a simple requirement in order for a grant of an exclusive license to be valid—put it in writing. If the parties really have reached an agreement, they can satisfy section 204(a) with very little effort."[4]*

Example. *A court concluded that the following special endorsement on the back of checks paid to writers did not amount to a transfer of copyright to the publisher: "Signature required. Check void if this endorsement altered. This check accepted as full payment for first-time publication rights to material described on face of check in all editions published by [the publisher] and for the right to include such material in electronic library archives." The court concluded that this did not amount to a valid assignment of online electronic rights by the writers. The court conceded that "a writing memorializing the assignment of copyright interests" can be brief, but this minimal requirement had not been met in this case because the language was unclear. It referred to the right to republish articles in "electronic library archives," and the court concluded that this language did not contemplate commercially sold CD-ROMs or online electronic databases. Further, the court pointed out that before the writers even signed their checks the articles had been republished in the online electronic databases.[5]*

Example. *In the PTL bankruptcy case, televangelists Jim and Tammy Bakker claimed that they were entitled to the value of all copyrights for music and books they had written while employed by PTL. In rejecting this claim, the court noted that "time and time again the Bakkers made representations to the general public that all such rights had been assigned to and were the property of PTL. The court has no basis upon which to make any finding to the contrary."[6]*

recording transfers The Copyright Office does not have any forms for transfers. Ordinarily, a transfer is in the form of a contract drafted by one of the parties. However, section 205 of the Copyright Act does permit transfers to be recorded in the Copyright Office. Although recording is not required for a valid transfer, it does provide certain legal advantages and sometimes is required to validate a transfer as against third parties with conflicting claims. The question of what terms should be included in a transfer agreement is considered later in this chapter.

termination of transfers

For works already under copyright protection on January 1, 1978, the copyright law contains special provisions allowing the termination of any grant of rights made by an author and covering any part of the period (usually 39 years) that has now been added to the end of the renewal copyright. This right to reclaim ownership of all or any part of the extended term is optional. It can be exercised only by certain persons (the author, or specified heirs of the author), and it must be exercised in accordance with prescribed conditions and within strict time limits.

Example. A federal court ruled that publishers could place the contents of magazines and other periodicals in online electronic databases and on CD-ROMs without obtaining the permission of writers whose articles were included in those periodicals.[7] Several authors sued the publishers, claiming that the inclusion of their articles in the online electronic databases and on CD-ROMs violated their copyright interests. The publishers disagreed, claiming that the writers had authorized the publication of their articles in an online electronic format, and that the republication of articles in "collective works" is permitted by the Copyright Act. The court concluded that none of the writers had legally transferred any rights to their publishers to republish the articles in an electronic format. It acknowledged that writers can assign all or any portion of the copyright in their works to a publisher by means of a written assignment. If they choose, they can transfer the right to republish their articles in an electronic format. But none of the writers had done so. However, the court concluded that the publisher had the right to republish the articles on the basis of 201(c) of the Copyright Act, which specifies that "[c]opyright in each separate contribution to a collective work is distinct from copyright in the collective work as a whole, and vests initially in the author of the contribution. In the absence of an express transfer of the copyright or of any rights under it, the owner of copyright in the collective work is presumed to have acquired only the privilege of reproducing and distributing the contributions as part of that particular collective work, any revision of that collective work, and any later collective work in the same series." According to this language, persons who contribute articles to collective works retain the copyright in their articles unless they have assigned them to the publisher. If they have not assigned the copyright in their articles to the publisher, then the publisher has the limited privilege of "reproducing and distributing the contributions as part of that particular collective work, any revision of that collective work, and any later collective work in the same series." Since the writers had not assigned any rights to the publishers other than the right to "first publish" their articles, the remaining question was whether the republication of the collective works in an electronic format was a "reproduction" or "revision" of the collective work. If so, then it was permissible according to section 201(c). The court concluded that the republication of the collective works (magazines and journals) on CD-ROMs and in online electronic databases met this test. It rejected the writers' argument that the individual magazines and periodicals lost their status as collective works when they were placed online and on CD-ROMs.

4.2 Publishing Contracts

Let's assume that you have completed (or are about to complete) a book, article, or song, and that you find a publisher that is willing to publish your work. What kind of contract should you sign? What terms should it contain? What rights should you transfer? These questions are of great importance to both authors and publishers, and they often are subject to negotiation. Consider the following points:

A. Attaching a Copyright Notice to Your Manuscript

copyright notice

Never submit a published work to a publisher for consideration without affixing a valid copyright notice. While a copyright notice is technically no longer required, there are important advantages to using such notices, and these are explained in chapter 1. Many authors and composers inadvertently "publish" their works before submitting them to publishers—for example, by circulating copies to several persons for review and comment. If you are not sure whether or not your work has been inadvertently published, then affix a copyright notice to any works that leave your control, including the copy that you submit to a publisher. If you are certain that the work is unpublished, then you can affix a notice reading "Unpublished work Copyright 2002 John Doe." It also is helpful to add the following notice: "Unpublished manuscript submitted for review purposes only; publication or reproduction is prohibited without the author's written consent; return to author when review completed."

B. What Rights Are You Transferring?

Determine what rights you are going to transfer to the publisher. Consider the following options:

rights that may be transferred to a publisher

• *All rights (i.e., copyright ownership).* Many publishers require that an author transfer or assign copyright ownership in a work, meaning that the author is left with no exclusive rights. Such arrangements are more common in book publishing than in the publishing of articles in periodicals. Authors who transfer copyright ownership in a book to a publisher typically receive in return a promise from the publisher to pay royalties at a predetermined rate and at specified intervals. Royalty agreements are also common in the transfer of copyright ownership in musical compositions. However, authors of books and composers of musical compositions sometimes agree to a specified fixed fee as their total compensation for conveying all rights in a particular work. Authors who transfer copyright ownership in an article to a periodical publisher typically receive a flat fee for their work. Note that an author who transfers all rights in a work to a publisher retains no legal rights whatever in the work. This can lead to unforeseen consequences.

> *Example. Linda writes a book and transfers her copyright ownership to a publisher in exchange for the publisher's commitment to pay Linda a royalty in the amount of 10% of the retail price of all books sold. If the retail price of the book is $20, and in 2002 the publisher sells 3,000 copies, Linda's royalty payments would be $6,000. By transferring copyright ownership, Linda retains none of the exclusive rights granted to a copyright owner under section 106. She may not, without authorization, make copies of her work, perform it, make derivative works (translations, abridgements, editions, etc.), or exercise any of the other exclusive rights. In addition, if the publisher is declared bankrupt, an author may never again be able to reclaim or reassert ownership in the copyright.*

> *Example. Lois writes an article for a religious periodical. The publisher asks for all rights, and a contract is signed conveying copyright ownership to the publisher. The article appears in January of 2002. In 2005, another publisher asks Lois for the right to publish the same article in its periodical. Lois has no right or ownership in the article, and so she must forward this request on to the original publisher. If Lois is unwilling to convey all her interests in her copyright, she should so inform the original publisher. Often, a publisher who otherwise would insist on receiving "all rights" in an article can be persuaded to accept a lesser interest.*

• *Exclusive license.* What if you are unwilling to part with copyright ownership in your book manuscript? How can you interest a publisher in publishing it? Ordinarily, the answer is an exclusive license, whereby you transfer to the publisher an exclusive license to publish the work in a specified geographical region (often the entire United States) for a specified period of time. Since such an agreement makes the publisher the sole supplier of the book, some publishers are perfectly willing to enter into such arrangements. Again, the author typically receives a royalty in exchange for granting the exclusive license. Like a transfer of copyright ownership, a transfer of an exclusive license must be in a writing signed by the person transferring the rights involved.

• *First rights (or first serial rights)*. An author who transfers first rights in an article to a periodical publisher gives the publisher the right to be the first to publish the article. The author retains all other rights in the work. First rights can be restricted to a particular country or region, such as "first United States serial rights" or "first North American serial rights."

> ***Example.*** *Pastor Larry writes an article for a religious periodical, and conveys first rights to the publisher. The article is scheduled to appear in the July 2002 issue. Pastor Larry has no legal right to publish the article in any other publication prior to July of 2002. However, once the article appears in the original publication, Pastor Larry owns all rights in the work, and can publish it in any other publication without the consent or knowledge of the original publisher. Note, however, that section 201(c) of the Copyright Act (discussed in Chapter 1) gives the publisher the right to reproduce the article in "any later collective works in the same series."*

• *One-time rights*. An author who transfers "one-time rights" in an article to a periodical publisher gives the publisher a nonexclusive right to publish the article on one occasion. There is no assurance that the publisher will be the first publisher to publish the article.

> ***Example.*** *In 1990, Peter wrote an article for a Sunday School publication that was published that same year. Peter transferred first rights to the publisher. In 2002, a religious periodical requests permission to publish the same article. Peter cannot transfer first rights to the second publisher, since the article already has been published. However, he can transfer "one-time rights," meaning that the second publisher is free to publish the article on one occasion without any assurance that it is the first to do so.*

• *Nonexclusive license*. "One-time rights" are in essence a transfer of a nonexclusive license to reproduce a work. This means that the publisher has legal authority to publish the work, but it does not have the exclusive right to do so. Book authors and composers of musical works who retain copyright ownership in their works occasionally transfer only a nonexclusive license to the publisher, meaning that the author remains free to publish the work with another publisher as well. Obviously, few publishers are interested in such an arrangement. One exception (discussed in sections 6.10 and 7.1) involves "blanket licenses" issued by publishers or some commercial companies representing several publishers. Such license agreements typically cover large repertories of sacred music. Churches that purchase such a license are authorized to make copies of listed music (e.g., transparencies, copies for the choir, bulletin inserts, and recordings) without violating the rights of copyright owners. However, a number of courts have held that such blanket licenses are legally enforceable only if they are nonexclusive. This means that a church must be able to purchase individual pieces of music without purchasing a blanket license, and it must be free to deal directly with the copyright owner rather than with the publisher or publisher's agent. Nearly all blanket license agreements are nonexclusive for this reason.

• *Simultaneous rights*. Let's assume that Anne writes an article for a Baptist Sunday School publication, and submits the same article for publication to a Methodist Sunday School publication. Both publishers agree to publish the work, and neither insists on a transfer of copyright ownership. Under these circumstances, Anne is said to have transferred "simultaneous rights" to the two publishers. Of course, this is merely another way of saying that she has transferred "one-time rights" to two publishers simultaneously. Such simultaneous transfers are common in religious periodicals, since there is relatively little overlapping in readership.

• *Subsidiary rights.* This term generally refers to many of the rights that the author of a book has in his or her work, other than publication. For example, the term includes the right to make derivative works (translations, dramatizations, abridgements, editions, etc.). Authors and publishers should carefully define which, if any, subsidiary rights are being transferred.

> ***Key point.*** *Note again that a transfer of copyright ownership, or of any one or more exclusive rights belonging to the copyright owner (under section 106 of the Copyright Act), is not valid unless "an instrument of conveyance, or a note or memorandum of the transfer, is in writing and signed by the owner of the rights conveyed . . . ." To the extent that any of the rights discussed above involves the transfer of copyright ownership or of an exclusive right, it must be in writing signed by the owner of the rights conveyed.*

> ***Key point.*** *Section 201(c) of the Copyright Act provides that "[i]n the absence of an express transfer of the copyright or of any rights under it, the owner of copyright in [a] collective work is presumed to have acquired only the privilege of reproducing and distributing the contribution as part of that particular collective work, any revision of that collective work, and any later collective work in the same series." This means that unless there has been an express transfer of more, the publisher of a periodical in which an article appears is presumed to have the privilege of reproducing the article in the periodical, in any revision of the periodical, or in later periodicals in the same series. This provision clarifies the rights of publishers of collective works (such as periodicals) in those all-too-common instances when the publisher and author fail to specify what rights are being transferred.*

> ***Example.*** *Mark writes an article for a religious periodical. The parties entered into no written agreement, and there was no understanding regarding what rights if any Mark was transferring. The publisher is presumed to have acquired the privilege of reproducing the article in the periodical, in revisions of the periodical, or in later periodicals in the same series. While no court has construed the meaning of the phrase "later collective work in the same series," it is likely that this means that the publisher has the privilege to reprint the article in future issues of the same periodical (in the same series), without Mark's authorization. This principle remains a source of considerable confusion in the publishing industry. Of course, as noted above, Mark can transfer more extensive rights to the publisher, but he apparently cannot transfer less than the basic republication "privilege" established by section 201(c).*

C. What Terms Should Be Included in a Contract with a Publisher?

terms to consider in a publishing contract

In most cases, the publisher provides a preprinted form and allows little if any variation. The courts have provided authors some relief by holding that standard publishing agreements drafted by publishers will be construed in favor of the author. This rule is based on (1) the general legal principle that ambiguities in a document should be construed against the party who drafted it (and who presumably could have avoided the ambiguities), and (2) the unfair bargaining power typically enjoyed by a publisher. Nevertheless, authors should consider the following terms when negotiating contracts with publishers:

a. Names and addresses of the parties.
b. Indicate whether or not the publisher (or author, in the case of a work made for hire) is a person, a corporation, a partnership, or an unincorporated association. In some states, an unincorporated association is not legally capable of contracting. Also, a corporation ordinarily can execute a contract only through authorized officers or representatives.
c. List the title of the work (and any alternative titles that have been used in connection with the work).

d. Indicate what kind of document is being executed (a transfer, license, assignment).

e. Describe the rights that are being transferred, and indicate whether they are exclusive or nonexclusive. This is one of the most important provisions in any publishing contract.

f. Define any geographical or time limitations. For example, is the publisher authorized to publish the work throughout the United States and in foreign countries? Is the publisher free to publish the work for the duration of the copyright?

g. Authors should consider requesting a "bail out" provision giving them the option of terminating a publishing agreement upon the occurrence of certain contingencies. For example, an author may want to reserve the right to terminate an agreement if sales of his or her work fall below a specified number in the course of a year. This is a very important right from an author's perspective.

h. Be sure to indicate who has the responsibility of renewing the copyright in a work in its first term as of January 1, 1978, if this has not already been done. Misunderstandings here can lead to a loss of some legal benefits. If the author is going to retain the copyright ownership in the work, then the agreement with the publisher should specify, for example, that the author is responsible for obtaining renewal registration. If, on the other hand, copyright ownership is being transferred to the publisher, then the agreement should indicate that the publisher is responsible for renewal registration. Works first copyrighted on or after January 1, 1978 are protected for a single copyright term, and accordingly no renewal registrations are necessary.

i. Designate the number of copies to be published in the first printing.

j. Define what, if any, subsidiary rights the publisher will have in the work (assuming that the author retains copyright ownership). For example, should the publisher have the right to make translations, abridgements, and future editions of literary works, or arrangements of musical works? What about movies, videos, and electronic publications (such as CDs and web sites)?

k. What compensation will the author receive for the rights transferred to the publisher, and how will it be paid? The author typically is given a right to periodic accountings that verify the accuracy of compensation being paid. Compensation ordinarily consists of either a flat fee or royalty payments. In either case, a fair amount should be negotiated. Also, consider whether or not advances should be paid. An advance is a prepublication payment by the publisher to the author, and usually is deducted from future royalty payments.

l. Determine what advertising and promotion the publisher will conduct, and how these expenses will be paid.

m. Many publishing contracts contain an author's warranty that he or she owns the copyright and that it does not infringe upon the rights of any other person (often called a "warranty of originality").

n. Arbitration clauses are common in publishing agreements. Such clauses require that any disputes between author and publisher be submitted to a panel of arbiters for resolution (rather than to the civil courts).

o. The agreement should be dated.

p. The parties must sign the agreement. If the publisher is a corporation, two duly authorized officers ordinarily sign on behalf of the corporation. The corporation's name must still be listed.

q. A notary's acknowledgement of each party's signature is desirable, but not required.

Endnotes

[1] Effects Associates, Inc. v. Cohen, 908 F.2d 557 (9th Cir. 1990).

[2] *See, e.g.,* Bateman v. Mnemonics, Inc., 79 F.3d 1532, 1537 n. 12 (11th Cir.1996).

[3] Papa's-June Music v. McLean, 921 F. Supp. 1154 (S.D.N.Y. 1996).

[4] Radio Television Espanola S.A. v. New World Entertainment, Ltd., 183 F.3d 922 C.A.9 1999).

[5] Tasini v. New York Times Co., 972 F. Supp. 804 (S.D.N.Y. 1997), *rev'd on other grounds,* 206 F.3d 161 (2nd Cir. 1999).

[6] In re Heritage Village Church and Missionary Fellowship, Inc., 92 B.R. 1000 (D.S.C. 1988).

[7] Tasini v. New York Times Co., 972 F. Supp. 804 (S.D.N.Y. 1997).

5

Exclusive Rights, Infringements, Remedies

5.1 Exclusive Rights

Section 106 of the copyright law gives the following six "exclusive rights" to a copyright owner:

(1) reproducing the copyrighted work in copies or phonorecords;

(2) preparing derivative works based upon the copyrighted work;

(3) distributing copies or phonorecords of the copyrighted work to the public by sale or other transfer of ownership, or by rental, lease, or lending;

(4) in the case of literary, musical, dramatic, and choreographic works, pantomimes, and motion pictures and other audiovisual works, performing the copyrighted work publicly;

(5) in the case of literary, musical, dramatic, and choreographic works, pantomimes, and pictorial, graphic, or sculptural works, including the individual images of a motion picture or other audiovisual work, displaying the copyrighted work publicly; and

(6) in the case of sound recordings, performing the copyrighted work publicly by means of a digital audio transmission.

> ***Key point.*** *Section 106A of the Copyright Act grants additional rights to authors of "works of visual art." These works include paintings, sculptures, and photographic images produced for exhibition purposes. Such works have little relevance to most churches and are not addressed in this text.*

These six exclusive rights are sometimes referred to as the rights of:

• reproduction

• adaptation

• publication

• performance

• display

These six rights comprise the "bundle of rights" that constitute or define copyright. As noted elsewhere in this book, each exclusive right may be subdivided indefinitely, and each subdivision of an exclusive right may be owned and enforced separately.

It is unlawful for anyone to violate any of the exclusive rights of a copyright owner. These rights, however, are not unlimited in scope. The approach of the Copyright Act is to set forth the copyright owner's exclusive rights in broad terms in section 106, and then to provide various limitations, qualifications, or exemptions in sections 107 through 122 of the Act. In some cases, these limitations are exemptions from infringement liability. One such limitation is the doctrine of "fair use." In other instances, the limitation takes the form of a "compulsory license" under which certain limited uses of copyrighted works are permitted upon payment of specified royalties and compliance with certain conditions. Many of the limitations on exclusive rights are discussed later in this chapter.

A. Reproduction

Section 106 of the Copyright Act gives the owner of a copyright in a work the exclusive right "to reproduce the copyrighted work in copies or phonorecords." This is perhaps the most important right that a copyright owner has, and it helps to explain the origin of the term "copyright"—i.e., the right to make copies. Read together with the relevant provisions of section 101, the right to reproduce a copyrighted work means the right to produce a material object in which the work is duplicated, transcribed, imitated, or simulated in a fixed form from which it can be "perceived, reproduced, or otherwise communicated, either directly or with the aid of a machine or device." A copyrighted work is infringed by reproducing it in whole or in any substantial part, and by duplicating it exactly or by imitation or simulation.

meaning of "reproduction"

The courts have helped to clarify the meaning of the term "reproduction." Consider the following: (1) It is now clear that the copying of a work into a different medium constitutes reproduction. To illustrate, copying a piece of sheet music onto a slide or transparency is a reproduction. (2) Copying can be done with a machine, or by hand. It is no defense to argue that a copy was made "freehand."[1] (3) Copying need not be verbatim to constitute reproduction. All that is required is that the infringing work is substantially similar to the copyrighted work, and that the infringing work was the product of copying rather than independent effort. (4) Copying constitutes a reproduction even if done for purely private purposes. It is the act of making the reproduction that violates the copyright owner's exclusive right, regardless of whether or not the infringer makes the copy for his or her own private use or distributes it publicly.[2] (5) The making of a single copy violates the copyright owner's exclusive right of reproduction. There is no requirement that multiple copies be reproduced.[3]

common church practices

It is the exclusive right of reproduction that poses the greatest risk of copyright infringement for most churches, since churches so commonly duplicate copyrighted materials. Consider just a few examples:

- fabricating transparencies

- duplicating copyrighted music for use by a choir, soloist, accompanist, or instrumental group

- printing the words of a chorus or hymn on a bulletin insert

- printing copyrighted materials in a church newsletter

- duplicating copyrighted materials in a church's educational program (e.g., Sunday School or private school)

- recording of worship services on audio and video tape and the distribution of such tapes

All of these acts, and many others, constitute potential infringements on a copyright owner's exclusive right of reproducing his or her copyrighted works. Whether infringement actually exists in a particular case will depend on the significance of the material copied both in terms of quantity and quality (see section 5.2), and the availability of one or more of the defenses to infringement discussed in Chapter 6. There is no doubt that most music publishers view the acts of copying described above to constitute copyright infringement.

> *Example.* *Pastor Mike is a minister of music. To save the church money, and to avoid copyright infringement, he transcribes by hand a copyrighted song and then makes copies for each member of the church choir. The fact that Pastor Mike made the copy by hand does not prevent the act from constituting copyright infringement.*

> *Example.* *Pastor Mike makes a transparency containing only the lyrics of a copyrighted song. He did not have authorization from the copyright owner. The making of the transparency infringes upon the copyright owner's exclusive right of reproduction.It does not matter that only the lyrics were copied (this is still a substantial reproduction of the copyrighted song), that a different "medium" was used (i.e., a transparency compared to a piece of sheet music), that the copy was made by hand, that only a single copy was made, or that Pastor Mike uses the transparency only in the course of worship services and does not otherwise distribute the work publicly.*

B. Adaptation

derivative works

Section 106 gives the copyright owner the exclusive right "to prepare derivative works based upon the copyrighted work." Section 101 defines derivative works to include "a translation, musical arrangement, dramatization, fictionalization, motion picture version, sound recording, art reproduction, abridgement, condensation, or any other form in which a work may be recast, transformed, or adapted." Only the copyright owner has the right to make a derivative work based on a copyrighted work. The making of a derivative work based on a copyrighted work without authorization from the copyright owner is an act of infringement.

> *Example.* *Dave composed a song (lyrics and music) in 1990. He owns the copyright in the work. Anne hears the song a few years later, and, without authorization, composes an arrangement using the same lyrics but different music. She has infringed upon Dave's exclusive right to make derivative works based on the original copyrighted work.*

> *Example.* *Dave writes a book in 1980. It is copyrighted in the name of the publisher that published the work. In 1990, Dave decides to write a second edition of the same*

work. He may not do so without authorization from the publisher, since only the publisher (as copyright owner) has the right to make derivative works based on the original.

C. Distribution

The copyright law gives the copyright owner the exclusive right to distribute copies or phonorecords of a copyrighted work to the public. This provision gives a copyright owner the right to control the first public distribution of an authorized copy or phonorecord of his or her work, whether by sale, gift, loan, rental, or lease. Likewise, any unauthorized public distribution of copies or phonorecords that were unlawfully made would be an infringement. As section 109 makes clear, however, the copyright owner's rights cease with respect to a particular copy or phonorecord once he or she has parted with ownership of it, meaning that a purchaser of an authorized copy of a work can later sell or in any other manner dispose of that particular copy.

D. Performance

A copyright owner has the exclusive right to publicly perform literary, musical, dramatic, and choreographic works, pantomimes, and motion pictures and other audiovisual works. To "perform" a work, according to the definition in section 101, includes reading a literary work aloud (book, article, etc.), singing or playing music, dancing a choreographic work, and acting out a dramatic work or pantomime. A performance is "public," according to section 101, if it takes place at a place open to the public or at any place where a substantial number of persons outside of a normal circle of a family and its social acquaintances is gathered. Performances in semipublic places such as schools, churches, and summer camps ordinarily are considered public performances.

broadcasts What about a live performance that is transmitted to the public via radio or television? For example, let's assume that the morning worship services at a church are broadcast over a local radio station. What is the effect of such an arrangement? There are two considerations to note. First, if there are no copyrighted songs or other copyrighted materials performed during the service, there ordinarily will not be a problem in broadcasting the service. Second, even if copyrighted music is performed during the service, such a performance is exempt from copyright infringement so long as it occurs in the course of a religious service at a church or other place of religious assembly. However, this exemption (which is discussed fully in Chapter 6) does not extend to public broadcasting over radio or television. Such transmission of the performance of copyrighted materials constitutes a separate performance, since under section 101 the concept of public performance covers not only the initial performance but also any further act by which that performance is transmitted or communicated to the public.[4] In most cases, such public broadcasts will not constitute an infringement upon the copyright owner's exclusive right of performance if the radio or television station has an appropriate license with ASCAP, BMI, SESAC, or some other performing rights society. It should be the broadcaster's responsibility to ensure that it can broadcast worship services containing live performances of copyrighted materials, though it would be prudent for churches that broadcast their services to question the broadcaster regarding the scope and coverage of its license agreements with the various performing rights societies.

E. Display

A copyright owner has the exclusive right to display publicly a copyrighted literary, musical, dramatic, or choreographic work, pantomime, or audiovisual work. Section 101 defines "display" as the showing of a copy of a work "either directly or by means of a film, slide, television image, or any other device or process . . . ." Note that this definition covers any showing of a "copy" of a work. Since "copies" are defined as including the material object in which the work is first fixed, the right of public display applies to original works as well as to reproductions of them. In addition to the direct showings of a copy of a work, a "display" would include the projection of an image on a screen or other surface by any method, the transmission of an image by electronic or other means, and the showing of an image on a cathode ray tube or similar apparatus connected with any sort of information storage and retrieval system (i.e., a computer monitor).

The exclusive right of the copyright owner extends only to public displays of the copyrighted work. As noted above, according to section 101, a performance or display is "public" if it occurs at a place open to the public or at any place where a substantial number of persons outside of a normal circle of a family and its social acquaintances is gathered. Performances in semipublic places such as schools, churches, and summer camps ordinarily will be public performances.

5.2 Infringement

Section 501 of the Copyright Act states that "[a]nyone who violates any of the exclusive rights of the copyright owner . . . is an infringer of the copyright." Of the six exclusive rights, the one causing the most difficulties for churches is the copyright owner's exclusive right to reproduce the work (i.e., make copies).

> *Key point. Copyright infringement does not require that the infringer "intends" to violate one or more of the copyright owner's exclusive rights. In many cases infringers "innocently" commit copyright infringement in the sense that they do not realize that what they are doing is wrong. This is no defense to liability.*

verbatim copying

similarity

Obviously, an infringement occurs when someone makes a verbatim copy of copyrighted material. But what if someone produces a work that is similar but not identical to another's copyrighted work? Can this constitute infringement on the copyright owner's exclusive right of reproduction? To illustrate, what if Joan writes an article that is published in a periodical in 2000, and that Gary submits an article to another periodical in 2002 that is very similar to Joan's work. Does Gary's article constitute infringement (i.e., an unauthorized reproduction of Joan's material)? The courts generally have resolved this question by applying the following presumption—access by the alleged infringer to the copyrighted material, plus substantial similarity between the allegedly infringing material and the copyrighted work, creates a presumption of infringement. The alleged infringer of course can claim that his work was an independent creation. However, the closer the similarity between the two works, the less likely it is that such a claim will prevail. Other relevant factors to consider in such a case would be the experience and training of the alleged infringer, his previous publishing record, the likelihood that he was capable of independently producing the work, and prior instances of infringement on his part. Some copyright owners intentionally insert errors in their works. The alleged infringer's claim of independent creation will seldom succeed if such errors are duplicated.

The House Report to the Copyright Act of 1976 specifies that "wide departures or variations from the copyrighted work would still be an infringement as long as the author's 'expression' rather than merely the author's 'ideas' are taken."[5]

> *Key point. Copying rarely is proven by direct evidence, since copiers usually deny that they were engaged in copying. Keep in mind two rules that the courts apply. First, a presumption of copying arises if there is proof of "access" by the alleged infringer to the original work, plus substantial similarity between the two works. Second, if access to the original work cannot be proven, then a presumption of copying may arise if the degree of similarity between the original work and the alleged copy is "striking."*

> *Key point. What is "substantial similarity"? Most courts apply the "ordinary person" test: Is the alleged copy so similar to the original that an ordinary reasonable person would conclude that the alleged copier unlawfully appropriated the owner's*

material? This test does not involve "analytic dissection and expert testimony," but depends rather on whether the alleged copy has captured the "total concept and feel" of the copyrighted work.[6]

paraphrasing

What about paraphrasing? If Gary's work (in the example used above) did not contain any "word-for-word" copying of Joan's material, but rather consisted of a paraphrase of it, can he prevail against Joan's charge of infringement? Probably not, since a number of courts have held that "paraphrasing is tantamount to copying in copyright law."[7] Another court has observed that copying "cannot be limited literally to the text, else a plagiarist would escape by immaterial variations."[8]

copying small portions

Another difficult question is the verbatim copying of only small portions of copyrighted material. When does such use constitute infringement on the copyright owner's exclusive right of reproduction? There is no easy answer to this question. Courts generally evaluate both the quantity of copyrighted material that is copied verbatim, and its quality. That is, what percentage of the copyrighted work was copied, and how much of the allegedly infringing work consisted of the copied material? Further, how significant was the "quality" of the copied material? Was it the essence of the work as a whole, or was it incidental or insignificant?

Copies violating the copyright owner's right of reproduction

examples of infringement

To illustrate, the courts have found copying of the following amounts of copyrighted material to constitute copyright infringement:

- two identical bars of a musical work[9]

- four notes and two words, which comprised the "heart of the composition"[10]

- three sentences (that were used for advertising purposes)[11]

- three sentences[12]

- eight sentences[13]

- less than one percent of the copyrighted work[14]

- the phrase "put on a happy face"[15]

- summaries of copyrighted reports, even though the copier cited the owner as the source of the information[16]

- 20 articles out of 90,000 (the court quoted from an opinion by a famous judge, "no plagiarist can excuse the wrong by showing how much of his work he did not pirate")[17]

Copies not violating the copyright owner's right of reproduction

examples of non-infringement

Copying of the following portions of copyrighted material was held not to constitute infringement upon the copyright owner's exclusive right of reproduction:

- a sentence and a half[18]

- sixteen words[19]

- two sentences[20]

- the musical notes comprising the melodies of the original song and the allegedly infringing song did not share significant amounts of either pitch or rhythm; at no place in the two songs were three musical notes in a row the same; the chord progressions of both songs, which are known as "I-IV-V progressions," are "the most common chord progressions in all of the music of Western civilization"; the chord changes are the same in only four out of twenty chord changes in the songs; no two melodic phrases in the two songs have the same rhythm; the lyrics of the songs have only six words in common, consisting of a phrase that is not unique or original to either song and that appears in at least eight songs that predate the songs involved in this case[21]

- 50 words copied from a 12,000-word book[22]

- direct quotations from a copyrighted biography comprised between .01% and .34% of the alleging infringing works, and were for "informational" rather than "creative" purposes[23]

- 5% of 12 works and 8% of 11 other works, each copy comprising only a few pages in length[24]

- "inclusion of 4.3% of published copyrighted work is not incompatible with a finding of fair use"[25]

church practices

Such precedent leaves little doubt that many reproductions of copyrighted materials by churches will constitute an infringement of the exclusive right of copyright owners to reproduce their works. To cite just a few examples, the copying of copyrighted chorus or hymn lyrics onto a transparency or bulletin insert ordinarily will amount to an infringement, since a substantial quantity of the original work is reproduced, the amount reproduced is significant in terms of quality, and the copy serves the same function as the original work.

To illustrate, in one case a publisher reproduced the chorus lyrics of two famous copyrighted songs in songsheet pamphlets, maintaining that the reproduction of only chorus lyrics of copyrighted songs was so trivial in nature and amount as to constitute noninfringing fair use. The court found such reproductions to be an infringement, and rejected the publisher's claim that its reproductions constituted fair use. Though only the chorus lyrics were reproduced (and not the regular verse lines or music), the court found that "the chorus of a musical composition may constitute a material and substantial part of the work and it is frequently the very part that makes it popular and valuable."[26] Similarly, another court found the reproduction of chorus lyrics in a song sheet magazine to be an infringement rather than fair use, since the reproduction "met the same demand on the same market" as the original.[27] The courts in each of these two cases gave a narrow interpretation of fair use because the function served by the infringing use directly satisfied a function that was served by the copyright owner's sheet music.

Obviously, verbatim copying of the lyrics and melody of a copyrighted musical work (for use by the choir, a soloist, an accompanist, or an instrumental group) would constitute infringement.

> *Key point.* One judge has observed, "Copyright law does not admit of simple, bright-line rules. . . . It is not possible to determine infringement through a simple word count; the quantitative analysis of two works must always occur in the shadow of their qualitative nature. For example, different quantities of use may be required to support a finding of substantial similarity depending on whether the use is a direct quotation of a fictional work, or a paraphrase of a factual compilation."[28]

5.3 Remedies

What legal remedies are available to a copyright owner whose copyrighted work has been infringed? This section will review the major remedies established under the Copyright Act.

A. Injunctions

Section 502 provides that a court may "grant temporary and final injunctions on such terms as it may deem reasonable to prevent or restrain infringement of a copyright." An injunction is a court order directing an individual to do or not to do some specified act. Noncompliance with such an order typically will constitute contempt of court.

A number of courts have held that a preliminary injunction is available if four factors are present: (1) a likelihood of success on the merits; (2) the copyright owner will suffer irreparable harm if injunctive relief is not granted; (3) the harm to the copyright owner if relief is denied is significantly greater than the harm to the alleged infringer if relief is granted; and (4) the public interest will be served by granting the relief. Permanent ("final") injunctions generally are available whenever copyright infringement has been established in a court of law, and there is a threat of continued acts of infringement.

B. Impounding and Disposition of Infringing Items

Section 503 specifies that a court, at any time after an infringement lawsuit is filed, "may order the impounding, on such terms as it may deem reasonable, of all copies or phonorecords claimed to have been made or used in violation of the copyright owner's exclusive rights . . . ." The same section further provides that if a court determines that infringement has occurred, it can "order the destruction or other reasonable disposition of all copies or phonorecords found to have been made or used in violation of the copyright owner's exclusive rights . . . ."

C. Actual Damages and Profits

Section 504(a) provides that "an infringer of copyright is liable for either (1) the copyright owner's actual damages and any additional profits of the infringer . . . or (2) statutory damages . . . ." Accordingly, the remedies of actual damages plus profits or statutory damages are in the alternative, and a copyright owner can choose to pursue only one of them. As was seen in a previous chapter, statutory damages will not be available to some copyright owners (e.g., owners of unregistered works), and in such cases the copyright owner has no choice under section 504 but to seek actual damages plus the infringer's profits. The remedy of actual damages plus profits will be summarized in this subsection, and the remedy of statutory damages in the following subsection.

Section 504(b) specifies that "[t]he copyright owner is entitled to recover the actual damages suffered by him or her as a result of the infringement, and any profits of the infringer that are attributable to the infringement and are not taken into account in computing the actual damages." How can a copyright owner compute actual damages? This has proven to be a very difficult task. In fact, the difficulty of proving actual damages prompted Congress to add the statutory damages provision. Copyright owners, in an attempt to prove actual damages, generally have tried to establish the fair market value of their copyright, and then base damages on the degree to which the copyright has been impaired by the act of infringement. Obviously, this is an inherently difficult task. In addition to actual damages, a copyright owner may recover any profits generated by the infringer that are attributable to the infringement. Proving the amount of such profits has proven as difficult a task as proving the copyright owner's actual damages. Section 504(b) specifies that "[i]n establishing the infringer's profits, the copyright owner is required to present proof only of the infringer's gross revenue, and the infringer is required to prove his or her deductible expenses and the elements of profit attributable to factors other than the copyrighted work." Some courts have awarded higher statutory damages in cases where infringement has occurred, but the amount of the copyright owner's damages and the infringer's profits cannot be established with sufficient certainty.

D. Statutory Damages

$750 to $30,000

A copyright owner whose work has been infringed may elect to recover statutory damages instead of actual damages plus the infringer's profits. Because of the difficulty in proving actual damages and infringer's profits, copyright owners frequently prefer to pursue statutory damages. Section 504(c) specifies that

> the copyright owner may elect, at any time before final judgment is rendered, to recover, instead of actual damages and profits, an award of statutory damages for all infringements involved in the action, with respect to any one work, for which any one infringer is liable individually, or for which any two or more infringers are liable jointly and severally, in a sum of not less than $750 or more than $30,000 as the court considers just. For the purposes of this subsection, all the parts of a compilation or derivative work constitute one work.

> In a case where the copyright owner sustains the burden of proving, and the court finds, that infringement was committed willfully, the court in its discretion may increase the award of statutory damages to a sum of not more than $150,000. In a case where the infringer sustains the burden of proving, and the court finds, that such infringer was not aware and had no reason to believe that his or her acts constituted an infringement of copyright, the court in its discretion may reduce the award of statutory damages to a sum of not less than $200.

Statutory damages are awarded in the discretion of the court whenever they are elected by a copyright owner who has established that one or more of his or her exclusive rights has been infringed. Perhaps the most important feature of statutory damages is that they are not dependent upon proof of actual damages. Rather, they are awarded automatically, in the discretion of a court, once infringement has been established. Section 504 establishes a maximum and a minimum amount of statutory damages, and authorizes the courts to choose whatever amount between and including such amounts that they consider to be "just". A number of important aspects of statutory damages are considered below:

(1) *general rule*

As a general rule, when a copyright owner elects to recover statutory damages, a court is obliged to award between $750 and $30,000.

(2) *minimum statutory damages*

$750

While minimum statutory damages generally are $750 for "all infringements involved in an action, with respect to any one work," section 504(c) goes on to provide that a court has the discretion to reduce the statutory damages from $750 to $200 if the infringer "sustains the burden of proving, and the court finds, that such infringer was not aware and had no reason to believe that his or her acts constituted an infringement of copyright . . . ." In addition, section 504(c)(2) provides that when a teacher, librarian, or archivist working for a nonprofit educational institution infringes copyrighted material in the honest belief that what he or she was doing constituted fair use, a court is prevented from awarding any statutory damages. The burden of proof with respect to an infringer's good faith rests with the copyright owner.

Example. A teacher at a religious school constituting a nonprofit educational institution makes copies of a copyrighted article for each member of her class in the honest belief that what she was doing constituted fair use. Unless the copyright owner can prove that the teacher was not in fact acting in good faith, the teacher's action, assuming that it constitutes copyright infringement, cannot be the basis for statutory damages.

(3) *maximum statutory damages*

$30,000 ($150,000 if intentional)

A court, in its discretion, may award statutory damages of up to $30,000 for "all infringements involved in an action, with respect to any one work." However, if a copyright owner proves, and a court agrees, that infringement was committed willfully, the court in its discretion may increase the award of statutory damages to $150,000. Unfortunately, "willfully" is not defined anywhere in the Copyright Act, but court rulings generally have interpreted the term to mean knowledge by the infringer that (a) his or her conduct amounts to infringement, and (b) no defenses are reasonably available.[29]

Example. A religious radio station that broadcasts copyrighted religious music without permission was found guilty of "willful infringement" and was assessed statutory damages of $52,500. The station manager admitted that he played copyrighted songs on the radio and that he had no license or permission to do so. He defended his actions by noting that "the artists have publicly stated their intent to minister through their Christian music" and that "their intent to minister is further accomplished by radio stations broadcasting their music to a listening audience." The court rejected this reasoning and assessed statutory damages of $52,500 against the station for willful copyright infringement. The court based this result on 15 proven infringements at $3,500 each. The court also ordered the station to pay the attorneys' fees the copyright owners incurred in maintaining their infringement lawsuit. This case serves as a useful reminder of the consequences associated with the willful infringement of another's copyright. It is common for church leaders to assume that they can infringe upon religious music or literature at will since the writers and composers of such material obviously had a religious motivation and in effect have "donated" their work to the church. Not only is this assumption inappropriate, but as this case demonstrates, it can lead to statutory damages for willful infringement.[30]

(4) *multiple infringements by one infringer of the same work*

Section 504(c)(1) specifies that a copyright owner may elect to recover statutory damages "for all infringements involved in the action, with respect to any one work, for which any one infringer is liable individually . . . ." The House Report to the Copyright Act of 1976 further specifies that "[a] single infringer of a single work is liable for a single amount between [$750] and [$30,000], no matter how many acts of infringement are involved in the action and regardless of whether the acts were separate, isolated, or occurred in a related series."[31] These statements seem to place beyond any doubt the principle that a copyright owner may recover only a single award of statutory damages despite repeated infringements of a particular copyrighted work by the same infringer.

To illustrate, if a church music director makes a copy (without authorization) of a copyrighted song for each of the 50 members of the church choir, and the copyright owner elects statutory damages, then apparently only a *single* award of statutory damages is available (assuming that the copyright owner brings an infringement action involving all of the allegedly infringing works). The copyright owner cannot receive a separate award for each of the 50 separate copies that were made of the same copyrighted work. Of course, a court is free to award a higher amount of statutory damages based on the number of copies that were made, and could award up to $150,000 if the copies were made willfully. However, only a single award of statutory damages would be available. This discussion assumes that the reference in section 504(c) to "all infringements involved in the action" refers to the lawsuit rather than to the transaction involved in the infringement. This seems to be the most sensible and natural interpretation, and it is certainly consistent with the provisions of the House Report quoted above.

A few courts have concluded that the reference in section 504(c) to "all infringements involved in *the action*" refers to the infringing transaction rather than to the lawsuit. Such an interpretation, though seemingly contrary to the wording of the House Report, would allow separate awards of statutory damages for each act of infringement.[32] Alternatively, a copyright owner in the example cited above could file 50 infringement lawsuits (i.e., 50 "actions") against the infringing party (the music director or the church), and elect statutory damages in each case. While not free from doubt, there is the possibility that this tactic could avoid the limitation on multiple awards of statutory damages for "all infringements involved in the same action, with respect to any one work, for which any one infringer is liable individually . . . ." And, it is possible that a court, in the interests of "judicial economy," would order all 50 lawsuits consolidated into a single action, while retaining the right of the copyright owner to seek multiple awards of statutory damages. Some courts have reached this very conclusion.[33] As a result, one cannot say that multiple infringements of a single copyrighted work by a single infringer will necessarily entitle the copyright owner to only a single award of statutory damages (assuming that statutory damages are elected). It is conceivable that a court would allow multiple awards based on the factors discussed above. If this is so, then the music director's act of making 50 copies of a copyrighted song (in the illustration described above) for each member of the church choir could result in statutory damages of $750 (or such other amount as the court deems just) times 50 ($37,500) rather than a single award. The possibility of such a result must be taken into account when evaluating the propriety of church copying activities.

(5) *compilations*

Section 504(c)(1) specifies that for the purposes of computing statutory damages, "all the parts of a compilation or derivative work constitute one work." This is a significant provision, and apparently was designed to prevent astronomical awards of statutory damages that otherwise would result from the unauthorized reproduction of compilations. For example, assume that XYZ Publishing Company prepared a hymnal containing 200 hymns, 125 of which are still protected by copyright. A church music director makes an unauthorized copy of the hymnal for her library. If XYZ Publishing Company sues the music director and a court awards the minimum amount of statutory damages, will XYZ receive a single award of $750 or an aggregate award of $93,750 ($750 times 125 copyrighted songs in the compilation)? Section 504(c)(1) seems to resolve this question unequivocally in favor of the single award of $750 because of its statement that "all parts of a compilation or derivative work constitute one work." But what if several copies of a compilation are made? For example, assume that XYZ Publishing Company publishes a chorus booklet containing 40 copyrighted songs, and that a church music director makes 100 unauthorized copies of the booklet on church duplicating equipment for use by the church congregation. While no court has addressed this question under the current copyright law, it is likely that the award of statutory damages in such a case would be limited to a single award of $750 based on the principles discussed in the preceding paragraphs. However, as noted before, it is conceivable that XYZ could avoid the limitations on statutory damages for multiple infringements by bringing 100 separate infringement suits.

chorus booklets

A common practice among churches is the fabrication of their own "compilations" consisting of chorus or song booklets containing several copyrighted musical works. To illustrate, assume that a church prepares a "chorus booklet" containing 50 popular copyrighted choruses, and then makes 200 copies of the booklet that are inserted in hymnal racks in the church sanctuary. Also assume that there is a different copyright owner for each of the 50 choruses. What would the statutory damages be in such a case, assuming that a court awards the minimum amount of $750? There are four possibilities: (1) a single award of $750 that must be apportioned among the 50 copyright owners whose works are represented in the compilation; (2) $37,500 ($750 per violation times 50 copyrighted works); (3) $150,000 ($750 per booklet times 200 unauthorized copies); or

(4) $7,500,000 ($750 times fifty copyrighted works times 200 unauthorized copies). Note carefully that the limitations applicable to compilations discussed above ordinarily would not apply in such a case since the church is not reproducing or otherwise infringing upon an existing compilation. Rather, it is independently making copies of individual copyrighted works and then compiling those copies in its own compilation. As a result, there seems to be little basis for applying the first option mentioned above (a single award of $750).

The second option ($37,500) appears to be the most consistent with the plain meaning of section 504(c)(1) of the Copyright Act, which specifies that a copyright owner may elect to recover a single award of statutory damages "for all infringements involved in the action, with respect to any one work, for which any one infringer is liable individually . . . ." The House Report to the Copyright Act of 1976 further specifies that "[a] single infringer of a single work is liable for a single amount between [$750] and [$30,000], no matter how many acts of infringement are involved in the action and regardless of whether the acts were separate, isolated, or occurred in a related series." As a result, it seems logical to conclude that the church will be liable, at a minimum, for statutory damages of $750 times the number of copyrighted works that were infringed (50).

The third approach ($150,000) is unlikely since it bases statutory damages on the number of unauthorized copies of a work that the infringer makes without reference to the number of works involved. This clearly contravenes section 504(c)(1). The fourth option ($7,500,000) is unlikely as well, since it also bases statutory damages upon the number of copies of a copyrighted work that the infringer unlawfully copies. This approach is in opposition to the principles outlined in the preceding section dealing with multiple infringements by one infringer of the same "work". As noted in that section, the House Report to the Copyright Act of 1976 specifies that "[a] single infringer of a single work is liable for a single amount between [$750] and [$30,000], no matter how many acts of infringement are involved in the action and regardless of whether the acts were separate, isolated, or occurred in a related series." These statements seem to place beyond any doubt the principle that a copyright owner may recover only a single award of statutory damages despite repeated infringements of a particular copyrighted work by the same infringer. Therefore, though the church made 200 unauthorized copies of each work, the copyright owners presumably cannot recover more than a single award of statutory damages apiece. However, as noted in the preceding section, it is possible that each of the 50 copyright owners in the example cited above could file 200 infringement lawsuits (i.e., 200 "actions") against the infringing party and elect statutory damages in each case. Under this approach, each copyright owner (50 in all) could collect $150,000 ($750 times 200), which would amount to a total of $7,500,000 in damages. While not free from doubt, there is the possibility that this tactic could avoid the limitation on multiple awards of statutory damages for "all infringements involved in the same action, with respect to any one work, for which any one infringer is liable individually . . . ." And, it is possible that a court, in the interests of "judicial economy," would order all 200 lawsuits consolidated into a single action, while retaining the right of the copyright owner to seek multiple awards of statutory damages. While this result is unlikely, it must be viewed as a possibility when evaluating the propriety of church practices and procedures.

(6) *multiple infringements by the same infringer of different works of the same owner*

Nothing in section 504 prevents a copyright owner from receiving separate awards of statutory damages from an infringer who infringes upon more than one of his or her copyrighted works. In this regard, the House Report to the Copyright Act of 1976 provides that "[w]here the suit involves infringement of more than one separate and independent work, minimum statutory damages for each work must be awarded. For example, if one defendant has infringed three copyrighted works, the copyright owner is entitled to statutory damages of at least [$2,250] and may be awarded up to [$90,000]." [34]

(7) *infringements of multiple exclusive rights*

Earlier in this chapter, the important point was made that each exclusive right may be subdivided indefinitely by the copyright owner. This raises the question of the proper manner of assessing statutory damages in cases where a copyright owner has transferred various exclusive rights in a particular work to two or more persons, and those exclusive rights are thereafter infringed upon by one or more individuals. Should each owner of an exclusive right in the same work be entitled to a separate award of statutory damages? The House Report to the Copyright Act of 1976 answers this question in the negative, by providing that "although the minimum and maximum amounts are to be multiplied where multiple 'works' are involved in the suit, the same is not true with respect to multiple copyrights, multiple owners, multiple exclusive rights, or multiple registrations. This point is especially important since, under a scheme of divisible copyright, it is possible to have the rights of a number of owners of separate 'copyrights' in a single 'work' infringed by one act of a defendant." [35]

(8) *registration*

Several benefits associated with copyright registration were summarized in Chapter 2. One of those benefits is eligibility for statutory damages. Section 412 specifies that "no award of statutory damages . . . shall be made for (1) any infringement of copyright in an unpublished work commenced before the effective date of its registration, or (2) any infringement of copyright commenced after first publication of the work and before the effective date of its registration, unless such registration is made within three months after the first publication of the work."

> **Example.** *A federal court in Massachusetts ruled that a trade show organizer was liable for copyright infringement occurring because of the unauthorized performance of copyrighted music by 6 of 2,000 exhibitors at a national trade show. This was so despite the fact that the organizer's contract with exhibitors contained a statement instructing exhibitors to comply with copyright law. This did not shift liability. The court concluded that the organizer retained sufficient control over the exhibitors to make it responsible for their copyright infringement. Control was demonstrated by (1) the rules and regulations that the organizer had established for exhibitors; (2) agents of the organizer circulated among the exhibitors to "ensure compliance" with the rules and regulations; (3) agents of the organizer were available during the convention to address exhibitor needs and respond to complaints; and (4) the organizer had the authority to restrict exhibits that were objectionable. The court stressed that the organizer could have prohibited exhibitors from playing or performing copyrighted music, but did not. The fact that exhibitors' contracts required them to comply with the copyright law did not prevent the organizer from liability for the exhibitors' copyright infringements, since the organizer "must shoulder responsibility when the instruction is not followed." The court awarded damages of $1,000 for each violation (a total of $6,000).* [36]

> **Example.** *A federal appeals court ruled that copyright infringement had occurred even though only lyrics were copied. The court observed: "Song lyrics enjoy independent copyright protection as literary works . . . and the right to print a song's lyrics is exclusively that of the copyright holder. . . . A time-honored method of facilitating singing along with music has been to furnish the singer with a printed copy of the lyrics. Copyright holders have always enjoyed exclusive rights over such copies. While projecting lyrics on a screen and producing printed copies of the lyrics, of course, have their differences, there is no reason to treat them differently for purposes of the Copyright Act." Many churches make unauthorized copies of song lyrics. Sometimes the lyrics are printed in a church bulletin. In other cases they are duplicated onto a transparency. In either case, or in any other case when lyrics are copied without authorization, copyright infringement has occurred. Church leaders need to understand that lyrics are entitled to copyright protection independently from the musical score.* [37]

Example. A federal appeals court ruled that a church violated the copyright law when it publicly distributed an unauthorized copy of copyrighted materials. The Church of Jesus Christ of Latter-Day Saints (the "Church") acquired a single copy of a copyrighted genealogical text and made several unauthorized copies which were distributed to the Church's "branch libraries." When the copyright owner learned of the Church's actions, it demanded that further distribution be stopped immediately. The Church recalled and destroyed many of the copies that it had made. It was concerned that nine libraries continued to possess unauthorized copies, and it wrote them each a letter asking them to locate and return any offending copies. The copyright owner visited a number of libraries, and found unauthorized copies at two locations. The owner sued the Church for copyright infringement. A federal appeals court ruled that the Church might be liable for copyright infringement. It observed: "A copyright infringement is a violation of any of the exclusive rights of the copyright owner. One of those exclusive rights is the right to distribute copies . . . of the copyrighted work to the public by sale or other transfer of ownership, or by rental, lease, or lending. Generally, as permitted by what is known as the first-sale doctrine, the copyright owner's right to distribute a copyrighted work does not prevent the owner of a lawful copy of the work from selling, renting, lending, or otherwise disposing of the lawful copy. For example, a library may lend an authorized copy of a book that it lawfully owns without violating the copyright laws. However, distributing unlawful copies of a copyrighted work does violate the copyright owner's distribution right and, as a result, constitutes copyright infringement. In order to establish distribution of a copyrighted work, a party must show that an unlawful copy was disseminated to the public." The court agreed with the copyright owner in this case that when a library "adds a work to its collection, lists the work in its index or catalog system, and makes the work available to the borrowing or browsing public, it has completed all the steps necessary for distribution to the public."[38]

Example. A federal appeals court ruled that Andrew Lloyd Webber may have engaged in copyright infringement of a religious song composed by Ray Repp, a composer of liturgical music. Ray Repp has written religious music for more than thirty years, and is a leading composer and performer of liturgical folk music. His music is included in many hymnals and songbooks, and has been published by the Lutheran, Episcopal, Presbyterian, and Catholic churches as well as by the Church of the Brethren. In 1978 he wrote the song "Till You." The song is liturgical in nature, and is based on passages from the Book of Luke commonly known as the "Magnificat." It has been distributed on albums, cassettes, and 25,000 copies of sheet music. Repp claimed that Andrew Lloyd Webber had access to this song and unlawfully copied it in writing the "Phantom Song" in his musical "The Phantom of the Opera." A federal district court dismissed the lawsuit largely on the basis of Webber's own testimony that he never heard the song, that he disliked "pop church music," and that his interest in church music was limited to the "English choral tradition." Repp appealed, and a federal appeals court reversed the district court's ruling and ordered the case to proceed to trial. The court noted that "if the two works are so strikingly similar as to preclude the possibility of independent creation, copying may be proved without a showing of access." The court continued: "While there was little, if any, evidence demonstrating access, there was considerable evidence that Phantom Song is so strikingly similar to 'Till You' as to preclude the possibility of independent creation and to allow access to be inferred without direct proof." In support of its conclusion, the court referred to two expert musicologists who had *testified that there was "no doubt" that Webber's "Phantom Song" was strikingly similar to and based upon "Till You."* [39]

E. Costs and Attorneys' Fees

Section 505 specifies that in any infringement lawsuit the court "in its discretion may allow the recovery of full costs by or against any party . . . [and] may also award a reasonable attorney's fee to the prevailing party as part of the costs."

F. Criminal Offenses

Section 506 lists four types of criminal offenses: willful infringement for profit, fraudulent use of a copyright notice, fraudulent removal of a copyright notice, and knowingly false representations in connection with a copyright application. Conviction of criminal infringement may result in a fine of up to $250,000, imprisonment for up to 5 years, or both. In addition, a court is empowered to order the seizure, forfeiture, and destruction or other disposition of infringing copies.

5.4 Liability of Churches for the Copyright Infringement of Employees

Can a church be liable for the copyright infringements of its staff? What about for the infringements of volunteers, such as youth workers and Sunday School teachers? Churches can be liable for copyright infringement in any of the following three ways:

(1) *direct copyright infringement*

direct infringement   A church may directly commit copyright infringement by its own actions. For example, if a church creates a web site that includes unauthorized copies of copyrighted material, the church would be directly liable for violating the copyright owner's exclusive right of reproduction. Or, if a church records worship services in which copyrighted music was performed, the church has infringed upon the copyright owners' exclusive right of reproduction.

(2) *contributory copyright infringement*

contributory infringement   The Copyright Act does not limit liability for copyright infringement to direct infringers. Section 501 states that "anyone who violates any of the exclusive rights of the copyright owner . . . is an infringer of the copyright." The courts have ruled that "third parties" can be liable for copyright infringement on the basis of either contributory or vicarious copyright infringement.

The most often-quoted definition of contributory infringement was provided by a federal appeals court:

> [O]ne who, with knowledge of the infringing activity, induces, causes or materially contributes to the infringing conduct of another, may be held liable as a contributory infringer. [40]

This definition demonstrates that contributory liability requires that the secondary infringer "know or have reason to know" of direct infringement. Knowledge of specific acts of infringement is not required. One court has observed that "if a computer system operator learns of specific infringing material available on his system and fails to purge such material from the system, the operator knows of and contributes to direct infringement." [41]

Contributory copyright infringement also requires that the secondary infringer "materially contribute" to the infringing conduct. Material contribution can include providing the "site and facilities" for the infringing conduct.

(3) *vicarious copyright infringement*

vicarious infringement

Vicarious copyright liability is an "outgrowth" of the doctrine of respondeat superior. Under this doctrine an employer is liable for the acts of its employees committed within the scope of their employment. Therefore, a church may be liable on the basis of vicarious copyright infringement for the acts of direct copyright infringement by its employees committed within the scope of their employment. However, the principle of vicarious copyright liability goes well beyond infringement by employees while at work. It also extends to cases in which an organization "has the right and ability to supervise the infringing activity and also has a direct financial interest in such activities." [42] Under this expanded definition, it is possible for churches to be liable for many acts of direct copyright infringement by their employees and others. All that is required is that a church have a right to supervise an infringing activity and a direct financial interest in that activity.

A right of supervision exists whenever a church has the authority to access and inspect its computers. Such authority often is expressly given in a computer use policy. One court has noted that "to escape imposition of vicarious liability, the reserved right to police must be exercised to its fullest extent. Turning a blind eye to detectable acts of infringement for the sake of profit gives rise to liability. . . . [F]ailure to police the conduct of the primary infringer leads to imposition of vicarious liability for copyright infringement." [43]

Vicarious liability is sometimes justified on the ground that it will create "a greater incentive for the enterprise to police its operations carefully to avoid unnecessary losses." [44]

Key point. *The Supreme Court has noted that the "lines between direct infringement, contributory infringement, and vicarious liability are not clearly drawn."* [45]

Example. *In 1987 a standard file format for the storage of audio recordings in a digital format was established that became known as MP3. With appropriate software, a computer operator can copy an audio compact disk (CD) directly onto a computer's hard drive by compressing the audio information on the CD into the MP3 format. The MP3's compressed format allows for rapid transmission of digital audio files from one computer to another by electronic mail. Napster is a company that promoted the sharing of MP3 files through a process called "peer-to-peer" file sharing. Users simply went to the Napster internet site, downloaded software, and then were able to transfer exact copies of the contents of MP3 files from one computer to another via the internet. This allowed users to "download" exact digital copies of a vast array of popular copyrighted songs. A group of music publishers sued Napster in federal court. The publishers claimed that Napster was a "contributory and vicarious" copyright infringer, and they asked the court to issue an injunction prohibiting Napster from "from engaging in, or facilitating others in copying, downloading, uploading, transmitting, or distributing" copyrighted music. The court issued the injunction, and Napster appealed. A federal appeals court ruled that Napster had engaged in copyright infringement, and it sustained the district court's injunction. The appeals court concluded that Napster users infringe at least two of the copyright holders' exclusive rights—the rights of reproduction and distribution. Napster users who upload files for others to copy violate the copyright holder's exclusive right of public distribution. And, Napster users who download files containing copyrighted music violate the copyright holder's exclusive right of reproduction. The court concluded that Napster was liable for the users' acts of copyright infringement on the basis of* *"contributory copyright infringement." It explained, "one who, with knowledge of the infringing activity, induces, causes or materially contributes to the infringing conduct of another, may be held liable as a contributory infringer. Put differently, liability exists if the defendant engages in personal conduct that encourages or assists the infringement." The court noted that Napster had "actual, specific knowledge of direct infringement" by its users, and concluded that "if a computer system operator learns of specific infringing material available on his system and fails to purge such material from the system, the operator knows of and contributes to direct infringement." The court also found Napster liable for its users' acts of copyright infringement on the basis of "vicarious copyright infringement." It defined vicarious infringement as infringement that is imputed to an employer because of acts of infringement by its employees in the course of their employment. But it concluded that vicarious liability also can be imputed to a defendant that "has the right and ability to supervise the infringing activity and also has a direct financial interest in such activities." The court ruled that this test was met in this case. Not only did Napster have a direct financial interest in the infringing activity of its users (its future revenue were directly dependent upon "increases in userbase"), but it also had the ability to supervise its users' conduct. The court noted that Napster's ability to block infringers' access for any reason was evidence of the right and ability to supervise, and that "to escape imposition of vicarious liability, the reserved right to police must be exercised to its fullest extent. Turning a blind eye to detectable acts of infringement for the sake of profit gives rise to liability."[46]*

Endnotes

[1] Universal Athletic Sales Co. v. Salkeld, 376 F. Supp. 514 (W.D. Pa. 1974).

[2] Sony Corp. v. Universal City Studios, Inc., 104 S. Ct. 774 (1984); Walt Disney Productions v. Filmation Associates, 628 F. Supp. 871 (C.D. Cal. 1986).

[3] House Report on the Copyright Act of 1976, p. 61.

[4] Schumann v. Albuquerque Corp., 664 F. Supp. 473 (D.N.M. 1987).

[5] House Report on the Copyright Act of 1976, p. 61.

[6] *See, e.g.,* Atari, Inc. v. North American Philips Consumer Electronics Corporation, 672 F.2d 607 (7th Cir. 1982).

[7] *See, e.g.,* Davis v. E.I. duPont de Nemours & Co., 240 F. Supp. 612 (S.D.N.Y. 1965).

[8] Nichols v. Universal Pictures Co., 45 F.2d 119 (2nd Cir. 1930).

[9] Robertson v. Batten, Barton, Durstine and Osborn, Inc., 146 F. Supp. 795 (S.D. Cal. 1956).

[10] Elsmere Music, Inc. v. National Broadcasting Co., 482 F. Supp. 741 (S.D.N.Y. 1980), *aff's,* 623 F.2d 252 (2nd Cir. 1980).

[11] Henry Holt & Co. v. Liggett & Myers Tobacco Co., 23 F. Supp. 302 (E.D. Pa. 1938).

[12] Amana Refrigeration, Inc. v. Consumers Union of the United States, Inc., 431 F. Supp. 324 (N.D. Iowa 1977).

[13] Martin Luther King, Jr. Center for Social Change, Inc. v. American Heritage Products, Inc., 508 F. Supp. 854 (N.D. Ga. 1981).

[14] Hedeman Products Copr. v. Tap-Rite Products Corp., 228 F. Supp. 630 (D.N.J. 1964).

[15] American Greetings Corp. v. Kleinfab Corp., 400 F. Supp. 228 (S.D.N.Y. 1975).

[16] Wainwright Securities, Inc. v. Wall Street Transcript Corporation, 558 F,2d 91 (2nd Cir. 1977).

[17] Nihon Keizai Shimbun, Inc. v. Comline Business Data, Inc., 166 F.3d 35 (2nd Cir. 1999) quoting Judge Learned Hand in Sheldon v. Metro-Goldwyn Pictures, Corp., 81 F.2d 49 (2nd Cir. 1936).

[18] Toulmin v. The Rike-Kumler Co., 316 F.2d 232 (6th Cir. 1963).

[19] Suid v. Newsweek Magazine, 503 F. Supp. 146 (D.D.C. 1980).

[20] Jackson v. Washington Monthly Co., 481 F. Supp. 647 (D.D.C. 1979).

[21] McCrae v. Smith, 968 F. Supp. 559 (D. Colo. 1997).

[22] Norse v. Henry Holt & Company, 847 F. Supp. 142 (N.D. Cal. 1994).

[23] Wright v. Warner Books, Inc., 748 F. Supp. 105 (S.D.N.Y. 1990).

[24] New Era Publications International v. Carol Publishing Group, 904 F.2d 152 (2nd Cir. 1990).

[25] Iowa State University Research Foundation, Inc. v. American Broadcasting Co., 621 F.2d 57 (2nd Cir. 1980).

[26] Johns & Johns Printing Co. v. Paull-Pioneer Music Corp., 102 F.2d 282 (8th Cir. 1939).

[27] Leo Feist, Inc. v. Song Parodies, Inc., 146 F.2d 400 (2nd Cir. 1944).

[28] Nihon Keizai Shimbun, Inc. v. Comline Business Data, Inc., 166 F.3d 35 (2nd Cir. 1999).

[29] *See, e.g.,* Blendingwell Music, Inc. v. Moor-Law, Inc., 612 F. Supp. 474 (D. Del. 1985).

[30] Meadowgreen Music Company v. Voice in the Wilderness Broadcasting, Inc., 789 F. Supp. 823 (E.D. Tex. 1992).

[31] House Report on the Copyright Act of 1976, p. 162.

[32] *See, e.g.,* Harris v. Emus Records Corp., 734 F.2d 1329 (9th Cir. 1984).

[33] *See, e.g.,* Harris v. Emus Records Corp., 734 F.2d 1329 (9th Cir. 1984). See also Nimmer on Copyright section 14.04E, n. 96.1.

[34] House Report on the Copyright Act of 1976, p. 162.

[35] *Id.*

[36] Polygram International Publishing, Inc. v. NEVADA/TIG, Inc., 855 F. Supp. 1314 (D. Mass. 1994).

[37] ABKCO v. Stellar Records, 96 F.3d 60 (2nd Cir. 1996).

[38] Hotaling v. Church of Jesus Christ of Latter-Day Saints, 118 F.3d 199 (4th Cir. 1997).

[39] Repp v. Webber, 132 F.3d 862 (2nd Cir. 1997).

[40] Gershwin Publishing Corp. v. Columbia Artists Management, Inc., 443 F.2d 1159 (2nd Cir. 1971). *See also* A&M Records, Inc. v. Napster, Inc., 239 F.3d 1004 (9th Cir. 2001); Fonovisa, Inc. v. Cherry Auction, Inc., 76 F.3d 259, 264 (9th Cir.1996).

[41] A&M Records, Inc. v. Napster, Inc., 239 F.3d 1004 (9th Cir. 2001).

[42] Gershwin Publishing Corp. v. Columbia Artists Management, Inc., 443 F.2d 1159 (2nd Cir. 1971).

[43] A&M Records, Inc. v. Napster, Inc., 239 F.3d 1004 (9th Cir. 2001).

[44] *Id.*

[45] Sony Corp. of America v. Universal City Studios, Inc., 464 U.S. 417 (1984).

[46] A&M Records, Inc. v. Napster, Inc., 239 F.3d 1004 (9th Cir. 2001).

6

Defenses to Copyright Infringement

A copyright owner's five exclusive rights are neither absolute nor unconditional. On the contrary, they are subject to a number of limitations, the more important of which are summarized in this chapter.

6.1 Fair Use

> **Key point.** *The Supreme Court has observed that the fair use doctrine "permits courts to avoid rigid application of the copyright statute when, on occasion, it would stifle the very creativity which that law is designed to foster."*[1]

Section 107 of the Copyright Act specifies that

four "fair use factors"   the fair use of a copyrighted work, including such use by reproduction in copies or phonorecords or by any other means specified [in section 106], for purposes such as criticism, comment, news reporting, teaching (including multiple copies for classroom use), scholarship, or research, is not an infringement of copyright. In determining whether the use made of a work in any particular case is a fair use the factors to be considered shall include—(1) the purpose and character of the use, including whether such use is of a commercial nature or is for nonprofit educational purposes; (2) the nature of the copyrighted work; (3) the amount and substantiality of the portion used in relation to the copyrighted work as a whole; and (4) the effect of the use upon the potential market for or value of the copyrighted work.

Fair use is one of the most common defenses invoked by persons charged with copyright infringement. Unfortunately, it is very difficult to define. Even section 107 does not define the term but rather recites "factors to be considered" in determining if a particular use is a fair use. Perhaps the best way to get a feel for the meaning of fair use is to review each of the four factors specified in section 107.

A. The Purpose and Character of the Use

first factor

The first factor to be considered in deciding whether or not a particular use of a copyrighted work is a fair use is "the purpose and character of the use, including whether such use is of a commercial nature or is for nonprofit educational purposes." The courts have focused on three aspects of a particular work's "purpose and character" in assessing this first factor.

(1) *was the use of copyrighted material commercially motivated?*

Clearly, the more "commercial" the motivation in exploiting the copyrighted work of another, the less likely that such use will be deemed "fair use." The Supreme Court has observed that "every commercial use of copyrighted material is presumptively an unfair exploitation of the monopoly privilege that belongs to the owner of the copyright," and therefore "any commercial use tends to cut against a fair use defense."[2] However, it is important to emphasize that the mere fact that a particular use of a copyrighted work is commercially motivated does not resolve the issue of fair use. Commercial motivation is but one factor to consider. Similarly, the mere fact that a particular use is not commercially motivated does not resolve the issue of fair use. In this regard, the Supreme Court has noted that "even copying for noncommercial purposes may impair the copyright holder's ability to obtain the rewards that Congress intended him to have."[3]

(2) *productive or "transformative" use*

A second aspect of a work's "purpose and character" that the courts have isolated is whether or not the work's use of another's copyrighted material is a "productive" or "transformative" use of the material. What the courts mean by this is that the "mere reproduction of a work in order to use it for its intrinsic purpose" cannot be a fair use of the copyrighted work.[4] Rather, in order for a particular work's use of copyrighted material to be a "fair use," it must go beyond mere reproduction and impart some productive or original material, or it must "transform" the original material. The Supreme Court has noted that the ultimate question is whether the new work

> adds something new, with a further purpose or different character, altering the first with new expression, meaning, or message . . . in other words, whether and to what extent the new work is "transformative." Although such transformative use is not absolutely necessary for a finding of fair use, the goal of copyright, to promote science and the arts, is generally furthered by the creation of transformative works. Such works thus lie at the heart of the fair use doctrine's guarantee of breathing space within the confines of copyright, and the more transformative the new work, the less will be the significance of other factors, like commercialism, that may weigh against a finding of fair use.[5]

(3) propriety

A third and final factor that some courts have cited in assessing the "purpose and character" of a particular use of copyrighted materials is the propriety of that use. This factor asks the question, "Was the use of the copyrighted material, under the circumstances, ethical and equitable?" To illustrate, the courts have held that verbatim copying of another's copyrighted materials without any attempt to obtain permission is an act of bad faith that precludes a fair use defense.[6] Similarly, use of copyrighted materials despite the copyright owner's refusal to grant permission is an unethical practice that, some courts have held, precludes a finding of fair use.

> ***Key point.*** *A Copyright Office cites the following examples of activities that courts have regarded as fair use: "Quotation of excerpts in a review or criticism for purposes of illustration or comment; quotation of short passages in a scholarly or technical work, for illustration or clarification of the author's observations; use in a parody of some of the content of the work parodied; summary of an address or article, with brief quotations, in a news report; reproduction by a library of a portion of a work to replace part of a damaged copy; reproduction by a teacher or student of a small part of a work to illustrate a lesson; reproduction of a work in legislative or judicial proceedings or reports; incidental and fortuitous reproduction, in a newsreel or broadcast, of a work located in the scene of an event being reported."*

B. The Nature of the Copyrighted Work

second factor

The second factor to be considered in deciding whether or not a particular use of a copyrighted work is a fair use is "the nature of the copyrighted work." This factor recites the basic principle that the nature of a copyrighted work is a relevant consideration in assessing whether another person's reproduction of some or all of its contents can constitute a fair use. To illustrate, compilations of factual materials (e.g., dictionaries, encyclopedias) are obviously more conducive to fair use than certain other works. The House Report to the Copyright Act of 1976 states that "the scope of the fair use doctrine should be considerably narrower in the case of newsletters than in that of either mass-circulation periodicals or scientific journals. The commercial nature of the user is a significant factor in such cases: Copying by a profit-making user of even a small portion of a newsletter may have a significant impact on the commercial market for the work."[7]

Further, the Senate Report on Copyright Act of 1976 provides that "textbooks and other material prepared primarily for the school markets would be less susceptible to reproduction for classroom use than material prepared for general public distribution."[8]

The Senate Report also provides that "a key, though not necessarily determinative, factor in fair use is whether or not the work is available to the potential user. If the work is 'out of print' and unavailable for purchase through normal channels, the user may have more justification for reproducing it than in the ordinary case . . . ."[9]

Out-of-print works

out-of-print works

What about out-of-print works? Obviously, if copyright protection has expired, then such works may be used without limitation. If an out-of-print work is still protected by copyright, then it cannot be copied or otherwise used without limitation. However, the scope of fair use is broader with out-of-print works. Consider the following: (1) A congressional committee report to the Copyright Act of 1976 states that "a key, though not necessarily determinative factor in fair use is whether or not the work is available to the potential user. If the work is out of print and unavailable for purchase through normal channels, the user may have more justification for reproducing it."[10] (2) Several courts have concluded that the scope of fair use is broader with out-of-print works.[11]

Example. Marty wants to use a portion of a copyrighted work in an article that he is writing. The copyright in the copyrighted work has not expired, but the work has been out of print for a number of years. The fact that a work is out of print does not mean that it is in the public domain and available for use by anyone without limitation. So long as the copyright has not expired, the copyright owner continues to enjoy all of the exclusive rights described in section 106, including reproduction in whole or in part. As a result, Marty must be concerned about the legal consequences of his action. However, in close cases, the fact that the copyrighted work is out of print may give Marty "more justification for reproducing it" than had the work still been available.

C. The Amount and Substantiality of the Portion Used

third factor

The third factor to be considered in deciding whether or not a particular use of a copyrighted work is a fair use is "the amount and substantiality of the portion used in relation to the copyrighted work as a whole." This factor asks the question, "How much of the copyrighted work was used?" Obviously, the more of a copyrighted work that is used, the less likely the use will be considered a fair use. Conversely, the less of a copyrighted work that is used, the more likely that the use will be considered a fair use. One thing is clear—verbatim or nearly verbatim reproductions of an entire copyrighted work will almost never be deemed a fair use.[12]

Some courts have held that in determining the amount and substantiality of the copyrighted work that is used, qualitative as well as quantitative considerations are relevant. That is, one should compare not only the actual physical percentage of the copyrighted work that is used, but also the significance of that portion in a qualitative sense to the whole. To illustrate, the United States Supreme Court has held that reproduction of a mere 200 words out of a 200,000-word copyrighted work did not constitute fair use, since the reproduced materials, while insignificant in terms of quantity, were very significant in terms of quality since they constituted the "heart of the work."[13]

Example. Joan is the music director at her church. She makes a transparency of a copyrighted song, reproducing both the music and lyrics. The transparency is used during morning worship services. Since this reproduction constitutes a verbatim reproduction of the entire copyrighted work, it is very doubtful that it will constitute fair use.

Example. Same facts as the preceding example, except that Joan reproduces only the lyrics, and not the music, of a copyrighted work. The lyrics comprise a substantial part of a copyrighted musical work, both quantitatively and qualitatively. As a result, it is doubtful that such a reproduction would be excused on the basis of the fair use defense. However, since the reproduction is not verbatim or nearly verbatim, the other three fair use factors should be considered.

Example. Jim frequently quotes biblical encyclopedias in articles that he writes for religious periodicals. The courts generally have held that the scope of fair use is greater when an informational work, such as an encyclopedia, is involved. Of course, one cannot automatically conclude that use of informational works constitutes fair use, even if credit is given to the source of the quotations. The other three fair use factors must be considered, as well as the amount and substantiality of the material actually used.

Key point. The courts have found that reproductions of the following amounts were insubstantial enough to be permissible fair use: (1) 5-8 percent, amounting to no more than a few pages in length;[14] (2) 4.3 percent;[15] (3) a parody of 29 seconds of a

40-minute copyrighted musical work, consisting of 6 out of a total of 38 bars of music;[16] *(4) less than 1 percent, with the copied material being used primarily for informational purposes;*[17] *(5) 4.3 percent.*[18]

Key point. *The courts have found that reproductions of the following amounts were substantial enough to constitute copyright infringement and were not fair use: (1) a commercial printer made "course packs" for college students that consisted of reproductions of 5-30 percent of the authors' original works;*[19] *(2) 52 percent of a copyrighted letter;*[20] *(3) 25-30 percent of a copyrighted work was copied verbatim, or through close paraphrasing, and the copied portion was the essence of the copyrighted work.*[21]

D. The Effect of the Use upon the Potential Market for or Value of the Copyrighted Work

fourth factor

The fourth factor to be considered in deciding whether or not a particular use of a copyrighted work is a fair use is "the effect of the use upon the potential market for or value of the copyrighted work." It must be emphasized that actual reduction in sales of the copyrighted material is not required to negate a claim of fair use. The United States Supreme Court has stated that all that is necessary is "proof either that the particular use is harmful, or that if it should become widespread, it would adversely affect the potential market for the copyrighted work. Actual harm need not be shown; such a requirement would leave the copyright holder with no defense against predictable damage. Nor is it necessary to show with certainty that future harm will result. What is necessary is a showing by a preponderance of the evidence that some meaningful likelihood of future harm exists."[22]

Key point. *A federal appeals court, in addressing the application of the fourth fair use factor in a case involving the alleged fair use of a church's religious publication, made the following observations: "This case presents a novel application of the fair use doctrine where the copyright owner is a not-for-profit organization. As might be expected, published case law deals with works marketed for profit. However, it cannot be inferred from that fact that the absence of a conventional market for a work, the copyright to which is held by a nonprofit, effectively deprives the holder of copyright protection. If evidence of actual or potential monetary loss were required, copyrights held by nonprofits would be essentially worthless. Religious, educational and other public interest institutions would suffer if their publications invested with an institution's reputation, and goodwill could be freely appropriated by anyone. The statute by its terms is not limited to market effect but includes also 'the effect of the use on the value of the copyrighted work. . . .' [C]opying for noncommercial purposes may impair the copyright holder's ability to obtain the rewards that Congress intended him to have. Those rewards need not be limited to monetary rewards; compensation may take a variety of forms. . . . [The infringer's] distribution of unauthorized version of [the text] harms [the church's] goodwill by diverting potential members and contributions from [it]."*[23]

the "different function" test

The four fair use factors summarized above provide only general guidance. In some cases, it is very difficult to determine whether a particular use of copyrighted material constitutes a fair use. Nevertheless, such a determination is critical, since a finding of fair use will avoid a claim of copyright infringement. Because of the importance of this issue, the courts have sought to provide additional clarification in resolving the fair use issue. A number of courts have formulated the following rule—a reproduction, even if substantial, of a copyrighted work may still constitute fair use if it performs a different function than the copyrighted work. To illustrate, one court held that the reproduction of the lyrics of a professional football team's 8-line theme song in a magazine article describing the history of the franchise was a noninfringing fair use. The court observed that the article that appeared in the magazine "was not intended to be a musical reproduction, nor was it related in any way to any musical endeavor. No element of competition was present between the article and the copyrighted song. . . . [I]t is safe to say that where the later work differs greatly in nature, scope, and purpose from the original, a larger liberty in making quotations and extracts will be permitted than in cases where the respective works are more or less competitive."[24] Similarly, a national magazine's publication of the lyrics to another chorus in an article paying tribute to a deceased actress was found to be a fair use for the same reasons,[25] as was reproduction of chorus lyrics in a humor magazine.[26]

In all of these cases, reproduction of the entire lyrics of a copyrighted song was held to be noninfringing fair use because such use served an entirely different function or purpose from the copyrighted musical work, and "had neither the intent nor the effect of fulfilling the demand for the original." The magazine articles were not intended to be music, or to compete with sales of the copyrighted works. In both cases, the courts indicated that it was extremely unlikely, if not impossible, that anyone would purchase the magazines in order to avoid purchasing copies of the copyrighted music. Magazine articles, though they contain the lyrics of copyrighted music, are sufficiently different in function and purpose from the music that such reproduction may in some instances constitute fair use.

chorus lyrics

However, it must be emphasized that not every reproduction of lyrics to copyrighted songs will amount to fair use. The reproduced lyrics must in fact serve a totally different function than the music itself. For example, in one case, a publisher reproduced the chorus lyrics of two famous copyrighted songs in songsheet pamphlets, maintaining that the reproduction of only chorus lyrics of copyrighted songs was so trivial in nature and amount as to constitute noninfringing fair use. The court found such reproductions to be an infringement, and rejected the publisher's claim that its reproductions constituted fair use. Though only the chorus lyrics were reproduced (and not the regular verse lines or music), the court found that "the chorus of a musical composition may constitute a material and substantial part of the work and it is frequently the very part that makes it popular and valuable."[27] Similarly, another court found the reproduction of chorus lyrics in a song sheet magazine to be an infringement rather than fair use, since the reproduction "met the same demand on the same market" as the original.[28] The courts in each of these two cases gave a narrow interpretation of fair use because the function served by the infringing use directly satisfied a function that was served by the copyright owner's sheet music.

> **Example.** *A church music director copies only the lyrics of a copyrighted song onto a transparency for use during worship services. The music director believes that this practice constitutes a permissible fair use of the copyrighted music. The transparency made by the church has the effect of fulfilling the demand for the original copyrighted work. Stated another way, it fulfills the same function as the original. According to the "function" or "purpose" test discussed above, such a use cannot be noninfringing fair use. This test is not a substitute for the four fair use factors, but it is helpful in resolving close cases.*

The courts have given the principle of fair use its broadest effect when the copyrighted material is reproduced for purposes of criticism, review, or comment, though substantial reproduction of copyrighted material is not necessarily permitted even for such purposes.

church practices

There is little doubt that many reproductions of copyrighted materials by churches will fail to constitute noninfringing fair use. Certainly any verbatim copying of an entire work will almost never constitute fair use. Examples of this type of copying include the duplication of a musical work for members of the choir, a bulletin insert, a soloist, an accompanist, an instrumental group, or for use as a transparency or slide. Even copying of a significant portion (in terms of either quantity or quality) of a copyrighted work ordinarily will fail to constitute noninfringing fair use. An example here would be the copying of only the lyrics (and not the melody) of a copyrighted chorus or hymn. In all of these cases, a finding of fair use will be unlikely because (1) such acts of copying fail the "productive purpose test" since they constitute mere reproductions of a work in order to use it for its intrinsic purpose; (2) the nature of the work involved does not suggest a broad definition of fair use; (3) the amount of copyrighted material that is copied is significant in terms of both quantity and quality; (4) similar acts of copying by other churches would "adversely affect the market for or value of the copyrighted work." In other words, none of the four fair use factors ordinarily will support a finding of fair use.

Example. A federal appeals court ruled that the use of several extended quotations of a religious leader reproduced without permission in an uncomplimentary biography constituted fair use. The court evaluated each of the 4 "fair use factors" and concluded that all of them supported the finding of fair use. With regard to the first factor, the court concluded that biographies, and particularly critical biographies, generally constitute fair use. The proposed book used quotations from the religious leader's published writings "for the entirely legitimate purpose of making his point that [the leader] was a charlatan and his church a dangerous cult." While the author no doubt expected to make a profit, this was a secondary purpose. As to the second factor, the court again emphasized that the proposed book was a biography, and that biographies generally constitute fair use. The court observed that "biographies, of course, are fundamentally personal histories and it is both reasonable and customary for biographers to refer to and utilize earlier works dealing with the subject of the work and occasionally to quote directly from such works." The third fair use factor asks how much of the copyrighted work is quoted—both in terms of quantity and quality. The court concluded that only small portions of several works were quoted, rather than larger selections of any one work. Further, the portions quoted were not "key portions" of any of the books. The court concluded that the fourth factor led to a finding of fair use, since the biography would have little if any impact on the sale of the copyrighted works. In conclusion, the court observed: "The book is a critical biography, designed to educate the public about [the deceased religious leader], a public figure who sought public attention, albeit on his own terms; the book quotes from merely a small portion of [his] works and from only those that have been published; and, it will cause no adverse impact protected by the copyright law on the market for [the copyrighted] writings. In these circumstances, we conclude that the book's use of passages from [the copyrighted] works is protected fair use."[29]

Example. Pastor Larry is the music minister at his church. He purchases a single copy of a copyrighted song and duplicates a copy for each of the 20 members of the church choir. Mary is the copyright owner of the song. Pastor Larry claims that his duplication of the music constitutes fair use, so it cannot be copyright infringement since it is the only one of Mary's works that the church has ever duplicated, and the minimal reproduction of 20 copies had no effect at all on the potential market for or value of the copyrighted work. This argument is incorrect. To negate a fair use claim, the copyright owner need not prove actual economic damage. Rather, all that is necessary is proof that if Pastor Larry's practice were to become widespread, it would adversely affect the potential market for the copyrighted work. Certainly, Mary would be able to make such a claim. Again, this will not necessarily negate Pastor Larry's fair use claim, since the other three fair use factors must be considered as well.

Example. Herbert W. Armstrong, the founder of the Worldwide Church of God (WCG), wrote a 380-page book entitled Mystery of the Ages. *The copyright of the book was in the Church's name. After Armstrong's death, the Church retired the book from further publication and distribution for several reasons, including the fact that the Church's positions on various doctrines (such as divorce, remarriage, and divine healing) had changed. Following Armstrong's death, a new religious organization (Philadelphia Church of God, or PCG) was founded that claimed to follow his teachings. This new church insisted that Armstrong's book was central to its religious practice and was required reading for all members hoping to be baptized. Until 1997 PCG relied on existing copies of Armstrong's book, but then began making thousands of verbatim copies of the entire text for its religious purposes. PCG ignored WCG's demand that it cease infringing its copyright. WCG thereafter sued PCG, claiming that its unauthorized duplication of the Armstrong book constituted copyright infringement. PCG argued that its actions were permitted by the first amendment guaranty of religious freedom, and constituted permissible "fair use" of the Armstrong book. A federal appeals court ruled that PCG's duplication of the book was not permissible fair use. The court noted that a copyright owner has the exclusive right to reproduce and distribute copies of a copyrighted work. Since WCG owned the copyright in the Armstrong book, it had the exclusive right to copy and distribute it. Further, this right "is not diminished or qualified by the fact that WCG is a not-for-profit organization [or by] the religious nature of its activity." The court then addressed each of the four use "factors" mentioned in the Copyright Act. The first factor calls for consideration of "the purposes and character of the use, including whether such use is of a commercial nature or is for nonprofit educational purposes." The court concluded that this factor did not support a finding of fair use, despite PCG's claim that its acts of copying was not "for profit." It concluded, "The crux of the profit/nonprofit distinction is not whether the sole motive of the use is monetary gain but whether the user stands to profit from exploitation of the copyrighted material without paying the customary price." The court noted that copying of the Armstrong text "unquestionably profits PCG by providing it at no cost with the core text essential to its members' religious observance, by attracting . . . new members who tithe ten percent of their income to PCG, and by enabling the ministry's growth." The second factor looks at "the nature of the copyrighted work." The court noted that the scope of fair use is broader when a "factual" or informational work is involved. It concluded that the "creativity, imagination and originality" embodied in the Armstrong text "tilt the scale against fair use." The third factor looks at "the amount and substantiality of the portion used in relation to the copyrighted work as a whole." The court noted that PCG copied the entire text verbatim, and that "we have found no published case holding that fair use protected the verbatim copying, without criticism, of a written work in its entirety." Nor did the religious nature of the work support a different conclusion, since PCG used the text as "a central element of its members' religious observance" and therefore "a reasonable person would expect PCG to pay for the right to copy and distribute [the text]." The fourth factor considers "the effect of the use upon the potential market for or value of the copyrighted work." The court noted that the WCG planned on publishing an annotated edition of Armstrong's text to reach out to those familiar with Armstrong's teachings and those in the broader Christian community. PCG's distribution of its unauthorized version of the text "thus harms WCG's goodwill by diverting potential members and contributions from WCG."* [30]

Example. *A nonprofit agency that provided services to public schools created a "library" of educational videos that it copied from a public television station and made available to several schools. The publisher of many of the programs that were copied sued the agency for copyright infringement. The agency insisted that its* *practices were a legitimate fair use of the copyrighted programs. A court disagreed, noting that the agency's "systematic practice" of making off-the-air videotapes of copyrighted works and the making of numerous copies of those works did not constitute fair use.[31]*

Example. *A federal court in New York ruled that a company's practice of making several copies of newsletters to distribute among employees constituted copyright infringement. The company subscribed to several newsletters and journals, and its employees frequently made photocopies of articles in these publications. Making copies "freed" the original publication to circulate among other employees; further, copying permitted employees to keep personal copies of the articles that they could take home and read at their own convenience, and that they could "mark up" without defacing the original. The court evaluated each of the 4 "fair use factors" and concluded that they did not support a finding of fair use. With regard to the first factor, the court concluded that the purpose and character of the copying was solely to duplicate the original articles, and that this objective is simply not compatible with fair use. As to the second factor, the court noted that "if cheap [copies] could be freely made and sold at a fraction of the subscription price, [the publisher] would not sell many subscriptions, it could not sustain itself, and articles of this sort would simply not be published." The third fair use factor asks how much of the copyrighted work is quoted, both in terms of quantity and quality. The court noted that entire articles and issues were copied, and that this was inconsistent with fair use. Finally, the court concluded that the fourth factor (market effect) did not support a finding of fair use.[32]*

6.2 Guidelines for Classroom Copying in Not-for-Profit Educational Institutions

educational copying

One of the most common fair use issues concerns the reproduction of copyrighted materials for educational purposes. In 1975, negotiating teams representing authors, publishers, and the "Ad Hoc Committee of Educational Institutions and Organizations on Copyright Law Revision" met informally in an attempt to reach a "meeting of the minds" concerning permissible educational uses of copyrighted material. The parties reached an agreement, known as the Agreement on Guidelines for Classroom Copying in Not-For-Profit Educational Institutions with Respect to Books and Periodicals. The House Report on the Copyright Act of 1976 reprinted the Agreement in full,[33] and further noted that the guidelines set forth in the Agreement "are a reasonable interpretation of the minimum standards of fair use." The guidelines contained in the Agreement are set forth below. It must be emphasized that the stated purpose of the guidelines was "to state the minimum and not the maximum standards of educational fair use," and that the parties acknowledged that "there may be instances in which copying which does not fall within the guidelines . . . may nonetheless be permitted under the criteria of fair use." The guidelines apply only to educational copying of literary works (books, articles, poetry, charts, etc.), and not to music.

"fair use guidelines" for classroom copying

Agreement on Guidelines for Classroom Copying in Not-For-Profit Educational Institutions with Respect to Books and Periodicals

I. Single Copying for Teachers

A single copy may be made of any of the following by or for a teacher at his or her individual request for his or her scholarly research or use in teaching or preparation to teach a class:

A. A chapter from a book;

B. An article from a periodical or newspaper;

C. A short story, short essay, or short poem, whether or not from a collective;

D. A chart, graph, diagram, drawing, cartoon, or picture from a book, periodical, or newspaper;

II. Multiple Copies for Classroom Use

Multiple copies (not to exceed in any event more than one copy per pupil in a course) may be made by or for the teacher giving the course for classroom use or discussion, provided that:

A. The copying meets the test of brevity and spontaneity as defined below;

B. The copying meets the cumulative effect test as defined below; and

C. Each copy includes a notice of copyright [Note: it is unclear whether or not the adoption of the Berne Convention eliminates this requirement. Accordingly, it should still be followed.]

Definitions of brevity, spontaneity, and cumulative effect

Brevity

(i) Poetry: (a) A complete poem if less than 250 words and if printed on not more than two pages or (b) from a longer poem, an excerpt of not more than 250 words.

(ii) Prose: (a) Either a complete article, story, or essay of less than 2,500 words, or (b) an excerpt from any prose work of not more than 1,000 words or 10% of the work, whichever is less, but in any event a minimum of 500 words.

[Each of the numerical limits stated in "i" and "ii" above may be expanded to permit the completion of an unfinished line of a poem or of an unfinished prose paragraph.]

(iii) Illustration: One chart, graph, diagram, drawing, cartoon, or picture per book or per periodical issue.

(iv) "Special" works: Certain works in poetry, prose, or in "poetic prose" which often combine language with illustrations and which are intended sometimes for children and at other times for a more general audience and fall short of 2,500 words in their entirety. Paragraph "ii" above notwithstanding such "special works" may not be reproduced in their entirety; however, an excerpt comprising not more than two of the published pages of such special work and containing not more than 10% of the words found in the text thereof, may be reproduced.

Spontaneity

(i) The copying is at the instance and inspiration of the individual teacher; and

(ii) The inspiration and decision to use the work and the moment of its use for maximum teaching effectiveness are so close in time that it would be unreasonable to expect a timely reply to a request for permission.

Cumulative Effect

(i) The copying of the material is for only one course in the school in which the copies are made.

(ii) Not more than one short poem, article, story, essay, or two excerpts may be copied from the same author, nor more than three from the same collective work or periodical volume during one class term.

(iii) There shall not be more than nine instances of such multiple copying for one course during one class term.

[The limitations stated in "ii" and "iii" above shall not apply to current news periodicals and newspapers and current news sections of other periodicals.]

III. Prohibitions as to I and II Above

Notwithstanding any of the above, the following shall be prohibited:

A. Copying shall not be used to create, replace, or become a substitute for anthologies, compilations, or collective works. Such replacement or substitution may occur whether copies of various works or excerpts therefrom are accumulated or reproduced and used separately.

B. There shall be no copying of or from works intended to be "consumable" in the course of study or of teaching. These include workbooks, exercises, standardized tests, test booklets, answer sheets, and other similarly consumable material.

C. Copying shall not:

(a) substitute for the purchase of books, publishers' reprints, or periodicals;

(b) be directed by higher authority;

(c) be repeated with respect to the same item by the same teacher from term to term.

D. No charge shall be made to the student beyond the actual cost of the photocopying.

The Guidelines for Classroom Copying in Not-for-Profit Educational Institutions are illustrated in the following examples.

> **Example.** *Randy, a teacher at a church-operated private school, copies a chapter from a reference book in preparation for teaching. This reproduction is considered to be a noninfringing fair use under the guidelines.*

> **Example.** *Same facts as the preceding example, except Randy makes copies of the chapter for each of the 30 students in his class. This act of copying is not necessarily noninfringing fair use. According to the guidelines, it will be fair use only if it meets the tests of brevity and spontaneity, meets the cumulative effect test, and each copy*

includes a notice of copyright. Stated another way, Randy's act of copying is permissible fair use if (1) the chapter copied contains not more than 1,000 words or 10% of the total work, whichever is less (a minimum of 500 words is allowed); (2) the decision to use the work and the moment of its use for maximum teaching effectiveness are so close in time that it would be unreasonable to expect a timely reply to a request for permission; (3) the copying is for only one course, and not more than two excerpts (three in the case of the same collective work) from the same author are copied during one class term, and no more than nine acts of multiple copying are performed for all works and authors for any one course during any class term; (4) all copies bear a notice of copyright, indicating the copyright owner's name, the year the work was published, and the word "copyright," the abbreviation "copr.", or the copyright symbol ©.

Example. *Same facts as the preceding example, except that Randy would like to make a copy of an article in a periodical for each member of his class. The copying in this case is permissible fair use, according to the guidelines, only if it satisfies the four requirements listed in the preceding example, with the following modifications: (1) the article is less than 2,500 words, or, if more than 2,500 words, then only 1,000 words or 10% of the total work, whichever is less, may be copied (in any event a minimum of 500 words is allowed); (2) not more than one article of the same author may be reproduced during one class term (except in the case of news periodicals, newspapers, or the current news sections of other periodicals).*

Example. *Randy makes a copy of a chart from a news magazine for each of the 30 members in his class. This copying is permissible fair use only if it meets the tests of brevity and spontaneity, meets the cumulative effect test, and each copy includes a notice of copyright. Note that with regard to the requirement of brevity, the guidelines specify that a teacher is permitted to copy, for each member of a class, one chart per periodical issue. The other requirements are discussed in the preceding examples.*

Example. *Same facts as the preceding two examples. Is Randy free to make copies of the same article and chart for each member of his class during subsequent school terms? The guidelines provide that "copying shall not . . . be repeated with respect to the same item by the same teacher from term to term."*

Example. *A Sunday School teacher would like to make copies of an article that appeared in a periodical for each member of her class. Do the guidelines apply to such a case? This question is not answered by either the guidelines themselves, or by court decisions. It is likely that the courts (and publishers) would apply the guidelines to the teaching activities of churches, since their application in this context is sensible, consistent with the purpose of the guidelines, and provides guidance and clarification that otherwise would be unavailable. Further, the House Report to the Copyright Act of 1976 specifies that "the same general standards of fair use are applicable to all kinds of uses of copyrighted material, although the relative weight to be given them will differ from case to case." On the other hand, it could be argued that the guidelines were designed solely for nonprofit educational institutions, and that Sunday Schools are integral parts of churches, which are primarily religious rather than educational in nature. At this time, it cannot be said with certainty that the guidelines apply to the teaching activities of churches, but this certainly seems to be the better and more reasonable conclusion.*

Example. *A federal court in California ruled that an instructor who made copies of copyrighted religious books and tapes for instructional purposes was guilty of copyright infringement. The court rejected the instructor's defense of "fair use." It concluded that she failed all four fair use factors. The purpose of the copying was commercial (the copied materials were sold to students); the nature of the copyrighted works were creative and thus entitled to a higher degree of protection; the amount copied (the entire copyrighted works) was substantial; and, the impact of the copying on the copyright owner's rights was significant since the instructor's act of unauthorized copying "fulfilled the demand for the original works and [will] diminish or prejudice their potential sale." Finally, the court rejected the instructor's claim that her copying met the standards for "fair use" as set forth in the so-called "fair use guidelines" for classroom copying of educational materials. The guidelines apply only to educational copying of literary works (books, articles, poetry, charts, etc.). Among other things, the guidelines specify that a teacher may make a single copy of a chapter from a book or an article from a periodical for use in teaching or in preparing to teach. The court observed that the instructor's copying in this case "was not restricted to one copy for her own use in teaching" and therefore was not eligible for a fair use exemption. The guidelines also permit teachers to make multiple copies of a copyrighted work for classroom use, but several restrictions apply. For example, a teacher may make multiple copies of an entire article of less than 2,500 words or an excerpt from a longer work so long as the excerpt is not more than the lesser of 1,000 words or 10 percent of the entire work. Further, the decision to use the work must be "spontaneous" in the sense that it is so close in time to the date the work is to be used that it would be unreasonable to expect a timely reply to a request for permission to reproduce it. There also are strict limitations on the number of times this exception can be used. The court concluded that this exemption did not apply: "[T]he undisputed evidence shows [that the instructor's] copying was not limited and spontaneous, but was extensive and methodical, and consisted of copying from the same author, time after time. This is clearly not within the letter or spirit of the congressional guidelines."* [34]

Example. *A federal appeals court ruled that a copyshop violated the copyright law by making "coursepacks" for sale to university students. The copyshop copied substantial sections of copyrighted texts, bound them into coursepacks, and sold them to students who needed them to fulfill reading assignments. The court ruled that none of the four fair use factors supported a finding of fair use in this case. The purpose and character of the unauthorized use was commercial exploitation. The nature of the copyrighted works was "creative" and "expressive." The amount of material copied from copyrighted texts ranged from 5 percent to 30 percent of the entire texts. Such percentages "are not insubstantial," the court concluded. Fourth, the market for the copyrighted texts would be significantly affected if copyshops routinely made unauthorized copies of copyrighted texts. The court noted that the Supreme Court has ruled that "one need only show that if the challenged use should become widespread, it would adversely affect the potential market for the copyrighted work." It concluded that "if copyshops across the nation were to start doing what the [copyshop has] been doing here . . . the potential value of the copyrighted works of scholarship . . . would be diminished accordingly." The court acknowledged that fair use "guidelines" were adopted by a coalition of authors, publishers, and educators in 1976 to assist in defining fair use in the academic context. These guidelines were accepted by congressional committees as part of their understanding of fair use. However, the court concluded that the copyshop's activities were "light years away from the safe harbor of the guidelines."* [35]

The guidelines specify that "copying shall not . . . substitute for the purchase of books, publishers' reprints, or periodicals." This statement seemingly contradicts every other provision in the guidelines. It makes sense only if read together with the "spontaneity" requirement that "the inspiration and decision to use [a] work and the moment of its use for maximum teaching effectiveness are so close in time that it would be unreasonable to expect a timely reply to a request for permission." In other words, if the article or chart that a teacher would like to copy for each member of a class appeared in a magazine a number of months or years previously, then the teacher cannot go out and purchase additional copies. Rather, he or she would have to purchase reprint copies from the publisher, a process that could take several weeks. This obviously would often destroy the teacher's objective in using the work, particularly if that objective was "spontaneous."

> *Key point. A separate set of guidelines for the use of multimedia materials by teachers has never been finalized.*

6.3 Guidelines for Educational Uses of Music

Shortly after the guidelines for books and periodicals were formulated, representatives of music publishers and music educators met to draft guidelines relative to music. It must be emphasized that the stated purpose of the guidelines, as with the guidelines for books and periodicals, was "to state the minimum and not the maximum standards of educational fair use." The parties acknowledged that "there may be instances in which copying which does not fall within the guidelines . . . may nonetheless be permitted under the criteria of fair use." Nevertheless, the House Report on the Copyright Act of 1976 reprinted the guidelines in full,[36] and further noted that the guidelines "are a reasonable interpretation of the minimum standards of fair use." The guidelines are set forth below:

Guidelines for Educational Uses of Music

"fair use guidelines" for music

A. Permissible Uses

1. Emergency photocopying to replace purchased copies which for any reason are not available for an imminent performance provided purchased replacement copies shall be substituted in due course.

2. (a) For academic purposes other than performance, single or multiple copies of excerpts of works may be made, provided that the excerpts do not comprise a part of the whole which would constitute a performance unit such as a section, movement, or aria, but in no case more than 10% of the whole work. The number of copies shall not exceed one copy per pupil.

(b) For academic purposes other than performance, a single copy of an entire performable unit (selection, movement, aria, etc.) that is (1) confirmed by the copyright proprietor to be out of print, or (2) unavailable except in a larger work, may be made by or for a teacher solely for the purpose of his or her scholarly research or in preparation to teach a class.

3. Printed copies which have been purchased may be edited or simplified provided that the fundamental character of the work is not distorted or the lyrics, if any, altered or lyrics added if none exist.

4. A single copy of recordings of performances by students may be made for evaluation or rehearsal purposes and may be retained by the educational institution or individual teacher.

5. A single copy of a sound recording (such as a tape, disc, or cassette) of copyrighted music may be made from sound recordings owned by an educational institution or an individual teacher for the purpose of constructing aural exercises or examinations and may be retained by the educational institution or individual teacher. (This pertains only to the copyright of the music itself and not to any copyright which may exist in the sound recording.)

B. Prohibitions

1. Copying to create, replace, or become a substitute for anthologies, compilations, or collective works.

2. Copying of or from works intended to be "consumable" in the course of study or of teaching such as workbooks, exercises, standardized tests, answer sheets, and like material.

3. Copying for the purpose of performance, except as in A(1) above.

4. Copying for the purpose of substituting for the purchase of music, except as in A(1) and A(2) above.

5. Copying without inclusion of the copyright notice which appears on the printed copy. [Note: it is unclear at this time whether or not the adoption of the Berne Convention eliminates this requirement. Accordingly, it should still be followed.]

The Guidelines for Educational Uses of Music are illustrated in the following examples.

Example. Diane teaches music at a church-operated school. The school choir is scheduled to give a performance on October 1. A few days before, several copies of the music are misplaced and cannot be located (all copies had been purchased by the school). Diane makes substitute copies on the school's duplicating equipment. This act of copying constitutes noninfringing fair use so long as Diane purchases replacement copies in due course.

Example. Diane makes a single copy of a section of a copyrighted musical work for use in her class preparation. No copies are made available to students. If the larger work which contained the copied section is confirmed by the copyright owner to be out of print, or if the section copied is not available except as a part of the larger work, then Diane's act of copying is permitted by the guidelines.

Example. Steve is a minister of music. He purchases a single copy of choral music that he reproduces on church duplicating equipment for each of the 30 members of the church choir. This practice clearly is not authorized by the guidelines, assuming that they apply, since: (1) such reproduction may not constitute "academic" purposes; (2) more than 10% of the work is duplicated; (3) it probably constituted "copying for the purpose of substituting for the purchase of music," which generally is never a permissible use; and (4) it probably constitutes prohibited "copying for the purpose of performance."

Example. Steve purchases 30 copies of a copyrighted choral work for the church choir. The work is musical only, without lyrics. Steve pencils in lyrics that he created himself on all 30 copies. This action violates the guidelines.

> *Example.* *Steve makes unauthorized transparencies of the choruses of several copyrighted religious songs and uses them during choir rehearsals and worship services. He claims that such uses are authorized by the guidelines. Steve's conclusion is incorrect for the same four reasons mentioned in the preceding example. Of course, the guidelines themselves acknowledge that "[t]here may be instances in which copying which does not fall within the guidelines . . . may nonetheless be permitted under the criteria of fair use." However, as noted previously in this chapter, it is very doubtful that the unauthorized fabrication of a transparency of the chorus of a copyrighted song could constitute a noninfringing "fair use" under the four factors described in section 107.*

application to churches

Since both sets of guidelines discussed above are intended for the teacher and classroom contexts, their application to church activities remains unclear. Certainly, they would apply to the activities of church-operated private schools, and a good case can be made that they should apply to church educational programs generally. Note, however, that the guidelines are very restrictive, and often will run counter to established church practices. Churches hoping that the guidelines will give them greater freedom to reproduce copyrighted materials ordinarily will be disappointed. If the guidelines do not apply to a particular church activity, then the question of fair use will be determined according to the four fair use factors mentioned in section 107 and summarized above.

> *Example.* *A church music director makes transparencies of copyrighted songs for use in worship services, and also makes copies of copyrighted music for use in choir rehearsals and performances. It is doubtful that the music guidelines would apply in the case of the transparencies, since it is unlikely that a court would construe congregational singing in a church service to constitute a "classroom" at a nonprofit "educational" institution. It is more likely, though not certain, that the guidelines would apply in the context of choir rehearsals. The point is this—even if the guidelines would apply in the context of church choir rehearsals, they will certainly not sanction or excuse the practice of reproducing entire copyrighted musical works. And, if the guidelines do not apply (as in the case of worship services), a church's practices will be judged according to the four fair use factors mentioned in section 107. As noted earlier in this chapter, the fabrication of transparencies of copyrighted music or lyrics ordinarily will not be deemed noninfringing fair use under an objective application of the four factors.*

One court has held that a choir director's duplication of 48 copies of a copyrighted musical work (the hymn "My God and I") for use by his choir did not constitute noninfringing fair use.[37] In rejecting the choir director's claim of fair use, the court observed that "[w]hatever may be the breadth of the doctrine of 'fair use,' it is not conceivable to us that the copying of all, or substantially all, of a copyrighted song can be held to be a 'fair use' merely because the infringer had no intent to infringe."

6.4 Reproductions by Libraries and Archives

Section 108 provides that under certain conditions it is not an infringement of copyright for a library or archives, or any of its employees acting within the scope of their employment, to reproduce or distribute not more than a single copy of a work, provided that (1) the reproduction or distribution is made without any purpose of direct or indirect commercial advantage, (2) the collections of the library or archives are open to the public or are available to researchers other than those affiliated with the library or archives, and (3) the reproduction or distribution of the work includes a notice of copyright that appears on the copy or includes a legend stating that the work may be protected by copyright if no such notice can be found on the copy.

The authorized reproductions are specified in sections 108(b) through 108(d). Section 108(b) authorizes the reproduction of up to three copies of an unpublished work solely for purposes of preservation and security, or for research use in another library if the work that is reproduced is currently in the collections of the first library and any copy made in digital format is not further distributed in that format or made available to the public in that format outside the premises of the library or archives.

Section 108(c) permits the reproduction of a published work solely for the purpose of replacement of a copy that is damaged, deteriorating, lost, stolen, or in a format that has become obsolete, if the library has determined, after a reasonable effort, that an unused replacement cannot be obtained at a fair price and any such copy reproduced in digital format is not made available to the public in that format outside the premises of the library or archives. A format is obsolete if the machine or device needed to view a work stored in that format is no longer manufactured or is no longer reasonably available in the commercial marketplace.

Section 108(d) authorizes reproduction of a copy of not more than one article or other contribution to a copyrighted collection or periodical issue, or of a copy of a small part of any other copyrighted work, at the request of a user or another library through an interlibrary loan request. The copy must become the property of the user, and the library must have no notice that the copy will be used for any purpose other than private study, scholarship, or research. Further, the library must display an appropriate warning (in at least 18-point type) in a location that would be clearly visible and legible to a casual observer at the place where reproduction orders are taken, and in print the warning in a box located prominently on the order form (in at least 8-point type). The warning prescribed by the Copyright Office is reproduced in Illustration 6-1.

Section 108(e) authorizes reproduction of a copy of an entire work under certain circumstances if it has been established that a copy cannot be obtained at a fair price if the copy becomes the property of the user and the library or archives has had no notice that the copy would be for any purpose other than private study, scholarship, or research; and the library or archives displays prominently, at the place where orders are accepted, and includes on its order form, the "Warning Concerning Copyright Restrictions" notice reproduced in this section.

Section 108(f) exempts a library or archives, and its employees, from liability for the unsupervised use of duplicating equipment located on its premises, provided that the equipment displays a notice that the making of a copy may be subject to the copyright law. Unfortunately, neither section 108 nor the Copyright Office regulations specify the content of such a notice. While not directly applicable, the "Warning Concerning Copyright Restrictions" notice reproduced in this section probably would suffice. Section 108(f) also specifies that the protection accorded to libraries, archives, and their employees, does not extend to the person making the copies to the extent that such copying exceeds fair use.

Illustration 6-1
NOTICE: WARNING CONCERNING COPYRIGHT RESTRICTIONS

The copyright law of the United States (Title 17, United States Code) governs the making of photocopies or other reproductions of copyrighted material.

Under certain conditions specified in the law, libraries and archives are authorized to furnish a photocopy or other reproduction. One of these specific conditions is that the photocopy or reproduction is not to be "used for any purpose other than private study, scholarship, or research." If a user makes a request for, or later uses, a photocopy or reproduction for purposes in excess of "fair use," that user may be liable for copyright infringement.

This institution reserves the right to refuse to accept a copying order if, in its judgment, fulfillment of the order would involve violation of copyright law.

Section 108(g) provides that the rights granted by section 108 extend only to the "isolated and unrelated reproduction of a single copy or phonorecord of the same material on separate occasions," and that no authorization is given to the related or concerted reproduction of multiple copies or phonorecords of the same material, whether made on one occasion or over a period of time and whether intended for aggregate use by one individual or for separate use by the individual members of a group.

Section 108(h) specifies that during the last 20 years of any term of copyright of a published work, a library or archives may reproduce, distribute, display, or perform in facsimile or digital form a copy of such work (or portions of it) for purposes of preservation, scholarship, or research, if the library or archives has first determined, on the basis of a reasonable investigation, that the work is not subject to normal commercial exploitation, a copy cannot be obtained at a reasonable price, and the copyright owner (or its agent) has not provided notice that either of the previous two conditions applies.

Section 108(i) specifies that the rights of reproduction under section 108 do not apply to a musical work or audiovisual work. Of course, these kinds of works continue to be protected under the concept of fair use.

> *Key point. Section 108 will have the greatest relevance to churches that operate a private school which contains a library.*

> *Example. A church music director routinely makes copies of copyrighted musical works for her office "library." Even if there is no further duplication of these works, this practice is not authorized by section 108 since musical works are not covered under section 108 and none of the protections provided under section 108 apply to such a practice.*

> *Example. A church operates a private school that contains a library. A duplicating machine located in the library is available to students. The library should post the "Warning Concerning Copyright Restrictions" notice that is reproduced in this section on or near the duplicating machine and on any written order form. Church leaders should be sure that the text of the notices meets the requirements summarized in this section.*

6.5 Displays

Section 109(c) provides that "the owner of a particular copy lawfully made . . . is entitled, without the authority of the copyright owner, to display that copy publicly, either directly or by the projection of no more than one image at a time, to viewers present at the place where the copy is located." Section 109(d) provides further that the privilege granted under section 109(c) does not, unless authorized by the copyright owner, "extend to any person who has acquired possession of the copy or phonorecord from the copyright owner, by rental, lease, loan, or otherwise, without acquiring ownership of it."

slides and transparencies

This section is of special relevance to many churches, and particularly to those that use transparencies and slides of copyrighted music in the course of worship services. Recall that one of the exclusive rights of a copyright owner is the right to display a copyrighted work publicly. Section 109(c) limits that exclusive right by adopting the general principle that the *lawful owner* of a copy of a copyrighted work should be able to put the copy on public display without the consent of the copyright owner.

The House Report to the Copyright Act of 1976 specifies that a copyright owner's exclusive right of public display

> would not apply where the owner of a copy wishes to show it directly to the public, as in a gallery or display case, or indirectly as through an opaque projector. Where the

copy itself is intended for projection, as in the case of a photographic slide, negative, or transparency, the public projection of a single image would be permitted as long as the viewers are "present at the place where the copy is located" . . . . [T]he public display of an image of a copyrighted work would not be exempted from copyright control if the copy from which the image was derived were outside the presence of the viewers. . . . Moreover, the exemption would extend only to public displays that are made "either directly or by the projection of no more than one image at a time."

The House Report specifies that section 109(d) qualifies the privilege granted in section 109(b) "by making it clear that [it does] not apply to someone who merely possesses a copy or phonorecord without having acquired ownership of it. Acquisition of an object embodying a copyrighted work . . . carries with it no privilege to . . . display it publicly under section 109(b)."

Let's illustrate the meaning of this important provision with some examples.

> **Example.** *Kelley is a church music director. She purchased a transparency of a copyrighted song that is projected on a screen during morning worship services as an aid to congregational singing. While this practice constitutes a "public display" of the copyrighted work, and ordinarily the copyright owner has the exclusive right to publicly display a copyrighted work, section 109(c) permits the projection of the transparency by Kelley since (1) the copy (transparency) was lawfully acquired, (2) it is displayed by projection at the place where the viewers are physically present, and (3) only one image at a time is projected.*

> **Example.** *Same facts as the preceding example, except that Kelley purchased a slide. The answer would be the same.*

> **Example.** *Instead of purchasing a transparency, Kelley makes one herself by printing the lyrics of a copyrighted song onto a piece of paper and then making a transparency of the copy on church duplicating equipment. The display of the transparency by means of projection during church worship services is not protected by section 109(c), since the copy that is being displayed by projection is not a "lawfully made" copy as required by section 109(c) and the House Report.*

> **Example.** *Kelley purchases a booklet containing 20 copyrighted songs. She projects these songs on a screen during choir rehearsals and church services by means of an opaque projector. This practice is permitted by section 109(c), since it constitutes the display, by projection, of no more than one image at a time, of a lawfully made copy to viewers present at the place where the copy is located.*

> **Example.** *A church purchases a reproduction of a copyrighted painting that is placed on a wall in the church. This "public display" is authorized by section 109(c).*

> **Example.** *A church's youth pastor rents a video tape for use at an evening youth meeting. The tape is rented from a local video outlet, and is licensed for private home viewing only. Section 109(c) does not protect the showing of the video to the church youth group, since section 109(d) provides that the privilege granted in section 109(c) does not extend to a person who obtains possession of a copyrighted work through rental or lease.*

6.6 Face-to-Face Teaching Activities

Section 110(1) of the Copyright Act provides that the following activities are not an infringement upon a copyright owner's exclusive rights:

> [P]erformance or display of a work by instructors or pupils in the course of face-to-face teaching activities of a nonprofit educational institution, in a classroom or similar place devoted to instruction, unless, in the case of [an] audiovisual work, the performance, or the display of individual images, is given by means of a copy that was not lawfully made under this title, and that the person responsible for the performance knew or had reason to believe was not lawfully made.

There are a number of important elements to note in section 110(1):

performances and displays only

First, it exempts from copyright infringement only *performances and displays* of copyrighted materials in the course of face-to-face teaching activities at an educational institution. Reproduction and duplication of copyrighted materials are not exempted.

Second, the exemption applies only to face-to-face teaching activities at a nonprofit educational institution, in a classroom or other similar place devoted to instruction. While church-operated schools ordinarily would satisfy this requirement, there is some question whether church educational activities would. Certainly a church's formal education program (e.g. a Sunday School) would be the most likely church activity to qualify under section 110(1), but there are no authoritative rulings or interpretations at this time that would make this conclusion free from doubt.

Third, the exemption contained in section 110(1) does not apply if the copy being displayed or performed was not lawfully made, and the person responsible for the performance or display knew or had reason to know that the copy was not lawfully made. This important provision will be illustrated by the following examples:

> **Example.** *A church's minister of education makes copies of copyrighted material for use in the church Sunday School program. This practice is not authorized by section 110(1), since that section authorizes only certain performances and displays, and not reproductions. The church of course can still maintain that its practice is justified by the principle of fair use, as explained earlier in this chapter.*

> **Example.** *A church's music director makes copies of copyrighted music for use during choir rehearsals. Even if this can be considered "face-to-face teaching activities of a nonprofit educational institution," the exemption provided by section 110(1) does not apply to reproductions. Rather, it exempts only certain performances and displays.*

> **Example.** *A church's music director purchases a single piece of sheet music containing a copyrighted song. Not wanting to violate the copyright law, the director does not make physical copies for the choir but rather makes a transparency of the song using church duplicating equipment. The transparency is used during choir rehearsals. Is this practice authorized under section 110(1)? The answer is clearly no. Even if church choir rehearsals can be considered "face-to-face teaching activities of a nonprofit educational institution," the exemption provided by section 110(1) does apply if the copy being displayed or performed was not lawfully made, and the person responsible for the performance or display knew or had reason to know that the copy was not lawfully made. This is probably the case here, since the music director probably will be deemed to have had reason to know that the copy (transparency)*

being displayed was not lawfully made. Note that the making of a transparency may be permitted by some copyright licenses. See section 6.10 in this chapter.

6.7 The Religious Services Exemption

As far as churches are concerned, section 110(3) ranks as one of the most important provisions in the entire Copyright Act. This section states that

> the following are not infringements of copyright . . . performance of a nondramatic musical work or of a dramatico-musical work of a religious nature, or display of a work, in the course of services at a place of worship or other religious assembly.

musical works of a religious nature

The exemption applies to "dramatico-musical" works of a "religious nature." This language is intended to exempt certain performances of sacred music that might be regarded as "dramatic" in nature, such as oratorios, cantatas, and choral services. However, the exemption is not intended to cover performances of secular operas, plays, or motions pictures, even if they have an underlying religious or philosophical theme and take place in the course of religious services.

course of services

To be exempted under section 110(3), a performance or display must be "in the course of services." This excludes activities at a place of worship that are for social, educational, fund raising, or entertainment purposes.

The exemption includes both performances of musical or dramatic works of a religious nature, or the display of a work, in the course of services at a place of worship or religious assembly.

> ***Key point.*** *The religious services exemption does not apply to the copying of religious music since copying is not a performance or a display.*

displays

All displays are covered by the exemption, regardless of the nature of the work being displayed. However, the definition of "display" does not extend to the sequential showing of motion pictures and other audiovisual works.

place of worship

Since the performance or display must occur "at a place of worship or other religious assembly," the exemption would not extend to religious broadcasts or other transmissions to the public at large, even where the transmissions were sent from the place of worship. On the other hand, as long as services are being conducted before a religious gathering, the exemption would apply if they were conducted in places such as an auditorium or outdoor theatre.

> ***Key point.*** *A federal court has observed that the religious services exemption is "a narrow exception to copyright protection," and that the Copyright Act "narrowly limits the privilege accorded religious uses to performance of a . . . literary or musical work . . . or display of a work, in the course of services at a place of worship or other religious assembly." The unauthorized copying and distribution of literature or music "falls outside of that narrow exception to copyright protection."[38]*

> ***Example.*** *A publisher of religious music can prevent churches from copying or publishing its copyrighted works, even if the churches only used the copies in nonprofit religious services. Neither the religious element nor the nonprofit element of a performance protects illegal copying or publishing.[39]*

Example. Rachel sings a copyrighted sacred song as a solo during a morning worship service at First Church. Since this constitutes a performance of the song, and since the copyright owner alone has the exclusive right to publicly perform a copyrighted work, Rachel's performance would constitute an infringement of copyright except for the exemption provided by section 110(3). Section 110(3) specifically provides that the performance of a musical work of a religious nature in the course of services at a place of worship or other religious assembly is exempt from copyright infringement. Therefore, neither Rachel nor the church has violated the copyright law.

Example. Same facts as the preceding example, except that the church broadcasts its morning worship services over a local radio station. The exemption provided by section 110(3) protects the live performance of the work in the course of the church service, but it does not extend to the radio transmission. The church should check with the radio station to be sure that it has a license that protects the transmission of the copyrighted music.

Example. Same facts as the two preceding examples, except that the church also prepares audio cassettes of its services for distribution to persons who were not able to attend the service. The exemption provided by section 110(3) does not extend to the making of audio tapes of the services in which copyrighted musical works were performed. The distribution of such tapes is governed by the compulsory license section of the copyright law (discussed later in this chapter).

Example. A church hosts a performance of the local symphony orchestra. The works performed during the concert include copyrighted contemporary musical works of a secular nature. The performance of these works is not protected from copyright infringement by section 110(3), although they may be protected under section 110(4), which is discussed later in this chapter.

Example. A church's music minister makes copies of copyrighted music for the members of her choir. This practice is not excused by section 110(3), since it does not constitute either a performance or a display.

Example. A church's music minister makes an unauthorized transparency of a copyrighted song and displays it on a screen during worship services. The making of the transparency is an infringement of copyright that is not protected by section 110(3), since it does not constitute a performance or a display.

Example. A youth pastor rents a video of a religious movie for use in an evening youth service. The showing of the video to the church youth group is an infringement of copyright if it were rented out only for private home viewing. Such an infringement is not excused by section 110(3) since it does not constitute either a performance or a display.

Example. During an overnight activity at church, a youth group watches a few programs on a television set brought by an adult sponsor. While the exemption available under section 110(3) will not apply, this activity is excused from infringement by section 110(5) of the Copyright Act, which exempts the mere reception in public of an ordinary radio or television receiving device of a kind commonly sold to members of the public for private use. This exemption assumes that the audience is not charged a fee to see the transmission.

6.8 The Nonprofit Performance Exemption

Section 110(4) contains a general exception to the exclusive right of a copyright owner to publicly perform his or her copyrighted work. It provides:

> [P]erformance of a nondramatic literary or musical work otherwise than in a transmission to the public, without any purpose of direct or indirect commercial advantage and without payment of any fee or other compensation for the performance to any of its performers, promoters, or organizers, [does not constitute copyright infringement] if—(A) there is no direct or indirect admission charge; or (B) the proceeds, after deducting the reasonable costs of producing the performance, are used exclusively for educational, religious, or charitable purposes and not for private financial gain, except where the copyright owner has served notice of objection to the performance under the following conditions; (i) the notice shall be in writing and signed by the copyright owner or such owner's duly authorized agent; and (ii) the notice shall be served on the person responsible for the performance at least seven days before the date of the performance, and shall state the reasons for the objection; and (iii) the notice shall comply, in form, content, and manner of service, with requirements that the Register of Copyrights shall prescribe by regulation.

Let's consider a number of important aspects of this important exemption.

requirements

1. *The performance must not have a profit motive.*

2. *No fee or compensation can be paid to the performers (or promoters or organizers) for the performance.* This condition does not prevent performers from receiving a salary for duties that include a particular performance. For example, performances by a school band do not lose the benefit of this exemption merely because the band conductor is a music teacher who receives an annual salary for performing his duties, so long as he receives no fee or payment for any particular performance.

3. *There must either be no direct or indirect admissions charge, or alternatively, if an admissions charge is assessed, then any amounts left after deducting the reasonable costs of producing the performance must be used solely for educational, religious, or charitable purposes.* If there is an admissions charge, then the copyright owner is given the authority to "veto" the performance by serving upon the person responsible for the performance a notice objecting to the performance. Such a notice must be in a writing that is signed by the copyright owner; it must be served upon the person responsible for the performance at least seven days before the date of the performance; and, it must state the reasons for the objection. The impact of this provision is limited severely by the fact that section 110(4) does not require that the copyright owner be notified that his or her work is going to be performed at a nonprofit event with an admissions charge.

> *Example. A professional musical group agrees to conduct a performance at a church on a Saturday night. The group will perform several copyrighted religious songs of other composers. An admissions fee of $5 per person will be charged, and the group will receive a guaranteed fee of $1,000 for the performance. Will the performance of these copyrighted works be exempt from copyright infringement under section 110(3)? The exemption provided by section 110(3) probably will not apply. Section 110(3) exempts from copyright infringement the performance of a religious work in the course of a services at a place of worship. It cannot be safely assumed that a court would conclude that a Saturday evening performance was "in the course of services" at a place of religious assembly, especially if religious services were not ordinarily scheduled or conducted at such a time. The House Report to the Copyright Act of 1976 states that*

the exemption provided by section 110(3) does not include performances "at a place of worship that are for social, educational, fund raising, or entertainment purposes." [40] *While it is possible that a court might regard such a performance to be in the course of a religious service, such a result cannot be safely assumed. If, on the other hand, the performance were conducted during a regularly scheduled morning or evening service, then there is much greater support for the applicability of section 110(3).*

Example. *Same facts as the preceding example. Assume that section 110(3) does not exempt the performance from copyright infringement. Will the performance be exempt from infringement under section 110(4)? The answer is no, since the performers will receive a fee for their performance. This result is not affected by a characterization of the compensation as a "donation" or "contribution" to the group.*

Example. *Same facts as the preceding two examples, except that no admissions fee will be charged, and the group will receive no compensation for its performance. Such a performance will qualify for exemption from infringement under section 110(4), since it is a nonprofit performance, the performers and promoters receive no compensation for the performance, and no admissions fee is charged.*

Example. *A musical group agrees to conduct a nonprofit performance of several copyrighted works at a church. The performance will not be conducted during a regularly scheduled service, but the group will receive no payment for its performance. An admissions fee of $5 per person will be charged, and all the proceeds will go toward a missions project of the church. The performance of a copyrighted work under these circumstances will not constitute a copyright infringement, so long as a copyright owner does not file a written notice of objection to the performance within seven days of the performance. As noted above, section 110(4) does not require the copyright owner to be apprised of an imminent performance of his or her work, and this fact renders the copyright owner's "veto" power largely ineffective. As a result, it is possible that a court may limit the application of section 110(4) to persons and organizations that have notified a copyright owner in advance of a scheduled performance of his or her copyrighted work. Churches wishing to rely on the exemption provided under section 110(4) should consider giving the copyright owner or owners notice of an imminent performance.*

6.9 Ephemeral Recordings

Section 112(c) provides that it is not an infringement of copyright for a nonprofit organization to make no more than one copy of a religious program containing performances of copyrighted musical works for each broadcast station carrying the program. The following conditions must be satisfied for this exemption to apply: (1) there is no charge for distribution of the copies; (2) none of the copies is used for any performance other than a single transmission by an organization possessing a license to transmit a copyrighted work; and (3) other than for one copy that may be preserved for archival purposes, the remaining copies must be destroyed within one year from the date the program was first transmitted to the public.

6.10 Compulsory Licenses

A. Background

Among the exclusive rights of a copyright owner are the rights to make copies of and distribute the copyrighted work. However, for copyright holders of nondramatic musical works, the exclusive rights of reproduction and distribution are limited by the compulsory license provisions of section 115 of the Copyright Act. Often referred to as the "mechanical license," section 115 grants third parties a nonexclusive license to make and distribute "phonorecords" of nondramatic musical works. The license can be invoked once a nondramatic musical work embodied in a phonorecord is distributed "to the public in the United States under the authority of the copyright owner." Unless and until such an act occurs, the copyright owner's rights in the musical work remain exclusive, and the compulsory license does not apply. Once it does occur, the license permits anyone to make and distribute phonorecords of the musical work provided, of course, that they comply with all of the royalty and accounting requirements of section 115.

It is important to note that the mechanical license only permits the making and distribution of phonorecords of a musical work, and does not permit the use of a sound recording created by someone else. Persons claiming a compulsory license must either assemble their own musicians, singers, recording engineers, and equipment, or obtain permission from the copyright owner to use a preexisting sound recording. One who obtains permission to use another's sound recording is eligible to use the compulsory license for the musical composition that is performed on the sound recording.

B. Application to Churches

tape recordings of church services

Can churches make and distribute tape recordings of worship services in which copyrighted music is performed? This is a significant concern of many churches, since it is a common practice for churches to make tape recordings of services available to members and nonmembers alike who either were not present for a particular service, or who for whatever reason desire a recording of a service. As noted in section 6.7 of this chapter, the Copyright Act exempts from copyright infringement the performance of a copyrighted musical work of a religious nature in the course of services at a church or other place of religious assembly. However, this exemption does not extend to the making of a copy of that performance. Churches can respond to this problem in a variety of ways.

options

• Obtain advance permission from copyright owners to make and distribute recordings of services in which copyrighted works are performed.

• Avoid the use of copyrighted music in recorded services.

• Turn off the recording device when copyrighted music is being performed during a recorded service (e.g., by a soloist, the choir, or the congregation). The finished recording will not contain any reproduction of copyrighted music. Some churches "splice in" prerecorded public domain musical works that were previously sung by the church choir for this purpose.

• Enter into a "blanket license agreement" with copyright owners (or their agents). This approach is discussed in section 6.10.

• Obtain a compulsory license (sometimes called a mechanical license)

compulsory license procedures

Let's turn our attention to this last option—a compulsory license. This technique avoids any infringement problem, but it remains relatively unknown to churches and church leaders. Here's how the compulsory license procedure works. Assume that a church records its services and distributes audio cassettes to anyone requesting one and paying a $5 "reproduction" fee. The morning worship service conducted on a particular day included the performance of one copyrighted song, and this song is included on the tapes of the service. The act of recording the service, as well as the making of additional tapes for distribution, ordinarily would constitute copyright infringement. However, if the copyright owner of the copyrighted song has authorized the distribution of phonorecords or tapes of the song to the public, and if the church's primary purpose in making the tapes was to distribute them to the public for private use, then the church's actions will not constitute copyright infringement if the church obtains a compulsory license.

It is important to note that the mechanical license only permits the making and distribution of phonorecords of a musical work, and does not permit the use of a sound recording created by someone else. Persons claiming a compulsory license must either assemble their own musicians, singers, recording engineers, and equipment, or obtain permission from the copyright owner to use a preexisting sound recording. One who obtains permission to use another's sound recording is eligible to use the compulsory license for the musical composition that is performed on the sound recording.

C. How Does One Obtain a Compulsory License?

The first step is to identify the copyright owner of the nondramatic musical work to be recorded. This may be done either by personally searching the records of the Copyright Office or by requesting that the Copyright Office conduct the search.

If the name and address of the copyright owner are found, then:

notice
- Before or within 30 days after making, and before distributing any phonorecords of the work, serve a Notice of Intention to Obtain a Compulsory License on the copyright owner by certified or registered mail.

royalties
- Make royalty payments, accompanied by a Monthly Statement of Account, to the copyright owner on or before the 20th day of each month for every phonorecord made and distributed in accordance with the license. See the table entitled "Compulsory License Royalty Rates" in this section.

annual statements
- File with the copyright owner a detailed Annual Statement of Account, certified by a certified public accountant.

If the name and address of the copyright owner are not found, then:

- File a Notice of Intention to Obtain a Compulsory License in the Library of Congress, Copyright Office, Licensing Division, 101 Independence Avenue, S.E., Washington, D.C. 20557-6400.

- Submit the statutory fee with each Notice of Intention. Upon receipt of such a Notice, the Licensing Division will provide the sender with a written acknowledgment of receipt and filing. Upon request and payment of an additional fee for each Notice of Intention, the Licensing Division will provide a Certificate of Filing.

- Make checks payable to Register of Copyrights.

> ***Key point.*** *The name and address of the copyright owner may appear in the records of the Copyright Office at a later time. Since royalty payments must be made after the copyright owner is identified in the Copyright Office records, a church claiming a compulsory license should periodically search these records to determine if the copyright owner has been identified. If the copyright owner is identified, the church should make royalty payments for phonorecords made and distributed after the copyright owner is so identified.*

The Copyright Office does not provide forms for the Notice of Intention, the Monthly Statement of Account, or the Annual Statement of Account.

> **Key point.** *The Copyright Act defines "phonorecords" as "material objects in which sounds, other than those accompanying a motion picture or other audiovisual work, are fixed." Since the compulsory license applies only to the making and distributing of phonorecords, and soundtracks are not "phonorecords," the compulsory license is not available to one wishing to record on a soundtrack.*

> **Key point.** *The person wishing to make and distribute phonorecords of a nondramatic musical work may negotiate directly with the copyright owner or his or her agent. But, if the copyright owner is unwilling to negotiate or if the copyright owner cannot be contacted, the person intending to record the work may use the compulsory licensing provisions of the copyright law.*

Table 6-1 Compulsory License Royalty Rates	
date	rate
after January 1, 2000	royalty rate payable with respect to each work embodied in the phonorecord shall be either 7.55 cents, or 1.45 cents per minute of playing time or fraction thereof, whichever amount is larger
after January 1, 2002	royalty rate payable with respect to each work embodied in the phonorecord shall be either 8.0 cents, or 1.55 cents per minute of playing time or fraction thereof, whichever amount is larger
after January 1, 2004	royalty rate payable with respect to each work embodied in the phonorecord shall be either 8.5 cents, or 1.65 cents per minute of playing time or fraction thereof, whichever amount is larger
after January 1, 2006	royalty rate payable with respect to each work embodied in the phonorecord shall be either 9.1 cents, or 1.75 cents per minute of playing time or fraction thereof, whichever amount is larger

As noted above, royalties are payable each month. This amount is computed, for each copyright owner, by multiplying the applicable royalty rate times the number of phonorecords or tapes made and distributed during the month times the number of times a copyrighted musical work of that owner was reproduced on the phonorecords or tapes. To illustrate, if a church records four services in a particular month, and makes and distributes 50 tapes of each service, and if it performed a copyrighted musical work of ABC Publishing Company in two of the monthly services, then the monthly royalty would be computed by multiplying the applicable royalty rate times 2 (copyrighted musical works) times 100 (tapes distributed containing the copyrighted work).

All compulsory licensees must keep in their possession all records and documents necessary to support fully the information set forth in an annual statement of account for a period of at least three years from the date an annual statement of account was served on a copyright owner.

Section 115(c) further provides that "if the copyright owner does not receive the monthly payment and the monthly and annual statements of account when due, the owner may give written notice to the licensee that, unless the default is remedied within thirty days from the date of the notice, the compulsory license will be automatically terminated. Such termination renders either the making or the distribution, or both, of all phonorecord [or tapes] for which the royalty has not been paid, actionable as acts of infringement . . . ."

Let's illustrate these requirements with several examples.

> *Example.* A church music director makes unauthorized copies of sheet music for members of the church choir. No compulsory license is available for such copies, since the compulsory license procedure is available only to the making of phonorecords (including tape recordings) of copyrighted musical works.

> *Example.* A church records worship services and distributes tapes upon request to anyone who pays a fee of $5. In the month of December, it performed a total of 12 copyrighted musical works in the 5 recorded services. These 12 works were owned by a total of 5 publishers. Phonorecords or tapes of each of the 12 works had previously been distributed to the public by the copyright owner. To obtain a compulsory license, the church must serve notice to each of the five copyright owners "before or within thirty days after making, and before distributing" phonorecords or tapes that include the copyrighted works. Then, by the following January 20, the church must submit a monthly statement of account to each copyright owner by registered or certified mail, along with the appropriate royalty fee. An annual statement of account must also be submitted to the copyright owners. How much will the church be required to pay in royalties? This depends on the number of tapes distributed. If a total of 10 tapes were distributed for each service (50 tapes for the month), then the royalties would be computed by multiplying the applicable royalty rate (see the table in this section) times the number of recorded services times the number of recorded songs protected by copyright. While compulsory licenses are an option that church leaders should consider, they are rarely used. As this example illustrates, most church leaders would find complying with the compulsory license requirements to be too burdensome. Other options that are available to church leaders are summarized at the beginning of this section.

> *Example.* A church music director makes an unauthorized transparency of a copyrighted song for use in the course of religious services. No compulsory license is available for such a copy, since the compulsory license procedure is available only to the making of phonorecords (including tape recordings) of copyrighted musical works.

> *Example.* A church does not charge for audio cassettes of church services that it distributes. The absence of a sales charge does not make the unauthorized copies exempt from infringement. The compulsory license procedure is available.

> *Example.* A church would like to pay compulsory license royalties to the copyright owner of a song that was performed in a church service that was recorded (100 tapes were distributed). However, the church cannot locate the copyright owner. If the owner is not identified in Copyright Office records, section 115 specifies that "it shall be sufficient to file the notice of intention in the Copyright Office."

> *Example.* A church has distributed tapes of its services for several years without authorization from any copyright owner and without complying with the compulsory license procedure. It learns of the compulsory license procedure, and would like to begin complying with it. Failure to have filed the prescribed notice with the copyright owner (or with the Copyright Office if the owner's whereabouts is unknown) "before

*or within thirty days after making, and before distributing" the phonorecords or tapes
of the church services will prevent the church from obtaining a compulsory license,
meaning that its actions will constitute copyright infringement unless authorization
has been previously obtained from the copyright owner.*

**alternatives to
compulsory
licenses**

Obviously, the compulsory license procedure is complex and cumbersome. Further, failure to have used it in the past may prevent its use in the future. As a result, most churches that distribute tape recordings of their services seek to avoid copyright infringement by selecting one of the other alternatives mentioned at the beginning of this section. Let's summarize them again. First, they may obtain advance permission from copyright owners to make and distribute recordings of services in which copyrighted works are performed. This approach may result in a church paying a modest fee. Second, they can avoid the use of copyrighted music. Third, they can turn off the recording device when copyrighted music is being performed (e.g., by a soloist, the choir, or the congregation). The finished tape will not contain any reproduction of copyrighted music. Some churches "splice in" prerecorded public domain musical works that were previously sung by the church choir for this purpose. Fourth, a church can enter into a "consensual agreement" or "blanket license agreement" with copyright owners. Such an agreement typically involves a compulsory license approach, with simplifications. For example, a music publisher may agree to dispense with the requirement that a church serve notice on the publisher "before or within thirty days after making, and before distributing" phonorecords or tapes that include copyrighted works. Further, a publisher may dispense with the monthly statements of account and the annual statement of account certified by a CPA. Instead, much less technical forms may be used.

Section 115 specifies that a compulsory license "includes the privilege of making a musical arrangement of the work to the extent necessary to conform it to the style or manner of interpretation of the performance involved, but the arrangement shall not change the basic melody or fundamental character of the work, and shall not be subject to protection as a derivative work . . . except with the express consent of the copyright owner."

6.11 Computer Programs

Section 117 of the Copyright Act provides that it is not an infringement for the owner of a copy of a computer program to make another copy of that program in either of the following two situations: (1) the intangible copy that is made in a computer's random access memory (RAM) when a piece of software is inputted into

---

The Digital Performance Act

In 1995, Congress passed the Digital Performance Right in Sound Recordings Act ("Digital Performance Act"), which amended section 115 of the Copyright Act to take account of technological changes which were beginning to enable digital transmission of sound recordings. The Act expanded the scope of the mechanical license to include the right to distribute, or authorize the distribution of, a phonorecord by means of a digital transmission which constitutes a "digital phonorecord delivery." A "digital phonorecord delivery" is defined as "each individual delivery of a phonorecord by digital transmission of a sound recording which results in a specifically identifiable reproduction by or for any transmission recipient of a phonorecord of that sound recording." As a result of the Digital Performance Act, the mechanical license applies to two kinds of disseminations of nondramatic musical works: (1) the traditional making and distribution of physical, hard copy phonorecords as described in this section, and (2) digital phonorecord deliveries, commonly referred to as DPDs. However, in including DPDs within section 115, Congress added a wrinkle by creating a subset of DPDs, commonly referred to as "incidental DPDs." It did this by requiring that royalty fees established under the compulsory license rate adjustment process distinguish between "(i) digital phonorecord deliveries where the reproduction or distribution of a phonorecord is incidental to the transmission which constitutes the digital phonorecord delivery, and (ii) digital phonorecord deliveries in general."

---

a computer, and (2) a single backup copy of a computer program can be made for archival purposes. Any other duplication of copyrighted computer software ordinarily constitutes copyright infringement, unless authorized by the copyright owner.

> ***Example.*** *A church purchases a single piece of software that is accessed simultaneously through a network of linked computers. This constitutes copyright infringement unless such use is authorized by a license or some other means (or, presumably, if the software is intended to serve a network).*

> ***Example.*** *A church owns one computer. It has purchased several pieces of software. It is not an infringement for the church to input its lawfully obtained software into its computer's random access memory, although this constitutes the making of a copy. The church may also make a single backup copy of each item of software for archival purposes. Note, however, that the backup copy must be for archival purposes only. It cannot be used on a minister's personal computer, or any other computer on the premises (unless the copyright owner has authorized additional duplication).*

> ***Example.*** *A church purchases a single piece of software that is used "one-at-a-time" (not simultaneously) by several computer operators. Such usage ordinarily will not constitute copyright infringement, since the owner of the software (the church) has the authority to use the software in any manner so long as unauthorized duplicates are not made.*

> ***Example.*** *A church obtains a piece of software from a local vendor on a trial basis. The church cannot make a copy of the software and then return the original to the vendor. Similarly, if an employee of the church brings a software program to work that she has purchased for her personal use, the church cannot make a copy of the software without authorization from the copyright owner.*

Many software makers are willing to provide additional copies of particular programs for greatly reduced prices, and in some cases do not even charge if duplicated copies are intended for nonprofit use. However, never assume that a church will be treated leniently. Always check with the software owner before any unauthorized duplication.

6.12 Authorization from the Copyright Owner

Even if none of the exceptions to copyright infringement discussed above is available, the use of copyrighted material may be authorized by the copyright owner. For example, assume that a church choir director wishes to perform a particular song during a worship service, he has a single octavo, he cannot obtain additional copies locally, and it is too late to order copies by mail. While this "emergency need" to make unauthorized copies is not a recognized exception to copyright infringement, the director is free to contact the copyright owner directly and request permission to make copies. If permission is granted, then the making of copies will not constitute infringement.

licenses
Many music publishers have very liberal policies with respect to church music. Some publishers grant "blanket licenses" to churches, authorizing them to make copies of any song in the publisher's repertory for an annual fee. Occasionally, several publishers and composers will assign the right to license the use of their works to a single company in return for the payment of a royalty. The company acts as a clearinghouse on behalf of the publishers and composers, granting blanket licenses to churches in exchange for a fee that is apportioned among the various publishers and composers. Perhaps the first such arrangement involving religious music

was implemented by F.E.L. Publications, Ltd., in the 1970s. F.E.L. obtained the rights to 1400 songs, and offered annual licenses to churches for a fee of $100. The annual license authorized a church to copy any of the listed songs. Further, the purchaser was granted the right to perform the music and text at not-for-profit performances for purposes of worship or classroom use. A church that wanted to use one of F.E.L.'s listed songs could not deal directly with any of the authors or composers whose musical works or copyrights had been exclusively assigned to F.E.L.

F.E.L.'s annual license differed from traditional marketing of music in that it did not distinguish between songs, but charged a lump sum for which the licensee received the use rights to all of F.E.L.'s 1400 available compositions, even though the purchaser desired to use only a few of the more popular songs. It also differed from usual marketing practices in that it relied heavily on the licensee to patrol its own use. On the anniversary date of the license, the customer had to destroy all copies made of the virtually unlimited number allowed, unless it elected to pay F.E.L another $100 for an additional annual license.[41]

A federal district court found the F.E.L. blanket licensing scheme to be a "tying contract" that was illegal under the Sherman Antitrust Act. Specifically, the court observed that

> by obtaining assignments of the songs with the right, on behalf of the composers, to license their use for an annual fee, and by obtaining assignment of copyrights for the same purpose, F.E.L. either absolutely controls or has ownership power over copyrights to hymnals, songbooks, and the 1400 religious songs listed in its master title index. A Catholic church or parish that wants to purchase the right to copy and use a song either in one of F.E.L.'s hymnals, songbooks, or those listed in its master title index, cannot deal directly with owners of the copyrighted works listed by F.E.L. In most instances, a church or parish does not desire permission to use all of F.E.L.'s listed songs; there is no interest in all of the songs in F.E.L.'s hymnals, songbooks, and listed in the master index. The most desired are about 25 or 30 of the more popular or "blockbuster" songs. Yet, F.E.L.'s policy has always been "all or nothing"; the church or parish desiring to purchase the right to copy and use some of the listed songs has to pay for permission to use all of them. The songs are different; in many instances, the composers are different, yet purchase of the right to use the more popular has been tied by F.E.L. to the purchase of all, including the less popular. It is now well known that a tying arrangement whereby a party agrees to sell one product but only on condition that the buyer also agrees to purchase a different or tied product is prohibited by the Sherman Act, and by the Clayton Act.

exclusive licenses The F.E.L. license was an exclusive license, meaning that a composer gave F.E.L. the sole right to market his or her song. While an in depth discussion of the legality of such licenses is beyond the scope of this book, it should be noted that a few courts have upheld the legal validity of nonexclusive licenses. For example, ASCAP and BMI operate in much the same manner as F.E.L. in the sense that members give ASCAP and BMI the right to license the performance or broadcast of members' copyrighted works. ASCAP and BMI in turn grant blanket licenses authorizing licensees, for a flat fee, to use any work in the ASCAP or BMI repertory. ASCAP and BMI have been the target of several lawsuits alleging violation of federal antitrust laws (because of "tying arrangements"). So far, ASCAP and BMI blanket licenses have been upheld on the ground that they are nonexclusive. This means that ASCAP's and BMI's members retain the right to directly license their works to third parties. Churches that obtained a license from F.E.L. were not afforded this right (they granted F.E.L. the exclusive right to license the performance and reproduction of their works).

Christian Copyright Licensing, Inc. (CCLI) A similar approach is used by Christian Copyright Licensing, Inc. (CCLI) of Portland, Oregon. CCLI has attempted to avoid the antitrust issue by having publishers and composers enter into nonexclusive assignments of their musical works with CCLI. While CCLI acts as a clearinghouse for several publishers and composers, the publishers and composers remain free to directly market and license their works to individual churches. Churches that purchase a blanket license from CCLI (called a "church copyright license") are authorized to make copies of copyrighted music in the CCLI repertory (which includes approximately 250,000 copyrighted works) in any of the following ways during the license term (some conditions apply):

• Make audio recordings of worship services in which copyrighted music is performed.

• Make video recordings of worship services in which copyrighted music is performed.

• Create and project songs from an overhead or slide projector during worship services, youth meetings, adult classes, and similar activities.

• Copy songs in bulletins that are distributed before worship services.

• Copy music onto songsheet handouts. Covered music can be copied from hymnals or songbooks or simply typed and duplicated.

• Copying songs from a variety of sources to create "customized" church songbooks.

• Maintain a database of songs on a church computer.

• Make audio or videotapes of weddings, camps, and special services.

The cost of the CCLI church copyright license is based on congregational attendance at the church's primary worship service during the week. For smaller churches, the cost of an annual license can be as low as $46. For larger churches the cost is greater, but most churches will pay no more than $200 for an annual license.

Churches that purchase a CCLI church copyright license must make a record of the songs they sing or perform in the course of a year, and file reports with CCLI. These reports help CCLI allocate royalties to the various publishers and composers.

For many churches, the CCLI license makes compliance with copyright law much easier. Churches wishing to contact CCLI may write them at the following address: Christian Copyright Licensing, Inc., 17201 NE Sacramento Street, Portland, Oregon 97230. The telephone number is 1-800-234-2446, and the web site is www.ccli.com.

> ***Key point.*** *Note that CCLI licenses only apply to limited cases of reproduction and performance of religious musical works. They do not convey any authorization with respect to duplication of literary works (books and articles), and they do not apply in all cases to reproduction or performance of music. For example, copying music for members of the church choir is not allowed. As a result, a CCLI license must not be viewed as a solution to all of a church's copyright concerns.*

Showing Videos to Groups at Church

Showing videos is a common church practice. Many churches show videos to children's and youth groups, and adult educational classes often show videos. This practice will constitute copyright infringement if the video is copyrighted and permission has not been granted (by license or direct authorization of the copyright owner) to show the video in church. Showing copyrighted videos to groups within the church usually constitutes an infringement of the copyright owner's exclusive right of public display. If the video was copied from a television broadcast or another video, there is also an infringement of the copyright owner's exclusive right of reproduction. It does not matter that no fee is charged to watch the video.

Some videos designed for church use allow their display to groups under specified conditions. It is imperative for church leaders to review the terms of the license, if any, that come with each video. Most are licensed solely for private, in-home viewing.

One way for churches to comply with the copyright law when showing videos is to purchase an annual license from Motion Picture Licensing Corporation, 5455 Centinela Avenue, Los Angeles, CA 90066-6970, telephone 1-800-462-8855 (web site mplc.com). MPLC is an independent copyright licensing service exclusively authorized by major motion picture studios and independent producers to grant "umbrella licenses" to nonprofit groups, including churches, to publicly display video licenses for private, in-home use. Over 50,000 organizations have obtained the MPLC license. The license allows unlimited use of all MPLC authorized motion picture titles within licensed facilities. The license period is generally one year and there is a low annual fee. The license does not cover showings where an admission is charged or where specific titles have been advertised or publicized. The fee for an annual license can be as low as $95. It is based on a number of factors, including the number of videos that will be shown during the year and the number of viewers.

Endnotes

[1] Stewart v. Abend, 495 U.S. 207 (1990).

[2] Sony Corp. v. Universal City Studios, Inc., 104 S. Ct. 774 (1984).

[3] *Id.*

[4] Universal City Studios, Inc., v. Sony Corp., 659 F.2d 963 (9th Cir. 1981), rev'd, 104 S. Ct. 774 (1984).

[5] Campbell v. Acuff-Rose Music, Inc., 510 U.S. 569 (1994).

[6] *See, e.g.,* Radji v. Khakbaz, 607 F. Supp. 1296 (D.D.C. 1985); Marcus v. Crowley, 695 F.2d 1171 (9th Cir. 1983).

[7] House Report on the Copyright Act of 1976, pp. 73-74.

[8] Senate Report on the Copyright Act of 1976, p. 64.

[9] *Id.* See also Sony Computer Entertainment America, Inc. v. Bleem, 214 F.3d 1022 (9th Cir. 2000).

[10] Senate Report on the Copyright Act of 1976. This language was quoted with approval by the United States Supreme Court in Harper & Row, Publishers, Inc. v. Nation Enterprises, 471 U.S. 539 (1985).

[11] *See, e.g.,* Maxtone-Graham v. Burtchaell, 803 F.2d 1253 (2nd Cir. 1986) (out-of-print status of copyrighted book supports fair use determination).

[12] *See, e.g.,* Walt Disney Productions v. Air Pirates, 581 F.2d 751 (9th Cir. 1978).

[13] Harper & Row, Publishers, Inc., v. Nation Enterprises, 471 U.S. 539 (1985).

[14] New Era Publications v. Carol Publishing Group, 904 F.2d 152 (2nd Cir. 1990).

[15] Maxtone-Graham v. Burtchaell, 803 F.2d 1253 (2nd Cir. 1986).

[16] Fisher v. Dees, 794 F.2d 432 (9th Cir. 1986).

[17] Wright v. Warner Books, Inc., 748 F. Supp. 105 (S.D.N.Y. 1990).

[18] Maxtone-Graham v, Burtchaell, 803 F.2d 1253 (2nd Cir. 1986).

[19] Princeton University Press v. Michigan Document Services, Inc., 855 F. Supp. 905 (E.D. Mich. 1994).

[20] Lish v. Harper's Magazine Foundation, 807 F. Supp. 1090 (S.D.N.Y. 1992).

[21] Robinson v. Random House, Inc., 877 F. Supp. 830 (S.D.N.Y. 1995).

[22] Sony Corp. v. Universal City Studios, Inc., 104 S. Ct. 774 (1984).

[23] Worldwide Church of God v. Philadelphia Church of God, Inc., 227 F.3d 1110 (9th Cir. 2000).

[24] Karll v. Curtis Publishing Co., 39 F. Supp. 836 (E.D. Wisc. 1941).

[25] Broadway Music Corp. v. F-R Publishing Corp., 31 F. Supp. 817 (S.D.N.Y. 1940).

[26] Berlin v. E.C. Publications, Inc., 219 F. Supp. 911 (S.D.N.Y. 1963).

[27] Johns & Johns Printing Co. v. Paull-Pioneer Music Corp., 102 F.2d 282 (8th Cir. 1939).

[28] Leo Feist, Inc. v. Song Parodies, Inc., 146 F.2d 400 (2nd Cir. 1944).

[29] New Era Publications International v. Carol Publishing Group, 904 F.2d 152 (2nd Cir. 1990).

[30] Worldwide Church of God v. Philadelphia Church of God, Inc., 227 F.3d 1110 (9th Cir. 2000).

[31] Encyclopedia Britannica Educational Corporation v. C.N. Crooks, 542 F. Supp. 1156 (W.D.N.Y. 1982).

[32] American Geophysical Union v. Texaco, Inc., 802 F. Supp. 1 (S.D.N.Y. 1992).

[33] House Report on the Copyright Act of 1976, pp. 68-70. Representatives of the American Association of University Professors and of the Association of American Law Schools strongly criticized the guidelines on the ground that they were too restrictive with respect to classroom situations at the college and graduate level.

[34] Bridge Publications, Inc. v. Vien, 827 F. Supp. 629 (S.D. Cal. 1993).

[35] Princeton University Press v. Michigan Document Services, Inc., 99 F.3d 1381 (6th Cir. 1996).

[36] House Report on the Copyright Act of 1976, pp. 70-71.

[37] Wihtol v. Crow, 309 F.2d 777 (8th Cir. 1962).

[38] Worldwide Church of God v. Philadelphia Church of God, Inc., 227 F.3d 1110 (9th Cir. 2000).

[39] F.E.L. Publications, Ltd. v. Catholic Bishop of Chicago, 214 U.S.P.Q. 409 (7th Cir. 1982).

[40] House Report on the Copyright Act of 1976, p. 84.

[41] F.E.L. Publications v. Catholic Bishop of Chicago, 506 F. Supp. 1127 (N.D. Ill. 1981).

7

The Catholic Bishop and Wihtol Cases

This chapter will summarize the two leading cases addressing the application of copyright law to the church. While both cases were decided under the copyright law that existed before the Copyright Act of 1976, they both continue to exert considerable influence.

7.1 F.E.L. Publications, Ltd. v. Catholic Bishop of Chicago[1]

The most significant case involving copyright infringement by a church is *F.E.L. Publications, Ltd. v. Catholic Bishop of Chicago.*

In response to the demand for Catholic liturgical music in the English language following the Second Vatican Council, F.E.L. Publications ("F.E.L.") began producing hymnals and songbooks. These publications consisted largely of public domain works, works composed by F.E.L., and works composed by other authors who had granted F.E.L. an exclusive license to sell their works in return for royalty payments. From the 1960s until 1976, Catholic parishes within the Chicago Archdiocese used F.E.L. hymnals and songbooks. Initially, F.E.L. granted churches a license to copy any of its copyrighted songs for two cents per copy. Because of unauthorized copying within the parishes, F.E.L instituted a new licensing program in 1972 which it called an "annual copying license" (ACL).

Under the new arrangement, churches could choose among three alternatives: (1) purchase a one-year ACL for $100 that gave a church a license (i.e., legal right) to "make unlimited numbers of copies from F.E.L.'s printed page or from user's own original master copy"; (2) purchase the right to use any song for any one occasion (such as a wedding or funeral) for a charge of two cents per copy per song (minimum charge of $10); and (3) churches could purchase F.E.L.'s hymnals and songbooks, regardless of whether they desired permanent copies of all or only a few selections. F.E.L. owned the rights to 1400 sacred songs, all of which were available to a church that purchased a one-year ACL for $100. Churches wanting to use any of these songs could not deal directly with the composer, since the composer had granted F.E.L. an exclusive license to market the work. Churches that purchased a one-year ACL for $100 were required to destroy all copies that were made pursuant to the license at the end of the term, unless an additional $100 was paid to renew the license for an additional year. F.E.L. also offered parishes a "prior copying release," which would excuse past copyright infringement for a single payment of $500.

The parishes' response to these arrangements was less than overwhelming, and, because of continued infringement, F.E.L. filed suit against the Catholic Bishop of Chicago in 1976. The lawsuit alleged that the Catholic Bishop infringed the copyrights owned by F.E.L. by "publishing, distributing, and selling songbooks including songs which were copied largely from F.E.L.'s work, and by allowing others to publish, distribute and sell songbooks on property owned, controlled and supervised by the Catholic Bishop."

F.E.L. alleged that it was entitled to actual damages of $190,400—the amount it would have received if each of the 238 infringing parishes had obtained F.E.L.'s $100 annual copying license for each of the three years in which infringement was proven, and had also obtained a $500 prior copying release for all previous unauthorized copying. After F.E.L. brought the lawsuit, the Catholic Bishop sent letters to local parishes and to bishops and archbishops throughout the United States, instructing them not to use F.E.L. materials until the lawsuit was completed. This action prompted F.E.L. to seek additional damages for the Catholic Bishop's alleged "tortious interference" with F.E.L.'s business relationships.

In 1981, a federal trial court acknowledged that the making of "xeroxed or typewritten hymnals from songs in copyrighted hymnals" constituted copyright infringement. However, the court dismissed the lawsuit on the ground that F.E.L.'s licensing scheme was a "tying contract" that was illegal under the Sherman Antitrust Act. Specifically, the court observed that

> by obtaining assignments of the songs with the right, on behalf of the composers, to license their use for an annual fee, and by obtaining assignment of copyrights for the same purpose, F.E.L. either absolutely controls or has ownership power over copyrights to hymnals, songbooks, and the 1400 religious songs listed in its master title index. A Catholic church or parish that wants to purchase the right to copy and use a song either in one of F.E.L.'s hymnals, songbooks, or those listed in its master title index, cannot deal directly with owners of the copyrighted works listed by F.E.L. In most instances, a church or parish does not desire permission to use all of F.E.L.'s listed songs; there is no interest in all of the songs in F.E.L.'s hymnals, songbooks, and listed in the master index. The most desired are about 25 or 30 of the more popular or "blockbuster" songs. Yet, F.E.L.'s policy has always been "all or nothing"; the church or parish desiring to purchase the right to copy and use some of the listed songs has to pay for permission to use all of them. The songs are different; in many instances, the composers are different, yet purchase of the right to use the more popular has been tied by F.E.L. to the purchase of all, including the less popular. It is now well known that a tying arrangement whereby a party agrees to sell one product but only on condition that the buyer also agrees to purchase a different or tied product is prohibited by the Sherman Act, and by the Clayton Act.

A federal appeals court reversed the lower court's ruling against F.E.L., and a trial was conducted. The jury agreed that copyright infringement had occurred, and returned a verdict (in April of 1984) of $190,400 in actual damages, $2 million in compensatory damages, and $1 million in punitive damages. The Catholic Bishop appealed this verdict, and a federal appeals court upheld the actual damages award of $190,400, but held that the other awards had to be reduced to the extent that they were based on the Bishop's encouragement of Chicago parishes to refrain from purchasing F.E.L.'s materials. The court observed that the Catholic Bishop of Chicago and the Chicago parishes comprise one legal entity, and accordingly the bishop could not be guilty of "interfering" in the business arrangements of others.

The *Catholic Bishop* decision is significant for the following reasons:

1. It recognizes that a church can be sued for copyright infringement.

2. It recognizes that making copies of copyrighted songs constitutes copyright infringement.

3. It demonstrates that typing only the lyrics of a copyrighted song is sufficient to constitute copyright infringement.

4. It indicates that certain "blanket license" agreements may be unlawful under federal antitrust law. The

license involved in the *Catholic Bishop* case was an exclusive license, meaning that a composer gave F.E.L. the sole right to market his or her song. While an in depth discussion of the legality of such licenses is beyond the scope of this book, it should be noted that a few courts have upheld the legal validity of nonexclusive licenses. For example, ASCAP and BMI operate in much the same manner as F.E.L. in the sense that members give ASCAP and BMI the right to license the performance or broadcast of members' copyrighted works. ASCAP and BMI in turn grant blanket licenses authorizing licensees, for a flat fee, to use any work in the ASCAP or BMI repertory. ASCAP and BMI have been the target of several lawsuits alleging violation of federal antitrust laws (because of "tying arrangements"). So far, ASCAP and BMI blanket licenses have been upheld on the ground that they are nonexclusive. This means that ASCAP and BMI members retain the right to directly license their works to third parties. Churches that obtained a license from F.E.L. were not afforded this right (authors and composers granted F.E.L. the exclusive right to license the performance and reproduction of their works).

7.2 Wihtol v. Crow [2]

In 1935, Austris Wihtol composed a song entitled "My God and I." The song achieved worldwide popularity, and became the chief source of income for its composer. It was performed largely in schools and churches. Nelson Crow was the choir director and organist at a Methodist church in Iowa. His duties included the selection of choral music for the choir and the furnishing of printed copies of music to its members. Mr. Crow found the song "My God and I" unsuitable for use by his choir, since the copyrighted song "was arranged for solo voice with piano score." Accordingly, he made a choral arrangement of the song which he duplicated for each member of his choir. His arrangement included a new four measure introduction, and contained the words "arranged by Nelson E. Crow." No reference was made to the composer, Mr. Wihtol.

Mr. Crow's church choir performed the new arrangement in a church service. He was so pleased with the result that he wrote Mr. Wihtol a letter advising him of the new arrangement and asking if he would be interested in buying it. When Mr. Wihtol's request to "inspect" a copy of the new arrangement was ignored, he sent Mr. Crow a letter advising him that "the plain fact is that you are guilty of copyright infringement and are subject to assessments and penalties that the law imposes on infringers." The letter continued: "For the present, we will not institute a criminal complaint for willful infringement (maximum penalty—one year in jail and $1,000 fine) because we wish to let you off as easily as possible. For the sake of a peaceful and pleasant settlement, please have all of the copies you made delivered to our office in California immediately." Crow immediately forwarded the copies that he had made. A few months later, Wihtol filed a lawsuit in federal district court alleging that Crow, and his church, were guilty of copyright infringement. The trial court concluded that Crow's arrangement was a noninfringing "fair use" of Wihtol's original; that the church was not guilty of infringement; and that Wihtol's threatening letter entitled Crow to an award of attorneys' fees. Wihtol immediately appealed this ruling.

The federal appeals court reversed the lower court's ruling and found Crow and the church guilty of copyright infringement. The court noted that Wihtol, the copyright owner, "had the exclusive right to copy his copyrighted song, and obviously Nelson E. Crow had no right whatever to copy it." The fact that Crow's copying "was done without intent to infringe" was of no help to him. In rejecting the trial court's conclusion that Crow's copying constituted noninfringing fair use of Wihtol's work, the court observed: "Whatever may be the breadth of the doctrine of 'fair use,' it is not conceivable to us that the copying of all, or substantially all, of a copyrighted song can be held to be a 'fair use' merely because the infringer had no intent to infringe." On the contrary, "the copying of [Wihtol's] song by Crow was, in our opinion, an infringement of [Wihtol's] copyright."

To constitute an invasion of copyright it is not necessary that the whole of a work should be copied, nor even a large portion of it in form or substance, but that, if so much is taken that the value of the original is sensibly

105

diminished, or the labors of the original author are substantially, to an injurious extent, appropriated by another, that is sufficient to constitute an infringement. The test of infringement is whether the work is recognizable by an ordinary observer as having been taken from the copyrighted source.

The court concluded that the church was also liable for copyright infringement since an employer is legally responsible for the actions of employees committed within the scope of their employment. The church had argued that it could not be responsible for Crow's infringement since he was an "independent contractor" rather than an employee. In rejecting this defense, the court observed that "it seems to us that the only reasonable inference that reasonably can be drawn from the evidence is that in selecting and arranging the song for use by the church choir, Crow was engaged in the course and scope of his employment by the church." The court also rejected the trial court's award of attorneys' fees to Crow as a result of Wihtol's intimidating letter. "Whatever may be thought of Wihtol," concluded the court, "the song is a copyrighted production which [he] can protect and defend against all infringements, intentional or otherwise." Further, the attorneys' fees never would have been awarded to Crow by the trial court had he been found guilty of infringement.

The Wihtol case is significant for the following reasons:

1. It recognizes that a church can be liable for the copyright infringement of its employees. Whether a particular individual is an employee of a church is often a difficult question to resolve. Generally, the "common law employee test" employed by the courts and the IRS in determining whether a particular taxpayer is an employee or self-employed for income tax reporting purposes is useful in making such a determination. See Richard Hammar's *Church and Clergy Tax Guide* for a complete explanation of this important test. The Wihtol case lends support to the conclusion that a church choir director and organist is an employee.

2. It recognizes that the unauthorized duplication of copyrighted music, even for performance by a church choir, constitutes copyright infringement.

3. It rejects the view that copying all, or substantially all, of a copyrighted musical work for use by a church choir constitutes noninfringing "fair use."

4. It recognizes that an unauthorized arrangement of a copyrighted musical work is an infringement of the copyright owner's exclusive rights. The arrangement involved in the Wihtol case involved a choral arrangement of a copyrighted song, together with a new four measure introduction.

Endnotes

[1] 506 F. Supp. 1127 (N.D. Ill. 1981), rev'd, 214 U.S.P.Q. 409 (7th Cir. 1982). See also 466 F. Supp. 1034 (N.D. Ill. 1978); 739 F.2d 284 (7th Cir. 1984); 754 F.2d 216 (7th Cir. 1985). This case will be referred to as the Catholic Bishop decision.
[2] 309 F.2d 777 (8th Cir. 1962).

8

Copyright in the Information Age

Copyright law in the United States was established at a time when the primary concerns were literary and musical works in written form. But we now live in the Information Age in which computers, software, electronic and digital modes of storage and communication, and the internet have led many to view paper publications as obsolete. How has copyright law responded to this strange new environment? That is the focus of this chapter.

8.1 Software

> *Key point. A report issued by the Software & Information Industry Association and the Business Software Alliance estimates that software "piracy" (the unauthorized duplication of copyrighted software) in 1999 cost U.S. software owners $3.2 billion. The report estimates that one in three uses of software by U.S. businesses in 1999 was from an unauthorized copy.*

Most churches own several software programs. Common examples are word processing, spreadsheet, database, financial, and audiovisual "presentation" software. It is common for many of these programs to be pre-installed on new computers, while other programs are purchased and installed after a computer is acquired.

copying software   There is much public confusion regarding the legality of making copies of software. This confusion is understandable. Consider the following factors:

- Software is a recent development unlike any previous medium or technology. This uniqueness has caused confusion regarding the legality of copying.

- Many software providers use "shrinkwrap licenses" that clearly describe the user's rights and obligations. But few users ever read these licenses because they consider them to be self-serving, or they find the language so technical as to be unintelligible. The "license" is quickly torn off the package and discarded.

- There are countless software programs that are freely available over the internet (often called "shareware") that are intended to be copied and shared. This practice has helped create the perception that software can be copied.

- The availability of all kinds of free information over the internet creates the perception that the public has a legitimate right to freely access and copy any information, whether subject to copyright protection or not.

As a result of these and other factors, many software users now view software as "different" from books and periodicals, and they assume that ordinary copyright principles do not apply. They believe they have a "right" to copy software and other forms of digital information. But as the landmark "Napster" case demonstrates, this perception is not always accurate and can lead to copyright infringement.[1]

What then do church staff need to know about copying software? This question is addressed in the following subsections.

A. Software Is Protected by Copyright Law

copyright covers software

Section 102 of the Copyright Act specifies that copyright protection "subsists . . . in original works of authorship fixed in any tangible medium of expression, now known or later developed, from which they can be perceived, reproduced, or otherwise communicated, either directly or with the aid of a machine or device." There is no question that this section allows software programs to be protected by copyright.[2] This means that the copyright owner of a software program has the same exclusive rights as any copyright owner, including the exclusive rights to copy and publicly distribute the program. As a result, it is a violation of copyright law for anyone who owns or possesses a software program to copy it, with the exceptions noted below.

> ***Key point.*** *A good rule to follow is that if a copyrighted software program can be used simultaneously by two or more persons then you have committed copyright infringement, because the only way that this can happen is for one or more copies to have been made.*

> ***Example.*** *Jay is a church staff member. He purchases a new computer at his home that came installed with the latest version of Microsoft Word. He brings the CD containing the software to work, and copies it on his church computer as well as the computers of three other staff members. Jay has committed copyright infringement if the copies he made at work were not authorized by Microsoft. This practice is sometimes called "softlifting."*

> ***Example.*** *Jay is a church staff member. He purchases a new computer at his home that came installed with the latest version of Microsoft Word. He installs the program on his laptop computer using the CD that came with his new computer. If Jay is the only person who uses both computers, then an argument can be made that no "simultaneous use" is possible, and therefore no copyright infringement has occurred.*

> ***Example.*** *Same facts as the previous example, except that Jay's wife often uses his home computer. Since simultaneous use of Microsoft Word is possible, Jay's act of*

installing the software on his laptop constitutes copyright infringement unless the copy was authorized by Microsoft.

Example. *Jay lets a friend borrow the CD containing the Microsoft Word program so she can install it on her computer. The friend returns the CD to Jay as soon as she installs the software on her personal computer. Jay has committed copyright infringement unless the copy was authorized by Microsoft.*

rationale

Some have argued that these rules are overly technical, and that persons who purchase computer software should be allowed to make copies so long as they realize no financial benefit. After all, cannot computer software be compared to a book that is purchased at a bookstore? The book owner is free to let anyone else borrow and read the book, and so why can't a purchaser of computer software do the same? Such an argument is unconvincing. Consider the following points:

• Book buyers who let others borrow and read their books *are not making unauthorized copies.* They are exercising their rights under what is called the "first sale doctrine." This doctrine, which is set forth in section 109(a) of the Copyright Act, specifies that the owner of a lawful copy "is entitled, without the authority of the copyright owner, to sell or otherwise dispose of the possession of that copy." But when a purchaser of computer software lets others borrow and download the software on their own computers, an unauthorized copy ordinarily is made that infringes on the copyright owner's exclusive right of duplication. A better analogy would be a book buyer who, rather than allowing others to borrow and read his book, makes copies for them. There is no question that this would amount to copyright infringement, and this is exactly what purchasers of computer software are doing when they allow others to download the software onto their own computers. Unauthorized copies are being made in violation of the copyright owner's exclusive rights.

• Computer software is a valuable property right. It is really no different in principle than computers themselves since both are examples of property. One is simply more tangible than the other. Would a church employee consider stealing a computer software program from a local office supply store without paying for it? Of course not. And yet, that is exactly what church employees are doing when they make unauthorized copies of a copyrighted software program. They are "stealing" from the copyright owner by acquiring a valuable property right without permission and without payment.

• Some church leaders evaluate whether or not to follow copyright law on the basis of the risk of detection and punishment. After all, if no one will ever know that church employees made a few unauthorized copies of computer software, who cares? But church leaders, more than anyone, should be guided in their judgments by ethical principles rather than the risk of punishment. Would a church employee walk out of a grocery store without paying for a cart of groceries because "no one was watching," or would he be guided by higher principles?

• In section 1.1 of this text we learned that the purpose of copyright law is "to promote the progress of . . . the useful arts, by securing for limited times to authors . . . the exclusive right to their respective writings." If authors and composers are given exclusive rights in their creative works, they will have little if any incentive to create them, and the public will be the loser. The United States Supreme Court stated the rationale as follows: "The economic philosophy behind the clause empowering Congress to grant . . . copyrights is the conviction that encouragement of individual effort by personal gain is the best way to advance public welfare through the talents of authors . . . in the useful arts. Sacrificial days devoted to such creative activities deserve rewards, commensurate with the services rendered."[3] If unauthorized copying of computer software becomes common enough, then companies and individuals will produce less of it because the financial rewards are too uncertain. In such a case, the entire society is the loser. Who, after all, is willing to work for extended periods of time without compensation? Jesus said that "the worker deserves his wages."[4]

B. Penalties for Unauthorized Duplication of Computer Software

As noted in section 5.3 of this text, a copyright infringer faces civil penalties of up to $150,000 per violation, and criminal penalties of up to $250,000 and a prison term of up to 5 years.

C. When Software Can Legally Be Copied

when software can be copied

In some cases, an owner of computer software can make a copy without committing copyright infringement. Consider the following examples:

(1) *the intangible copy made in a computer's random access memory (RAM)*

Section 117 of the Copyright Act specifies that it is not an infringement for the owner of a software program to make the "intangible copy" of the program in a computer's random access memory (RAM) that is needed to operate the program.

(2) *archival copies*

Section 117 of the Copyright Act specifies that it is not an infringement for the owner of a software program to make a single backup copy for archival purposes.

(3) *authorization by the copyright owner*

Copyright owners may authorize the duplication of computer software. Examples include (1) "site" licenses (sometimes called "concurrent use" licenses) that authorize employers to make up to a specified number of copies for their employees; (2) "shareware," which is software that users are allowed to copy on the condition that they pay the copyright owner a fee; (3) "freeware," which is the same as shareware except that no fee is expected or required; (4) a "shrinkwrap license" that comes with computer software and that in some cases may authorize a purchaser to make a limited number of copies under specified circumstances.

> ***Tip.*** *Some computer software licenses permit the purchaser to download the software on a computer at a place of employment and at home. Be sure to read your software license carefully since it will specify permitted uses.*

(4) *software in the public domain*

Software in the public domain has either lost its copyright protection, or never had it. This will be rare for any software created since March of 1989 when the Berne Treaty became effective, since a copyright notice is no longer required to maintain copyright protection. This means that the omission of a copyright notice on software will not result in the loss of copyright protection.

> ***Example.*** *A church has a computer network for all of its office computers. The church purchases a "Local Area Network" (LAN) version of a software program that is installed on the network and is accessible by all users. This practice is permissible so long as the terms of the license agreement are followed. For example, some licenses only permit access by a specified number of users. If this number is exceeded, copyright infringement occurs.*

> ***Example.*** *Same facts as the previous example, except that the church purchases a software program designed for use by an individual user (not a network). The software is installed on the church's computer network and is accessible by all users.*

This constitutes copyright infringement unless such use is authorized by the license agreement.

Example. A church owns one computer. It has purchased several pieces of software. It is not an infringement for the church to input its lawfully obtained software into its computer's random access memory, although this constitutes the making of a copy. The church may also make a single backup copy of each item of software for archival purposes. Note, however, that the backup copy must be for archival purposes only. It cannot be used on a minister's personal computer, or any other computer on the premises (unless the copyright owner has authorized additional duplication).

Example. A church has 2 pastors and 6 nonminister employees who have church-provided computers. One of the pastors purchases a new software program that works so well that he allows all of the other church employees to download the software onto their computers. Unless specifically authorized by the copyright owner (for example, in a license agreement) this practice constitutes copyright infringement since it violates the copyright owner's exclusive right of reproduction.

Example. Pastor Greg has a computer in his church office. In order to enable him to perform work while at home, the church permits him to copy onto his home computer three software programs that were purchased for his church computer. Is this practice permissible? After all, the only reason the copies are being made is to enable Pastor Greg to perform work at home. If the software can legally be used at church, why can't it be used at home? Copying the software onto Pastor Greg's home computer infringes on the copyright owners' exclusive right of reproduction, unless the copying is authorized by license.

Key point. Church staff should avoid purchasing software through internet auctions. It is common for persons to offer expensive software programs at a small fraction of their retail price. The low price makes the software very attractive, and can result in quick profits to the seller. In many cases, the software being offered represents an unauthorized copy. A recent survey conducted by the Software Information & Industry Association shows that 91% of all software sold over internet auctions is illegitimate. Unbelievable "bargains" are a good sign that the software is an unauthorized copy.

D. Reducing a Church's Liability Through a Software Policy

software policy

Employers are liable for the copyright infringement of their employees committed within the scope of their employment.[5] As a result, it is advisable for churches to take steps that will reduce the risk of liability for their employees' infringing acts. Here are two steps that can reduce a church's risk of liability: (1) adopt a software policy, and (2) have all staff sign a statement acknowledging their receipt, comprehension, and acceptance of the policy. A sample software policy and employee acceptance are set forth in Illustration 8-2.

8.2 E-mail

Most churches now have computers that are connected by modem or cable to the internet. This has opened a whole new mode of communication which has come to be known as "e-mail." It is now common for church staff members to communicate with other staff members, congregation members, vendors, and a host of other persons and organizations by means of e-mail. But church staff should recognize that the use of e-mail can lead to copyright infringement in some cases.

Illustration 8-1
Software Policy

Most software programs available for use on computers owned by the church are protected by federal copyright law. Churches are not exempt from these laws. In addition, software is normally protected by a license agreement between the purchaser and the software seller. The software provided by the church for use by staff may be used only as specified in the applicable software license. It is the policy of the church to respect the copyright protections given to software owners by federal law. As a result, the church expects all staff to abide by this policy.

1. Prohibitions. Church staff are prohibited from engaging in any one or more of the following acts:

    (a) Making unauthorized copies of church-provided software, including the downloading of church-owned software programs on an employee's personal computer at his or her home. The making of one archival copy of a software program is allowed so long as it is made by the user of the original program, kept with the original program, not further duplicated, and not used as a working copy unless the original is lost or destroyed. Staff are permitted to download a software program on a replacement computer so long as the program is deleted on the previously used computer.

    (b) Making unauthorized copies of software owned by a staff member for use on a church computer.

    (c) Using unauthorized copies of software programs.

    (d) Allowing persons who are not church staff members to make duplicate copies of church-provided software without the express written permission of the copyright owner.

    (e) Using church equipment to make unauthorized copies of software.

    (f) Using unauthorized copies of software on church-owned computers or on personal computers on church property.

    (g) Modifying a program to enable several persons to simultaneously access the program by means of a network or otherwise without the express written permission of the copyright owner.

    (h) Modifying the contents of a computer program without the express written permission of the copyright owner.

2. Reporting of known or suspected violations. Church staff shall report to the senior pastor or business administrator any known or suspected violations of this policy.

3. Violations of this policy. Any staff member who violates this policy is subject to disciplinary action. In addition, persons who violate U.S. copyright law and software licensing agreements may be subject to civil and criminal liability.

4. Responsibilities of the church. The church will investigate any known or suspected violation of this policy. It also will apprise all current and future staff (having access to church-owned computers) of this policy.

5. Definitions. As used in this policy, the term "staff" refers to employees, independent contractors, volunteers, members, and others who are allowed to use a computer owned by the church. The term "unauthorized copy" refers to copies of copyrighted software that are made without the express authorization of the copyright owner, whether made on discs, CDs, tapes, or in a computer's permanent memory. The term "unauthorized copy" does not refer to software that is in the public domain or that is "freeware."

Illustration 8-2
Employee's Acceptance of Software Policy
I have been given a copy of the church's Software Policy; I have read and understand all of its provisions; I agree to comply fully with the Software Policy; and in consideration of my continuing employment I understand and agree that any violation on my part of the Software Policy may result in my discipline, including dismissal.

_____   _____
employee signature   date

---

copyright law and e-mail

To illustrate, assume that Esther is a church employee, and that she has access to the internet on her church-provided computer. Esther occasionally comes across articles and other items that she thinks would be of interest to others, and she downloads the material and "attaches" it to e-mail messages. If Esther downloads and sends copyrighted material by means of e-mail, she has committed copyright infringement by violating the copyright owners' exclusive right of reproduction. When Esther sends copyrighted material with her e-mail, she is making a number of unauthorized copies. First, the material is stored, at least temporarily, in the internet service provider's (ISP's) random access memory (RAM). When Esther sends her e-mail, the ISP makes another copy that is stored in her "out box." The e-mail is then forwarded to the designated recipient, which often results in additional copies being made "en route" by intermediate providers. Eventually, a copy is made in the recipient's "in box." Other copies may be made if Esther makes "back up" copies of her computer memory. As this example illustrates, the use of e-mail can lead to copyright infringements if copyrighted materials are transmitted. As a result, church staff who have access to e-mail should be warned (in writing, through an appropriate policy) not to transmit any copyrighted material.

8.3 The Internet

Most churches now have at least one computer with access to the internet either through a phone modem or cable connection. This section will review the history of the internet, summarize how it works, and then address four potential copyright issues that are associated with church use of the internet.

A. History of the Internet

The "internet" is a collection of tens of thousands of networks linking millions of computers worldwide. What we now refer to as "the internet" grew out of an experimental project of the Department of Defense's Advanced Research Projects Administration ("ARPA") designed to provide researchers with direct access to supercomputers at a few key laboratories and to facilitate the reliable transmission of vital communications. ARPA supplied funds to link computers operated by the military, defense contractors, and universities conducting defense-related research through dedicated phone lines, creating a "network" known as ARPANet. Programs on the linked computers implemented a technical scheme known as "packet-switching," through which a message from one computer to another would be subdivided into smaller, separately addressed pieces of data, known as "packets," sent independently to the message's destination and reassembled upon arrival. Each computer on the network was in turn linked to several other computers, creating any number of routes that a communication from one computer could follow to reach its destination. If part of the network were damaged, a portion of the message could be re-routed automatically over any other path to its ultimate destination, a characteristic of the network intended initially to preserve its operability in the event of enemy attack.

Having successfully implemented a system for the reliable transfer of information over a computer network, ARPA began to support the development of communications protocols for transferring data between different types of computer networks. Universities, research facilities, and commercial organizations began to develop and link together their own networks implementing these protocols. These networks included a high-speed "backbone" network known as NSFNet, sponsored by the National Science Foundation, smaller regional networks, and, eventually, large commercial networks run by organizations such as Sprint, IBM, and Performance Systems International (commonly known as "PSI").

As faster networks developed, most network traffic shifted away from ARPANet, which formally ceased operations in 1990. What we know as "the internet" today is the series of linked, overlapping networks that gradually supplanted ARPANet. Because the internet links together independent networks that merely use the same data transfer protocols, it cannot be said that any single entity or group of entities controls, or can control, the content made publicly available on the internet or limits, or can limit, the ability of others to access public content. Rather, the resources available to one with internet access are located on individual computers around the world. It is estimated that as many as 200 million individuals had access to the information and tools of the internet by the year 1999.

Access to the internet can take any one of several forms. First, many educational institutions, businesses, libraries, and individual communities maintain a computer network linked directly to the internet and issue account numbers and passwords enabling users to gain access to the network directly or by modem. Second, "internet service providers" (ISPs) offer modem access to computers or networks linked directly to the internet for a fee. Third, commercial "on-line services"—such as America Online, CompuServe, Prodigy, and Microsoft Network—allow subscribers to gain access to the internet while providing extensive content within their own proprietary networks. Finally, organizations and businesses can offer access to electronic bulletin-board systems—which, like national on-line services, provide certain proprietary content; some bulletin-board systems in turn offer users links to the internet.

B. Categories of Internet Use

There are two overlapping categories of internet use. First, an individual who has secured access to the internet can correspond or exchange views with one or many other internet users. Second, a user can locate and retrieve information available on other computers. For any communication to take place over the internet, two pieces of software, adhering to the same communications protocol, are required. A user must have access to certain kinds of "client" software, which enables a computer to communicate with and make requests of remote computers where information is stored. These remote computers must be running "server" software, which provides information in response to requests by client software.

Communicating with other internet users

Perhaps the most widely used internet service is electronic mail, or "e-mail." Using any one of dozens of available "mailers" (client software capable of reading and writing e-mail), a user is able to address and transmit a message to one or more specific individuals. A user can also "subscribe" to an electronic mailing list on a topic of interest; the user receives a copy of messages posted by other subscribers and, in turn, can post messages for forwarding to the full mailing list. Once a mailing list is established, it is typically maintained using a "mail exploder"—a program such as "listserv" running on the server on which the list resides—that automatically (i.e., without human intervention) responds to a user's request to be added to or removed from the list of subscribers and retransmits messages posted by a subscriber to others on the mailing list. Some mailing lists are "closed": a user's request to join the list requires the approval of an individual who maintains the list. Mailing lists (both open and closed) may also be "moderated": all messages posted to the list are forwarded to a moderator, who approves certain messages and retransmits them to subscribers.

An individual sending a message that will be retransmitted by a mail exploder program has no way of knowing the e-mail addresses of other subscribers. Even if the user could obtain an e-mail address for each subscriber to a particular list, those addresses alone would provide no information about subscribers. There is no directory that identifies persons using a certain e-mail address. In addition, a user can avoid disclosing his true e-mail address by developing an e-mail "alias" or by using an "anonymous remailer"—a server that purges identifying information from a communication before forwarding it to its destination. Internet users may also transmit or receive "articles" posted daily to thousands of discussion groups, arranged by subject matter and known as "newsgroups," available through an electronic bulletin-board system known as "Usenet." When a user with access to a Usenet server—that is, a computer participating in the Usenet system—posts an article to a particular newsgroup, the server automatically forwards the article to adjacent Usenet servers, which in turn forward it to other servers, until the article is available on all Usenet sites that furnish access to the newsgroup in question.

Once a message reaches a particular Usenet site, it is temporarily stored there so that individual users—running client software, known as a "newsreader," capable of sorting articles according to header information identifying the newsgroup to which the article was posted—can review and respond to the message. Some Usenet newsgroups are moderated; messages to the newsgroup are forwarded to an individual who selects those appropriate for distribution. Because Usenet articles are distributed to (and made available on) multiple servers, one who posts an article to a newsgroup has no way of knowing who will choose to retrieve it, or whether or not the newsgroup is moderated. There is no newsgroup equivalent of a "closed" mailing list: access to a particular newsgroup can only be limited by restricting the number of servers participating in the newsgroup.

The internet also offers opportunities for multiple users to interact in real time. Using a program called "Talk," two users can exchange messages while they are both on line; a message typed on one user's computer will appear almost immediately on the other's screen. Servers running so-called "chat" software, such as Internet Relay Chat ("IRC"), permit multiple users to converse by selecting one of many discussion "channels" active at any time. Commercial on-line services such as America Online, CompuServe, Prodigy, and the Microsoft Network offer their own chat systems for their members. Having joined a channel, the user can see and read messages transmitted by other users, each identified by a name the user selects upon joining the channel. Individual participants in IRC discussions know other participants only by the names they choose upon entering the discussion; users can participate anonymously by using a pseudonym.

Locating and retrieving information on the internet

Individuals with internet access can take advantage of a number of tools for locating and retrieving information and resources stored on remote computers. One who wishes to make certain articles, files, or software available to other users will set up a server, adhering to certain communications protocols, capable of retrieving and presenting stored information in response to a request from client software using the same communications protocol.

(1) *File-Transfer Protocol ("FTP")*. One type of software implements a set of conventions for copying files from a host computer known as "file-transfer protocol" ("FTP"). With appropriate client software, a user with an account on the host computer can contact the server, view a directory of available files, and copy one or more of those files to his own computer. In addition to making files available to users with accounts, thousands of content providers also make files available for "anonymous" retrieval by users who do not possess an account on the host computer. A content provider who makes files available for retrieval by anonymous FTP has no way of discerning who gains access to the files.

(2) *"Gopher " Servers*. A second type of server software capable of making available the resources of a host computer is known as a "gopher" program. A gopher server presents information in a set of menus, enabling a user who gains access to the server to select a series of increasingly narrow menu items before locating a

desired file that can be displayed on or copied to the user's computer. A content provider who maintains a gopher server ordinarily has no way of knowing who will gain access to the information made available.

world wide web

(3) *The World Wide Web.* The third and perhaps best known method of locating and accessing information on the internet is by exploring the World Wide Web. Documents available on the Web are not collected in any central location; rather, they are stored on servers around the world running Web server software. To gain access to the content available on the Web, a user must have a Web "browser," which is software such as Netscape Navigator, Mosaic, or Internet Explorer, that is capable of displaying documents formatted in "hypertext markup language" ("HTML"), the standard Web formatting language. Each document has an address, known as a Uniform Resource Locator ("URL"), identifying, among other things, the server on which it resides. Most documents also contain "links," which are highlighted text or images that, when selected by users, permit them to view another, related Web document.

Because Web servers are linked to the internet through a common communications protocol, known as hypertext transfer protocol ("HTTP"), a user can move seamlessly between documents, regardless of their location; when a user viewing a document located on one server selects a link to a document located elsewhere, the browser will automatically contact the second server and display the document. Some types of Web client software also permit users to gain access to resources available on FTP and gopher sites.

search engines

A number of "search engines"—such as Yahoo, Magellan, Alta Vista, WebCrawler, and Lycos—are available to help users navigate the World Wide Web. For example, the service Yahoo maintains a directory of documents available on various Web servers. A user can gain access to Yahoo's server and type a string of characters as a search request. Yahoo returns a list of documents whose entries in the Yahoo directory match the search string and organizes the list of documents by category. Search engines make use of software capable of automatically contacting various Web sites and extracting relevant information. Some search engines, such as Alta Vista, store the information in a database and return it in response to a user request. Others, such as Yahoo, employ a group of individuals to determine whether and how a site should be categorized in the Yahoo directory.

As the growth in internet use and the wide availability of tools and resources to those with access to the internet suggest, the internet presents extremely low entry barriers to those who wish to convey internet content or gain access to it. In particular, a user wishing to communicate through e-mail, newsgroups, or Internet Relay Chat need only have access to a computer with appropriate software and a connection to the internet, usually available for a low monthly fee. The user then in a sense becomes a public "speaker," able to convey content, at relatively low cost, to users around the world to whom it may be of interest. Those who possess more sophisticated equipment and greater technical expertise can make content available on the internet for retrieval by others (known or unknown) by running a server supporting anonymous FTP, a gopher server, or a Web server. Yet content providers need not necessarily run their own servers or have the programming expertise to construct their own sites; they can lease space on a Web server from another or create a "home page" through an on-line commercial service.

C. Church Use of the Internet

A connection to the internet raises several potential copyright issues, including the following:

e-mail

(1) *e-mail*

The application of copyright law to e-mail is addressed in section 8.2 of this text.

browsing

(2) *browsing*

Browsing refers to the viewing of Web pages with a Web browser. To view a Web page the Web browser needs the URL of the desired document. This can be provided by either typing the information in the "URL window" on the browser's home page, or by using a pre-existing link on a pre-existing Web page (a "bookmark"). While browsing technically creates unauthorized copies of what is being viewed in the random access memory (RAM) of the user's computer, the question is whether these transitory copies are permanent enough to constitute a violation of the copyright owner's exclusive right of reproduction.

Some courts have reached the extraordinary conclusion that browsing the internet results in the making of unauthorized copies because of the temporary copies of web pages that are created in the random access memory (RAM) of the user's computer. For example, one court ruled that a computer repair person, who was not authorized to use the computer owner's licensed operating system software, committed copyright infringement when he turned on the computer and loaded the operating system into RAM memory long enough to check an "error log."[6] According to this case, the loading of data from a storage device into RAM constitutes copying because that data stays in RAM long enough for it to be perceived.

Other courts have concluded that the transitory "copies" of copyrighted web pages and materials that are created in the RAM memory of a user's computer are not permanent enough to constitute unauthorized copying, and so no copyright infringement occurs. To illustrate, in a case involving the unauthorized copying of copyrighted religious texts by a computer bulletin board service, a federal court ruled that browsing does not constitute a copyright infringement even though it involves the making of unauthorized copies. The court observed:

> Browsing technically causes an infringing copy of the digital information to be made in the screen memory. . . . The temporary copying involved in browsing is only necessary because humans cannot otherwise perceive digital information. It is the functional equivalent of reading, which does not implicate the copyright laws and may be done by anyone in a library without the permission of the copyright owner. However, it can be argued that the effects of digital browsing are different because millions can browse a single copy of a work in cyberspace, while only one can read a library's copy at a time. Absent a commercial or profit-depriving use, digital browsing is probably a fair use; there could hardly be a market for licensing the temporary copying of digital works onto computer screens to allow browsing. Unless such a use is commercial, such as where someone reads a copyrighted work online and therefore decides not to purchase a copy from the copyright owner, fair use is likely. Until reading a work online becomes as easy and convenient as reading a paperback, copyright owners do not have much to fear from digital browsing and there will not likely be much market effect. Additionally, unless a user has reason to know, such as from the title of a message, that the message contains copyrighted materials, the browser will be protected by the innocent infringer doctrine, which allows the court to award no damages in appropriate circumstances. In any event, users should hardly worry about a finding of direct infringement; it seems highly unlikely from a practical matter that a copyright owner could prove such infringement or would want to sue such an individual.[7]

In other words, even if browsing constitutes the making of unauthorized copies, no copyright infringement occurs in most cases because of the fair use defense[8] and the innocent infringer defense.[9]

downloading

(3) *downloading*

> ***Key point.*** *To download means to receive information (usually a file) from another computer by means of a modem. The opposite is an upload, which means to send a file to another computer.*

The downloading of materials from web sites is a common practice. Pastors may download information to use in preparing sermons, and other church staff members may download information for use in church classes, programs, and publications. If the material that is downloaded is not copyrighted, then there is no problem with infringement. For example, if a staff member downloads forms from the IRS website, this is permissible. But downloading copyrighted material is another story. There is no question that downloading copyrighted information infringes upon the copyright owner's exclusive right of reproduction. If the user uploads the copyrighted material to others, then the copyright owner's exclusive right of public distribution may be infringed.[10] However, the fair use defense often prevents downloading from constituting copyright infringement.[11] In other words, downloading copyrighted information for the user's personal reference or research often will constitute permitted fair use. Examples include downloaded news items, product reviews, travel schedules, research information, and weather reports. These items often will constitute permissible fair use under the four-factor analysis contained in the Copyright Act since the purpose of the downloading is noncommercial, the nature of the downloaded material is factual, the amount downloaded is small, and there is little if any impact on the market for the copyrighted work.

But some downloading will not qualify as fair use. For example, if a user downloads a copyrighted computer program, or music, this cannot be considered fair use. Further, when users upload information to others, this weakens the availability of the fair use defense.

> ***Example.*** *Individuals who downloaded copies of video games "to avoid having to buy video game cartridges" were guilty of copyright infringement. The fair use defense did not apply.*[12]

> ***Example.*** *In the "Napster" case, a federal appeals court ruled that users who downloaded copyrighted music were engaging in copyright infringement. MP3 is a standard file format for the storage of audio recordings in a digital format. With appropriate software, a computer user can copy an audio compact disk (CD) directly onto a computer's hard drive by compressing the audio information on the CD into the MP3 format. The MP3's compressed format allows for rapid transmission of digital audio files from one computer to another by electronic mail. Napster is a company*

The Audio Home Recording Act

Digital audio tape (DAT) technology was introduced to the consumer-electronics world in 1986. With this new technology, consumers for the first time could make home copies of prerecorded music as good as the commercial originals. Moreover, the technology allowed consumers to make copies not only from the commercial originals but from "copies of copies." From a single work, thousands of copies could be made that would be virtually indistinguishable from the original. The music recording industry became concerned that the DAT recorder's "perfect" copying capabilities could significantly decrease consumer demand for commercially prerecorded music products because there would be significantly more illegal "perfect" copies in circulation. The Audio Home Recording Act (AHRA) was enacted by Congress in 1992 to address this concern. AHRA contains the following provisions: (1) consumers are permitted to make copies directly from a lawfully purchased prerecorded tape for personal use but, due to digital code that is inserted into any initial copy, are prevented from making further copies from the initial copy; (2) a royalty is imposed on digital recorders, which are deposited with the Copyright Office for distribution by the Copyright Royalty Tribunal; (3) consumers are given immunity from liability for making analog musical recordings or digital musical recordings on a device covered by the AHRA royalty provisions. Note that computers and CD-R drives are not covered devices, and so AHRA does not provide legal immunity to persons who copy music onto their computer's hard drive or a CD.

that promoted the sharing of MP3 files through a process called "peer-to-peer" file sharing. Users simply went to the Napster internet site, downloaded software, and then were able to transfer exact copies of the contents of MP3 files from one computer to another via the internet. This allowed users to "download" exact digital copies of a vast array of popular copyrighted songs. A group of music publishers sued Napster in federal court. The court primarily addressed the liability of Napster for copyright infringement, but in so doing it also addressed the liability of individual users who downloaded copyrighted music using Napster. Napster insisted that its users were not engaging in copyright infringement because they were simply downloading MP3 files to "sample" the music in order to decide whether to purchase the recording, and that this is a permissible fair use. In rejecting this argument, the court concluded that sampling remains a commercial use even if some users eventually purchase the music.[13]

Key point. *According to one survey, 73% of college students used Napster at least monthly to download unauthorized copies of copyrighted music. Another survey found that persons 18 to 24 years of age download copyrighted music at least once each week.*

(4) *web sites*

church web sites

Churches can commit copyright infringement when creating and maintaining their own web sites. Here are some examples:

• *Images.* The use of someone else's image on your own web site without permission is a potential copyright infringement. Some "clip art" providers allow the use of their work on a web site for a fee. Before using clip art, be sure to read carefully the terms of the license.

• *Text.* The use of copyrighted text on a web site without permission will infringe upon the copyright owner's exclusive rights of reproduction and public distribution.

• *Linking.* Most web pages are written in computer languages, chiefly HTML, which allow the programmer to prescribe the appearance of the web page on the computer screen and, in addition, to instruct the computer to perform an operation if the cursor is placed over a particular point on the screen and the "mouse" is clicked. Programming a particular point on a screen to transfer the user to another web page when the point (referred to as a hyperlink) is clicked is called *linking*. Web pages can be designed to link to other web pages on the same site or to web pages maintained by different sites. For example, a web page maintained by a church may provide a hyperlink to its parent denomination's site, or to the site of a church literature supplier. Links bear a relationship to the information superhighway comparable to the relationship that roadway signs bear to roads. Like roadway signs, they point out the direction. Unlike roadway signs, they take one almost instantaneously to the desired destination with the mere click of an electronic mouse. The courts have ruled that linking in itself does not constitute copyright infringement. To illustrate, one court observed,

> Links are what unify the World Wide Web into a single body of knowledge, and what makes the Web unique. They are the mainstay of the internet and indispensable to its convenient access to the vast world of information. They often are used in ways that do a great deal to promote the free exchange of ideas and information that is a central value of our nation. Anything that would impose strict liability on a web site operator for the entire contents of any web site to which the operator linked therefore would raise grave constitutional concerns, as web site operators would be inhibited from linking for fear of exposure to liability. And it is equally clear that exposing those who use links to liability . . . might chill their use, as some web site operators . . . may be more inclined to remove the allegedly offending link rather than test the issue in court.[14]

119

Church web sites should not contain links to other web sites without first obtaining permission from the provider of the other site. Also, never create links that do not clearly reveal the source of the linked information.

• *Miscellaneous issues.* There are other legal concerns associated with the establishment and maintenance of church web sites having nothing to do with copyright law. These concerns, which are beyond the scope of this book, include the selection and protection of domain names, defamation, and trademark infringement.

The Napster Case

In 1987 a standard file format for the storage of audio recordings in a digital format was established that became known as MP3. With appropriate software, a computer operator can copy an audio compact disk (CD) directly onto a computer's hard drive by compressing the audio information on the CD into the MP3 format. The MP3's compressed format allows for rapid transmission of digital audio files from one computer to another by electronic mail. Napster is a company that promoted the sharing of MP3 files through a process called "peer-to-peer" file sharing. Users simply went to the Napster internet site, downloaded software, and then were able to transfer exact copies of the contents of MP3 files from one computer to another via the internet. This allowed users to "download" exact digital copies of a vast array of popular copyrighted songs. A group of music publishers sued Napster in federal court. The publishers claimed that Napster was a "contributory and vicarious" copyright infringer, and they asked the court to issue an injunction prohibiting Napster from "from engaging in, or facilitating others in copying, downloading, uploading, transmitting, or distributing" copyrighted music. The court issued the injunction, and Napster appealed. A federal appeals court ruled that Napster had engaged in copyright infringement, and it sustained the district court's injunction. The appeals court concluded that Napster users infringe at least two of the copyright holders' exclusive rights—the rights of reproduction and distribution. Napster users who upload files for others to copy violate the copyright holder's exclusive right of public distribution. And, Napster users who download files containing copyrighted music violate the copyright holder's exclusive right of reproduction. The court concluded that Napster was liable for the users' acts of copyright infringement on the basis of "contributory copyright infringement." It explained, "one who, with knowledge of the infringing activity, induces, causes or materially contributes to the infringing conduct of another, may be held liable as a contributory infringer. Put differently, liability exists if the defendant engages in personal conduct that encourages or assists the infringement." The court noted that Napster had "actual, specific knowledge of direct infringement" by its users, and concluded that "if a computer system operator learns of specific infringing material available on his system and fails to purge such material from the system, the operator knows of and contributes to direct infringement." The court also found Napster liable for its users' acts of copyright infringement on the basis of "vicarious copyright infringement." It defined vicarious infringement as infringement that is imputed to an employer because of acts of infringement by its employees in the course of their employment. But it concluded that vicarious liability also can be imputed to a defendant that "has the right and ability to supervise the infringing activity and also has a direct financial interest in such activities." The court ruled that this test was met in this case. Not only did Napster have a direct financial interest in the infringing activity of its users (its future revenue was directly dependent upon "increases in userbase"), but it also had the ability to supervise its users' conduct. The court noted that Napster's ability to block infringers' access for any reason was evidence of the right and ability to supervise, and that "to escape imposition of vicarious liability, the reserved right to police must be exercised to its fullest extent. Turning a blind eye to detectable acts of infringement for the sake of profit gives rise to liability."[15]

D. Internet Usage Policy

See Illustration 8-3 for a sample employee internet usage policy, developed by the Software & Information Industry Association.

Illustration 8-3
Employee Internet Usage Policy

Note: This policy was prepared by the Anti-Piracy Division of the Software & Information Industry Association (SIIA). It is reprinted with permission. SIIA permits the use of this policy in church employee manuals, and authorizes churches to modify the policy.

As part of this organization's commitment to the utilization of new technologies, many/all of our employees have access to the Internet. In order to ensure compliance with the copyright law, and protect ourselves from being victimized by the threat of viruses or hacking into our server, the following is effective immediately:

1. It is [Organization's] policy to limit Internet access to official business. Employees are authorized to access the Internet, for personal business, after-hours, in strict compliance with the other terms of this policy. The introduction of viruses, or malicious tampering with any computer system, is expressly prohibited. Any such activity will immediately result in termination of employment.

2. Employees using [Organization's] accounts are acting as representatives of the [Organization]. As such, employees should act accordingly so as not to damage the reputation of the organization.

3. Files which are downloaded from the Internet must be scanned with virus detection software before installation or execution. All appropriate precautions should be taken to detect for a virus and, if necessary, to prevent its spread.

4. The truth or accuracy of information on the Internet and in email should be considered suspect until confirmed by a separate (reliable) source.

5. Employees shall not place company material (copyrighted software, internal correspondence, etc.) on any publicly accessible Internet computer without prior permission.

6. Alternate Internet Service Provider connections to [Organization's] internal network are not permitted unless expressly authorized and properly protected by a firewall or other appropriate security device(s).

7. The Internet does not guarantee the privacy and confidentiality of information. Sensitive material transferred over the Internet may be at risk of detection by a third-party. Employees must exercise caution and care when transferring such material in any form.

8. Unless otherwise noted, all software on the Internet should be considered copyrighted work. Therefore, employees are prohibited from downloading software and/or modifying any such files without permission from the copyright holder.

9. Any infringing activity by an employee may be the responsibility of the organization. Therefore, this organization may choose to hold the employee liable for their actions.

10. This organization reserves the right to inspect an employee's computer system for violations of this policy.

I have read [organization's] anti-piracy statement and agree to abide by it as consideration for my continued employment by [organization]. I understand that violation of any above policies may result in my termination.

_____   _____
user signature   date

Endnotes

[1] A&M Records, Inc. v. Napster, Inc., 239 F.3d 1004 (9th Cir. 2001). The Napster case is addressed later in this chapter,

[2] The earliest court case recognizing the copyrightability of software was a 1983 decision by a federal appeals court. *Apple Computer, Inc. v. Franklin Computer Corp., 714 F.2d 1240 (3rd Cir. 1983)*. In the Apple case, the argument was made by Franklin Computer Corporation that computer software was not copyrightable since it was designed to be read by machines rather than humans. The court rejected this argument. It concluded that the "source code" that comprises a computer program is a "literary work" that can be copyrighted.

[3] Mazer v. Stein, 347 U.S. 201 (1954).

[4] Luke 10:7 (NIV).

[5] *See, e.g.,* A&M Records, Inc. v. Napster, Inc., 239 F.3d 1004 (9th Cir. 2001), Fonovisa, Inc. v. Cherry Auction, Inc., 76 F.3d 259 (9th Cir. 1996); Shapiro, Bernstein and Co. v. H.L. Green Co., 316 F.2d 304 (2nd Cir, 1963); Polygram International Publishing, Inc. v. Nevada/ TIG, Inc., 855 F. Supp. 1314 (D. Mass. 1984).

[6] MAI Systems Corp. v. Peak Computer, Inc., 991 F.2d 511 (9th Cir.1993).

[7] Religious Technology Center v. Netcom, Inc., 907 F.Supp. 1361 (N.D. Cal. 1995).

[8] *See* section 6.1, *supra.*

[9] *See* section 1.3, *supra.*

[10] *See* section 5.1, *supra.*

[11] *See* section 6.1, *supra.*

[12] Sega Enterprises, Ltd. v. MAPHIA, 857 F.Supp. 679 (N.D.Cal.1994).

[13] A&M Records, Inc. v. Napster, Inc., 239 F.3d 1004 (9th Cir. 2001).

[14] Universal City Studios, Inc. v. Reimerdes, 111 F.Supp.2d 294 (S.D.N.Y. 2000).

[15] A&M Records, Inc. v. Napster, Inc., 239 F.3d 1004 (9th Cir. 2001).

9

The Application of Copyright Law to the Church—A Glossary

The previous eight chapters explained in detail the application of copyright law to most church practices. This chapter will summarize, by topic and in alphabetical order, the major issues. You can use this chapter to obtain a quick answer to most questions. However, if you would like a more complete explanation of any particular issue, please refer back to the earlier chapters. References to specific sections or chapters are provided at the conclusion of each topic.

ACCOUNTINGS [see Compulsory Licenses]

ARCHIVAL COPIES

Can a church make a copy of any copyrighted work for archival purposes without violating the copyright law? The answer is no. However, some duplication may be authorized. Section 108 authorizes "libraries and archives" to make a single archival copy of a copyrighted work if no commercial benefit is intended, the collections of the library or archives are open to the public or are available to researchers not associated with the library or archives, and the copies contain a copyright notice. Section 108 also allows libraries and archives to make an archival copy of a damaged, lost, or stolen copyrighted work if an unused replacement copy cannot be obtained at a fair price. Interpreted broadly, section 108 may authorize churches to make a single copy of a copyrighted work for a church library or archives if the conditions summarized above are satisfied. No court has addressed the application of section 108 to churches. A library maintained by a church-operated private school would much more clearly qualify under section 108. Note that section 108 does not apply under any circumstances to musical works or audiovisual works (except in the case of copies made to replace damaged, lost, or stolen works). Further, section 108 applies only to "isolated and unrelated reproductions of a single copy" on separate occasions. As a result, a church choir director could not make 25 copies of a copyrighted octavo and claim that the making of these copies is authorized by section 108.

Section 117 allows the lawful owner of a computer program to make a "backup" copy for archival purposes.

[See sections 6.4, 6.11, and 8.1(C).]

ARRANGEMENTS (musical)

A musical arrangement is an adaptation of a musical composition. Arrangements may adapt a composition to fit another medium of performance (i.e., an instrumental arrangement of choral music, or of a piano composition), or they may simply modify an existing composition while retaining the character of the original. Whatever its form, an arrangement ordinarily is considered to be a "derivative work." Section 106 gives to a copyright owner the exclusive right to "prepare derivative works based upon the copyrighted work." Therefore, it is important to recognize that only the copyright owner has the authority to make arrangements of a copyrighted musical composition. Persons wanting to make an arrangement of a copyrighted musical work must obtain permission in advance from the copyright owner.

[See section 5.1(B).]

ARTICLES

Articles appearing in periodicals raise a number of important copyright questions: (1) are articles copyrightable independently of the periodical itself (and if so, how is this accomplished); (2) must copyrighted articles contain a separate copyright notice; (3) what right does the publisher of a periodical have to reprint an article that appeared previously in its publication; (4) how much of an article can be copied or quoted without infringing on the rights of the copyright owner? Let's answer each of these questions briefly. First, an article can be copyrighted separately from a publication in which it appears. Section 103(b) provides that the copyright in a periodical is independent of, and does not affect, any copyright in the preexisting materials that make up the periodical. Second, unless the author of an article transfers greater rights in a signed writing, it is presumed that he or she gives a publisher only the limited authority to publish the article in a single issue, plus in later issues "in the same series." Third, how much of a copyrighted article can be copied without infringing on the rights of the copyright owner? This question is answered fully in sections 5.1(A) and 6.1. For a brief discussion, see the topic "Copies" in this chapter.

[See sections 1.2 and 1.4.]

ASSIGNMENTS [see Transfers]

AUTHOR UNKNOWN

Occasionally a church will print a poem or quotation in a church bulletin or newsletter with the notation "author unknown." If the church cannot ascertain the identity of the author after a reasonable search, it is free to publish the work with the citation "author unknown," so long as it can establish that it was misled by the omission of notice.

[See section 1.3(B).]

AUTHORS

Section 201(a) of the Copyright Act specifies that a copyright in a particular work vests initially in the author. However, the term "author" is not defined. Note that the author of a "work made for hire" is the employer of the person who created the work.

[See section 1.4.]

BERNE CONVENTION

The Berne Convention is an international copyright convention established a century ago and endorsed by most nations. The United States became a party to the Berne Convention on March 1, 1989. Participation by the United States in this significant convention increases the international protections available to American authors. To become a party to the convention, Congress had to make various changes in our copyright law (unwillingness to make the required changes was one of the major reasons that it took the United States a century to join the convention). Among the notable changes in our copyright law were the following: (1) mandatory notice of copyright was abolished for works published for the first time on or after March 1, 1989; (2) registration of a copyrighted work whose "country of origin" is not the United States is no longer necessary in order to sue for infringement; (3) the penalties for copyright infringement were increased significantly; (4) the works of American authors and composers receive "automatic" legal protection in most foreign countries; (5) the recording of copyright "transfers" or assignments is no longer required prior to suing for infringement. These important changes, among others, are reflected throughout this text.

BIBLES

The King James Version is in the public domain, meaning that anyone can quote it as extensively as desired. Therefore, it is perfectly permissible to print the lyrics (but not the music) of "scripture choruses" using the

King James Version. However, all of the more recent translations and paraphrased versions of the Bible are copyrighted. As a result, these works cannot necessarily be quoted or reproduced without raising the possibility of copyright infringement. Most modern translations and paraphrased versions of the Bible contain an authorization (usually on or near the title page) for specified uses. For example, the New International Version permits users to quote from or reprint "up to and inclusive of one thousand verses without express written permission of the publisher, providing the verses quoted do not amount to a complete book of the Bible nor do the verses quoted account for 50% or more of the total work in which they are quoted." To illustrate, there are five books of the Bible that contain only one chapter (Obadiah, Philemon, Jude, 2 John, and 3 John). Technically, a pastor could not read the NIV translation of any of these books in a sermon without first obtaining permission from Zondervan Bible Publishers, the copyright owner. The reading of a copyrighted translation or version in the course of worship services is not exempted from copyright infringement by virtue of the "religious services exemption" set forth in section 110(3) of the Copyright Act, since this exemption only applies to religious music. However, the principle of "fair use" will justify the reproduction of portions of copyrighted translations and versions in many situations.

[See sections 5.1(A), 5.1(D), and 6.1.]

BLANKET LICENSES

A blanket license is a convenient way for a church to avoid infringing upon the copyrights of certain publishers and composers. Generally, a blanket license authorizes a church to use specified copyrighted music for certain purposes during the term of the license. The church pays a fee for the license. Blanket licenses are offered by some music publishers, and by a few companies that have obtained the legal right to license the copyrighted works of certain publishers and composers. Blanket licenses cannot ensure that a church will never violate the copyright laws, since (1) such licenses only authorize the making of certain types of copies and certain recordings and broadcasts (the terms vary from company to company), and (2) not all of the music that a church uses will be covered by blanket licenses. Christian Copyright Licensing, Inc. has developed a large repertory of songs that it is authorized to license to local churches. Churches that are not willing to obtain a blanket license should contact directly the publishers of the music that they enjoy performing, since individual publishers remain free to license the use of their works directly to churches even though they have agreed to allow CCLI or any other clearinghouse to act as their agent in licensing their works. In other words, CCLI has only a "nonexclusive" right to license copyrighted works in its repertory.

[See sections 6.12 and 7.1.]

BOOKS

Books raise a number of copyright issues that are summarized elsewhere in this chapter. See the following topics—Bibles, Copies, Classroom Instruction, Fair Use, Hymnals, Libraries, Registration.

BROADCASTS

Some churches broadcast their services over radio or television stations. In some cases the broadcasts are "live," while in others tape recordings of prerecorded services are utilized. What copyright questions are raised if a church's services are broadcast over a radio or television station? Performances of copyrighted musical works of a religious nature in the course of religious services at a church or other place of religious assembly are exempt from copyright infringement. However, this exemption does not extend to broadcasts of those performances. Whether such broadcasts constitute copyright infringement will depend upon whether or not the broadcaster has obtained a license to broadcast the copyrighted works performed in the course of the religious services. While this ordinarily is the responsibility of the broadcasting station, it would be appropriate for a church to confirm that the broadcaster in fact has a valid license authorizing broadcasts of the copyrighted religious works performed in the church services. These same rules generally apply to special programs produced by churches that are broadcast over radio or television stations. Examples include a short weekly or daily programming, or a holiday special. Also note that a church that records its services for future broadcasts has the right to make a recording (an "ephemeral recording") for each transmitting station if certain conditions are satisfied.

[See sections 5.1(A), 5.1(D), 5.1(E), 5.2, 6.1, 6.5, 6.7, and 6.9.]

BULLETINS

Churches often reprint poetry, cartoons, or the lyrics to copyrighted songs in their weekly bulletins and newsletters. If all or a significant portion of the lyrics to a copyrighted song are reproduced, or all or a significant portion of a copyrighted poem, or a copyrighted cartoon, such practices ordinarily would constitute copyright infringement. This is true even if proper credit is given to the author or composer.

[See sections 5.1(A), 5.2, and 6.1.]

CARTOONS

Church bulletins and newsletters often contain cartoons. However, if a copyrighted cartoon is reproduced, such a practice ordinarily will constitute copyright infringement. If you see a cartoon in a copyrighted periodical that you would like to reprint in a church bulletin or newsletter, be sure to obtain advance permission from the copyright owner.

[See sections 5.1(A), 5.2, and 6.1.]

CHOIR

The activities of church choirs often raise questions under copyright law. The major areas of concern are as follows: (1) choir directors cannot make unauthorized copies of copyrighted music for members of the choir without infringing upon the copyright owner's exclusive right to make copies of his or her work; (2) choir directors cannot make unauthorized transparencies of copyrighted music for use during choir rehearsals; (3) choirs are free to perform copyrighted music in the course of church services, but if the service is recorded and copies of the recording are sold or otherwise distributed to others without authorization from the copyright owner, infringement may occur; (4) choir directors should not alter or make arrangements of copyrighted works, since such actions may constitute an infringement upon the copyright owner's exclusive right to make derivative works. Note that the so-called "fair use guidelines" for educational uses of music (see "Classroom Teaching Activities—Making Copies") do not authorize the duplication of choral music. However, they do permit emergency photocopying to replace purchased copies that for any reason are not available for an imminent performance provided that purchased replacement copies are later substituted.

[See sections 5.1(A), 5.1(B), 5.1(D), 5.2, 6.1, 6.7, 6.10, 7.1, and 7.2.]

CHORAL WORKS [see Choir]

CHORUS BOOKLETS

Many churches have prepared "chorus booklets" to facilitate the singing of contemporary music during worship services. Typically, these booklets consist of the lyrics of a variety of copyrighted and public domain choruses. If the chorus lyrics are subject to copyright protection, then their unauthorized reproduction for use in church chorus booklets will constitute copyright infringement. It is no defense that only the lyrics (and not the music) are reproduced, since the lyrics comprise a significant portion (both in terms of quantity and quality) of the whole work. Further, the unauthorized reproduction of chorus lyrics is not justified because their use will be limited to religious worship services. Such a practice was found to constitute copyright infringement in the Catholic Bishop decision summarized in Chapter 7.

[See sections 5.1(A), 5.1(B), 5.1(D), 5.2, 6.1, 6.7, 6.10, 7.1, and 7.2.]

CHORUSES

Many church congregations sing choruses during worship services. Choruses are musical compositions consisting of both lyrics and music, and they ordinarily are either integral parts of a copyrighted hymn containing one or more verses or independent works not associated with another piece of music. Choruses raise a number of copyright issues. First, copyright protection can extend to either the lyrics, the music, or both. For example, both the lyrics and music of many choruses are subject to copyright protection. However, with older works, the lyrics and original score often are in the public domain (i.e., they have lost their copyright protection). Churches need to be careful here, since a new musical arrangement of a public domain chorus can be separately copyrighted. In such a case, the lyrics remain in the public domain, but the music is protected against infringement. This means that a church is free to copy in any manner the lyrics to such a chorus, but it cannot copy the music without authorization. Second, there is no doubt that the chorus of a copyrighted hymn constitutes a substantial enough part of the original that a church cannot copy it without infringing upon the copyright owner's exclusive right to make copies. The same rule applies to a chorus that is independent of any other musical work. This means that a church cannot make copies of copyrighted choruses, without authorization, for any purpose. This includes copies for the choir, copies inserted in "chorus booklets" utilized during congregational singing, and transparencies fabricated by church staff for use during choir rehearsals, church services, or instruction. Third, copyrighted choruses can be performed during church services—meaning that they can be sung by a choir or by the congregation. This assumes that lawful copies are being used for the performance. If the service in which choruses are performed is being recorded and copies of the recording are sold or otherwise distributed to others without authorization from the copyright owner, infringement may occur. Fourth, choir directors should not alter or make arrangements of copyrighted choruses, since such actions may constitute an infringement upon the copyright owner's exclusive right to make derivative works. Fifth, chorus lyrics (if copyrighted) cannot be reproduced in church bulletins or bulletin inserts, even if intended for just a single use, without authorization.

[See sections 5.1(A), 5.1(B), 5.1(D), 5.2, 6.1, 6.7, 6.10, 7.1, and 7.2.]

CHURCH LIABILITY

Churches can be liable for copyright infringement in any of the following three ways: (1) A church may directly commit copyright infringement by its own actions. For example, if a church creates a web site that includes unauthorized copies of copyrighted material, the church would be directly liable for violating the copyright owner's exclusive right of reproduction. (2) A church may be liable for an employee's acts of copyright infringement on the basis of the principle of contributory copyright infringement. Liability exists if a church "knew or had reason to know" of direct infringement by a staff member. Knowledge of specific acts of infringement is not required. Contributory copyright infringement also requires that the secondary infringer "materially contribute" to the infringing conduct. Material contribution can include providing the "site and facilities" for the infringing conduct. (3) Under the principle of vicarious copyright liability an employer is liable for the acts of its employees committed within the scope of their employment. It also imposes liability on an organization that "has the right and ability to supervise the infringing activity and also has a direct financial interest in such activities." Under this expanded definition, it is possible for churches to be liable for many acts of direct copyright infringement by their employees and others. All that is required is that a church have a right to supervise an infringing activity and a direct financial interest in that activity.

[See section 5.4.]

CHURCH SERVICES [see Religious Services]

CLASSROOM TEACHING ACTIVITIES—MAKING COPIES

Can a teacher make copies of copyrighted materials for each of the students in a class? If so, how does this protection apply to churches? These are two very important questions. In 1975, a group of publishers and educators drafted a set of guidelines specifying various types of classroom copying that they considered to be noninfringing "fair use." These guidelines pertained to copying of books and periodicals by nonprofit educational institutions for classroom use, and they were later included in the House Report on the Copyright Act of 1976 as "a reasonable interpretation of the minimum standards of fair use." These guidelines are reproduced in full in section 6.2. Generally, they authorize the making of copies for each member of a class if the copying meets tests of brevity, spontaneity, and "cumulative effect." Review the actual guidelines carefully. It is not yet clear whether the guidelines apply to churches, though there is little doubt that they will apply to church-operated private schools, and they logically should apply to religious instructional activities that occur in classroom facilities within a church. Also note that representatives of music publishers and music educators developed another set of guidelines that apply to educational uses of music. These guidelines were also approved by the House of Representatives in its report on the Copyright Act of 1976, and they are reproduced in full in section 6.3 of this book. Like the guidelines that apply to the copying of books and periodicals for classroom use, strict conditions apply with regard to the amount of music that can be copied. Further, it is unclear whether the music guidelines apply to churches. However, it is reasonably certain that they will apply to church-operated private schools, and they logically should apply to religious instructional activities that occur in classroom facilities within a church.

[See sections 6.2 and 6.3.]

CLASSROOM TEACHING ACTIVITIES—PERFORMANCES AND DISPLAYS

The performance or display of copyrighted works in the course of face-to-face teaching activities in a classroom at a nonprofit educational institution are permissible activities. Church-operated schools would qualify for this special protection, and it is arguable that instructional activities within a church would also qualify (though no court has so ruled). Note that only performances and displays are permitted—this rule does not authorize the making of copies. Second, only displays of lawfully acquired copies are covered. For the guidelines applicable to making copies for classroom use, see "Classroom Teaching Activities—Making Copies."

[See section 6.6.]

COMPULSORY LICENSES

A copyright owner has the exclusive right to publicly perform his or her works. However, the Copyright Act permits musical works of a religious nature to be performed in the course of services at a church or other religious assembly. This exception does not extend to recordings made of services, and accordingly a church commits copyright infringement by making and distributing recordings of services in which copyrighted music is performed. Churches can avoid this problem by obtaining a compulsory license (previously called "mechanical licenses") from the copyright owner. Such a license is available to any church that satisfies several conditions (including the filing of a timely notice with the copyright owner prior to distributing the tapes, the filing of monthly and annual statements of account with the copyright owner, and the payment of royalties). Failure to comply with these conditions (unless excused by the copyright owner) prevents a church from obtaining a compulsory license, and ordinarily makes the recording of services in which copyrighted music is performed a copyright infringement.

[See section 6.10.]

COMPUTERS

Many churches have grown dependent upon computers. While computers can save churches a substantial amount of time, they also create potential copyright problems. In particular, church employees must not make copies of copyrighted software without permission (other than a single copy for archival purposes). This includes software obtained for review or trial purposes from a local dealer, and also software owned privately by a church employee or church member. Also, church staff should be instructed not to modify copyrighted software without written permission.

See also E-Mail, Internet, and Software.
[See sections 6.11, 8.1, 8.2, and 8.3.]

COPIES

Many churches make copies of various literary and musical works for a variety of purposes. Examples include reproductions of (1) song lyrics in a church bulletin or homemade song booklet or on a transparency or slide, (2) both lyrics and music of choral music for members of the choir, (3) excerpts from books or magazines for use in the church educational program, or in church newsletters, (4) tape recordings (audio and video) of church services that contain performances of copyrighted songs, and (5) computer programs. These, and many other church copying practices, are potential infringements upon one of the most significant "exclusive rights" of a copyright owner—the right to make copies of his or her work. Verbatim copying of an entire work is not required in order for copyright infringement to occur. Reproductions of portions of a copyrighted work that are substantial either in terms of quantity or quality will suffice. It ordinarily is no defense that the infringer merely paraphrased the copyrighted work, or that copies were made for "nonprofit" or religious purposes. Nevertheless, the copyright owner's exclusive right to make copies is subject to a number of exceptions, including the following: (1) Fair use. Copying will not infringe upon the copyright owner's exclusive right of reproduction if it amounts to a "fair use" of the work. The following four factors must be considered in determining whether a particular use is a noninfringing fair use: (i) the purpose and character of the use, (ii) the nature of the copyrighted work, (iii) the amount and substantiality of the portion used in relation to the copyrighted work as a whole, and (iv) the effect of the use upon the potential market for or value of the copyrighted work. Fair use is ordinarily very difficult to establish. It will not be available if the amount of a copyrighted work that is copied is significant either in terms of quantity or quality, the copies serve the same function as the copyrighted work, and the copying is made in lieu of purchasing lawful copies of the work. Copying is permitted in limited situations for classroom instruction (see "Classroom Teaching Activities—Making Copies"). (2) The making of a copy for "archival" purposes is permitted in some situations (see "Archival Copies"). (3) Recording a religious service containing copyrighted music is in some cases permitted if the recording is to be submitted to a television or radio station for public broadcasting. (4) Recording a religious service containing copyrighted music is in some cases permitted if the church obtains a compulsory license. (5) The making of copies may be permitted under the terms of a blanket license agreement executed by the copyright owner or a company acting on behalf of the copyright owner.

[See sections 5.1(A), 5.2, 6.1, 6.2, 6.3, 6.4, 6.9, 6.10, 6.11, and 6.12.]

COPYRIGHT NOTICE [see "Notice of Copyright"]

DEPOSIT REQUIREMENTS

In general, a copyright owner has a legal obligation to deposit two copies of his or her work with the Copyright Office within three months of publication for the use of the Library of Congress. Failure to make the deposit can result in fines and other penalties, but will not affect copyright protection.

[See section 2.4.]

DERIVATIVE WORKS

One of the exclusive rights belonging to a copyright owner is the right to make "derivative works" that are based on the original work. Examples of derivative works include translations, musical arrangements, editions, and abridgements. This is a significant consideration for church musicians, for some of them are not aware that they have no legal right to make arrangements of copyrighted music.

[See section 5.1(B).]

DUPLICATING EQUIPMENT

Most churches have a duplicating machine. The making of copies of copyrighted materials (literary or musical) often will constitute copyright infringement. Exceptions do exist. (See "Copies.") Churches should place a copyright notice near any church-owned duplicating machine, advising users of their legal responsibility not to make unauthorized copies or copyrighted material. A similar notice should be placed in the vicinity of any duplicating equipment owned by a church-operated private school. School libraries may make copies of copyrighted materials under limited circumstances.

[See section 6.4.]

DURATION OF COPYRIGHT PROTECTION

How long does copyright protection continue? This is a significant question not only for copyright owners, but also for churches wishing to duplicate older materials. Once the term of copyright protection expires, a work ordinarily falls into the "public domain" and may be used for any purpose without authorization. Works created on or after January 1, 1978 ordinarily are protected for a term consisting of the author's life plus an additional 70 years. Works published or copyrighted before January 1, 1964 were protected for an initial term of 28 years, and could be renewed for a second term of 67 years by filing a renewal form with the Copyright Office during the 28th year of the first term of copyright. Works copyrighted between January 1, 1964 and December 31, 1977 are protected by copyright for the 28-year original term and a 67-year renewal term without the need for a renewal registration. Copyrights in their second term on January 1, 1978 were automatically extended to a combined term of 95 years (the renewal term was increased from 28 years to 67 years).

[See Chapter 3.]

EDUCATIONAL USES OF COPYRIGHTED MATERIALS [see Classroom Teaching Activities]

E-MAIL

Most churches now have computers that are connected by modem or cable to the internet. This has opened a whole new mode of communication which has come to be known as "e-mail." It is now common for church staff members to communicate with other staff members, congregation members, vendors, and a host of other persons and organizations by means of e-mail. Church staff members may commit copyright infringement by downloading copyrighted material from a web site and attaching it to an e-mail message that they send.

[See section 8.2.]

EMERGENCY COPIES

The "Guidelines for Educational Uses of Music," adopted by a group of music publishers and educators (and approved by the House of Representatives in its report on the Copyright Act of 1976), permit "emergency photocopying to replace purchased copies which for any reason are not available for an imminent performance provided purchased replacement copies shall be substituted in due course." This provision only applies to musical works.

[See sections 6.2, and 6.3.]

EMPLOYEE-MADE WORKS [see Works Made for Hire]

EXCLUSIVE RIGHTS

The copyright law gives a copyright owner the following five exclusive rights: (1) to reproduce the copyrighted work in copies or phonorecords; (2) to prepare derivative works based upon the copyrighted work; (3) to distribute copies or phonorecords of the copyrighted work to the public by sale or other transfer of ownership, or by rental, lease, or lending; (4) in the case of literary, musical, dramatic, and choreographic works, pantomimes, and motion pictures and other audiovisual works, to perform the copyrighted work publicly; and (5) in the case of literary, musical, dramatic, and choreographic works, pantomimes, and pictorial, graphic, or sculptural works, including the individual images of a motion picture or other audiovisual work, to display the copyrighted work publicly. These five exclusive rights are sometimes referred to as the rights of reproduction, adaptation, publication, performance, and display. They comprise the "bundle of rights" that constitute or define copyright. It is unlawful for anyone to violate any of the exclusive rights provided to the owner of a copyright. These rights, however, are not unlimited in scope. The approach of the Copyright Act is to set forth the copyright owner's exclusive rights in broad terms, and then to provide various limitations, qualifications, or exemptions.

[See section 5.1.]

FAIR USE

Section 107 of the Copyright Act specifies that "the fair use of a copyrighted work . . . for purposes such as criticism, comment, news reporting, teaching (including multiple copies for classroom use), scholarship, or research, is not an infringement of copyright. In determining whether the use made of a work in any particular case is a fair use the factors to be considered shall include—(1) the purpose and character of the use, including whether such use is of a commercial nature or is for nonprofit educational purposes; (2) the nature of the copyrighted work; (3) the amount and substantiality of the portion used in relation to the copyrighted work as a whole; and (4) the effect of the use upon the potential market for or value of the copyrighted work." Fair use is one of the most common defenses invoked by persons charged with copyright infringement. However, it ordinarily is very difficult to establish. It will not be available if the amount of a copyrighted work that is copied is significant either in terms of quantity or quality, the copies serve the same function as the copyrighted work, and the copying is made in lieu of purchasing lawful copies of the work. Copying is permitted in limited situations for classroom instruction (see "Classroom Teaching Activities— Making Copies").

[See sections 6.1, 6.2, and 6.3.]

FAIR USE GUIDELINES [see Classroom Teaching Activities—Making Copies]

FORMS [see Appendix 2]

HYMNALS

Hymnals raise a number of copyright issues. First, a hymnal ordinarily is a "collective work," meaning that it is eligible for copyright protection. Such protection extends only to the material contributed by the compiler (such as a foreword, any editing, and the arrangement or order of the individual works included in the hymnal). The fact that the hymnal is copyrighted does not in any way extend or affect the copyright protection of any work included in the hymnal. A public domain work remains a public domain work, even though it appears in a copyrighted hymnal. Further, the copyright term of a song first published in 1950 is not extended by its inclusion in a hymnal published in 2001. Second, the individual works contained in a hymnal need not bear separate copyright notices. A single copyright notice applicable to the copyrighted work as a whole is sufficient to satisfy the requirements of copyright notice with respect to the separate contributions (first published before March 1, 1989) that it contains. No copyright notice is needed to preserve the copyright in a work first published on or after March 1, 1989. Therefore, the fact that a particular song found in a hymnal does not have a separate copyright notice does not mean that it is in the public domain. Third, churches are not free to create without permission their own "hymnals" or songbooks by making copies of copyrighted songs (even if only the lyrics are copied).

[See sections 1.2, and 5.1(A).]

INFRINGEMENT

The copyright law defines "infringement" as any violation of one or more of the five exclusive rights of the copyright owner (see "Exclusive Rights").

[See section 5.2.]

INTERNET

Most churches now have at least one computer with access to the internet either through a phone modem or cable connection. Downloading copyrighted material from internet web sites infringes upon the copyright owner's exclusive right of reproduction. If the user uploads the copyrighted material to others, then the copyright owner's exclusive right of public distribution may be infringed. The fair use defense often prevents downloading from constituting copyright infringement. But some downloading will not qualify as fair use. For example, if a user downloads a copyrighted computer program, or music, this cannot be considered fair use. Further, when users upload information to others, this weakens the availability of the fair use defense.

Churches can commit copyright infringement when creating and maintaining their own web sites in several ways, including (1) the use of someone else's images or artwork on your own web site without permission, and (2) the use of copyrighted text on your web site without permission.

[See sections 8.2 and 8.3.]

LIBRARIES

The copyright law permits libraries to make copies of copyrighted works under certain conditions. Examples include copies made for preservation or security and copies made to replace damaged or lost copies (if unused replacements cannot be obtained at a fair price). Additional conditions apply.

[See section 6.4.]

LICENSES

A license is an authorization, usually in writing and for a fee, by which a copyright owner (or an agent acting on behalf of the owner) authorizes another (the licensee) to use copyrighted works in a way that would otherwise constitute infringement. Compulsory licenses (see "Compulsory Licenses") permit churches to distribute recordings of services in which copyrighted music is performed. Blanket licenses (see "Blanket Licenses") permit churches to copy (and sometimes to perform or record) any musical works listed in the repertory of the copyright owner or its agent.

[See sections 6.10 and 6.11.]

LYRICS

Copyright protection can extend to both lyrics and music. Therefore, it is no defense for a church employee to argue that he or she "copied only the lyrics." Of course, once a song enters the public domain, the lyrics and original music are no longer protected. Subsequent arrangements of the same work can be copyrighted, but such arrangements protect only the new musical composition and not the original lyrics.

[See sections 1.2, 5.1(A), 5.2, and 6.1.]

MECHANICAL LICENSES [see Compulsory Licenses]

NONPROFIT PERFORMANCES

Performances of copyrighted literary or musical works in the course of "nonprofit performances" will not constitute copyright infringement if certain conditions are satisfied. These conditions include the following: (1) The performance must not have a profit motive. (2) No fee or compensation can be paid to the performers (or promoters or organizers) for the performance. This condition does not prevent performers from receiving a salary for duties that include a particular performance. For example, performances by a school band do not lose the benefit of this exemption merely because the band conductor is a music teacher who receives an annual salary for performing his duties, so long as he receives no fee or payment for any particular performance. (3) There must either be no direct or indirect admissions charge, or alternatively, if an admissions charge is assessed, then any amounts left after deducting the reasonable costs of producing the performance must be used solely for educational, religious, or charitable purposes. If there is an admissions charge, then the copyright owner is given the authority to "veto" the performance by serving upon the person responsible for the performance a notice objecting to the performance. Such a notice must be in a writing that is signed by the copyright owner; it must be served upon the person responsible for the performance at least seven days before the date of the performance, and it must state the reasons for the objection. The impact of this provision is limited severely by the fact that section 110(4) does not require that the copyright owner be notified that his or her work is going to be performed at a nonprofit event with an admissions charge.

[See section 6.8.]

NOTICE OF COPYRIGHT

When a work is published, a notice of copyright should be placed on all publicly distributed copies. Failure to comply with this notice requirement can result in the loss of copyright protection for a work first published before March 1, 1989. The contents and placement of a valid copyright notice are described in sections 401(b) and 401(c) of the Copyright Act. A valid notice consists of three elements: (1) the symbol (†(the letter C in a circle), the word "Copyright," or the abbreviation "Copr."; and (2) the year of first publication of the work (in the case of compilations and derivative works incorporating previously published material, the year date of first publication of the compilation or derivative work is sufficient); and (3) the name of the owner of copyright in the work, or an abbreviation by which the name can be recognized, or a generally known alternative designation of the owner. Works first published on or after March 1, 1989 are not required to display a valid copyright notice in order to preserve their copyright protection. However, such a valid notice is still recommended with respect to such works, since it will prevent infringers from claiming an "innocent infringement" defense.

[See section 1.3.]

OPAQUE PROJECTORS

Many churches project the lyrics of copyrighted choruses and other religious songs onto screens or walls during the course of congregational worship. If the lyrics consist of a transparency or slide made by church employees without authorization of the copyright owner, then the act of making the transparency or slide ordinarily will constitute an infringement. Section 109(c) provides that "the owner of a particular copy lawfully made . . . is entitled, without the authority of the copyright owner, to display that copy publicly, either directly or by the projection of no more than one image at a time, to viewers present at the place where the copy is located."

This section generally allows the display of lawfully made copies of religious music in the course of religious services. Lawfully made copies include transparencies or slides that were purchased by the church from the copyright owner. They do not include copies made by church staff without authorization. However, note that if the church purchases a copy of a piece of music and then projects it on a screen during worship services by means of opaque projection, no copyright infringement has occurred since the church is displaying a lawfully obtained copy. An unauthorized copy is not being displayed. As a result, churches that use unauthorized slides and transparencies should consider the option of purchasing and using an opaque projector to display religious music during congregational singing.

[See section 6.5.]

OUT-OF-PRINT WORKS

Out-of-print works have not necessarily lost their copyright protection because the copyright term of most works far exceeds their useful life. Nevertheless, the House Report to the Copyright Act of 1976 states that the fact that a copyrighted work is out-of-print gives a user "more justification for reproducing it than in the ordinary case." This simply means that one who copies an out-of-print work will have a somewhat easier task in establishing noninfringing fair use than otherwise would be the case.

[See section 6.1.]

PENALTIES

An array of potential penalties confront the copyright infringer. These include injunctions prohibiting further infringement, confiscation and destruction of the infringing items, actual damages, statutory damages, and attorneys' fees. Fines and prison sentences are imposed for criminal offenses.

[See section 5.3.]

PERFORMANCES—RELIGIOUS [see Religious Services]

PERIODICALS

A periodical is a literary work that is published at regular (e.g., monthly) intervals. Examples include religious journals, devotional magazines, and newspapers. Periodicals raise a number of copyright issues. First, it should be assumed that all articles and contributions to a periodical are copyrighted. This means they cannot be reproduced without authorization. Remember that an individual contribution to a periodical need not bear its own copyright notice so long as (1) the contribution was first published before March 1, 1989 and the periodical as a whole contains a valid notice, or (2) the contribution was first published on or after March 1, 1989. Therefore, the fact that an individual entry does not have its own separate copyright notice does not mean that it is in the public domain. Second, the periodical publisher acquires no more than the bare right to publish the article one time (or in future issues of the same periodical) unless the author conveys additional rights by means of a signed writing. Third, excerpts of copyrighted articles contained in periodicals can be quoted (orally or in written materials) only with authorization of the copyright owner or if the quotation constitutes a noninfringing fair use.

[See sections 1.3, 1.4, and 6.1.]

PHONORECORDS

A technical term that includes records and tape recordings.

[See section 1.3.]

POETRY

Churches often reprint poetry in church bulletins and newsletters. This practice constitutes copyright infringement if the poetry is copyrighted, and if authorization from the copyright owner has not been obtained. If the author of a poem cannot be ascertained after a reasonable search, the poem can be printed with the caption "author unknown." In this case, the church will not be guilty of copyright infringement even if the poem is copyrighted, so long as it can prove that it was "misled" by the omission of a valid copyright notice containing the author's name.

[See sections 1.3, 5.1(A), 5.2, and 6.1.]

PROJECTORS [see Opaque Projection, Transparencies]

PUBLICATION

"Publication" is a very important concept under the copyright law. Among other things, it determines when a copyright notice must be affixed to copies of a work. Distribution of copies of a work following its publication, without a valid copyright notice, can result in the loss of copyright protection. Publication is a technical term that must not be confused with commercial publishing.

Publication is defined as "the distribution of copies or phonorecords of a work to the public by sale or other transfer of ownership . . . ." Authors and composers may inadvertently lose their copyright protection by circulating too many copies of their work (for review purposes) without affixing a valid copyright notice, since at some point the circulation of an unpublished work will constitute publication. Precautionary measures are discussed in the text.

[See sections 1.3, 2.2, and 4.2.]

PUBLIC DOMAIN

Works that have lost their copyright protection, or that never were eligible for copyright protection, are said to be in the "public domain," which is another way of saying that they may be copied, performed, or used in any other way without anyone's authorization. A word of caution is in order. Do not assume that a particular work is in fact in the public domain without adequate proof. For example, as noted under "Periodicals," the mere fact that an article in a periodical does not contain a separate copyright notice does not mean that it is in the public domain. The same rule applies to individual songs in a hymnal (see "Hymnals"). Further, the lyrics of a hymn may be in the public domain, but a particular arrangement of the hymn may still be covered by copyright protection. Finally, the adoption of the Berne Convention by Congress effective March 1, 1989 resulted in the elimination of all "copyright formalities"—including copyright notice. Accordingly, works first published on or after March 1, 1989 need not display a valid copyright notice. Section 401(d) of the Copyright Act suggests that an infringer can avoid or at least reduce legal liability for infringing on a copyrighted work (that did not contain a valid notice) by asserting that the absence of a copyright notice made his or her infringement "innocent." Such a defense is not available if a valid copyright notice is displayed on the work (even though not required). Accordingly, copyright notices should still be displayed even though they technically may not be required.

[See sections 1.2, 3.1, and 3.2.]

RADIO [see Broadcasts]

RECORDINGS [see Tape Recordings]

REGISTRATION

In general, copyright registration is a legal formality intended to make a public record of the basic facts of a particular copyright. While registration is not required, it does provide certain benefits, including the following: it establishes a public record of the copyright claim; it ordinarily is necessary before any infringement suits may be filed in court; if made within three months after publication of a work, or prior to publication, statutory damages and attorneys' fees will be available to the copyright owner in a court action. Registration is a fairly simple procedure that requires the submission of a form (and a small fee) to the Copyright Office.

[See sections 2.1, 2.2, and 2.3.]

REHEARSAL TAPES

Taped accompaniments are becoming increasingly common for choral works in lieu of the traditional organ or piano. Some choir directors, in an effort to assist choir members in learning their parts, make copies of the accompaniment tape for choir members to take home with them. Clearly, such a practice infringes upon the copyright that exists in the underlying work and perhaps in the sound recording as well, unless authorization is obtained in advance.

[See sections 1.3, 5.1(A), and 5.2.]

RELIGIOUS SERVICES

Performances of religious music, and displays of works, are exempted from copyright infringement if the performance or display occurs "in the course of services at a place of worship or other religious assembly."

The term "display" does not cover the showing of motion pictures or videos. Also note that the religious services exemption does not extend to any act of unauthorized copying. To illustrate, the exemption does not protect the unauthorized duplication of a slide or transparency that is then displayed during a worship service. It is the unauthorized duplication that constitutes the copyright infringement, and this conclusion is not affected by the exemption of displays. The religious services exemption protects the performance of religious music in the course of worship services by a congregation, soloist, choir, orchestra, or any other person or group. Note that the exemption does not extend to recordings or broadcasts of such services (see "Broadcasts" and "Tape Recordings").

[See section 6.7.]

RESEARCH

In 1975, a group of publishers and educators drafted a set of guidelines specifying various types of copying that they considered noninfringing "fair use" when done by teachers. These guidelines were later included in the House Report on the Copyright Act of 1976 as "a reasonable interpretation of the minimum standards of fair use." These guidelines are reproduced in full in section 6.1. Generally, they permit a teacher to make a single copy of a chapter from a book, an article from a periodical, a short story, or a poem, for purposes of scholarly research or for use in preparing to teach a class.

[See section 6.2.]

ROYALTIES [see Compulsory Licenses]

SCHOOLS [see Classroom Teaching Activities—Making Copies; Classroom Teaching Activities—Performances and Displays; Libraries; Research]

SCRIPTURE CHORUSES

Many churches enjoy singing choruses consisting of scriptural passages set to music. Often, the lyrics of these choruses are reproduced on a songsheet, in a chorus booklet, or on a transparency. So long as the lyrics are from a public domain translation of the Bible (such as the King James Version), these practices are all permissible. Of course, the music accompanying the lyrics may be copyrighted, and accordingly the reproduction of the music may constitute copyright infringement.

[See sections 1.2, 1.3, 3.1, 3.2, 5.1(A), 5.1(B), 5.1(D), 5.2, 6.1, 6.7, 6.10, 7.1, and 7.2.]

SHEET MUSIC

Churches use sheet music in a variety of ways, including choral, instrumental, and solo performances. Copyrighted sheet music cannot be duplicated without authorization from the copyright owner. Copyright protection extends to both lyrics and music, so it is no defense that "only the lyrics were copied." Duplication can take a variety of forms, including the making of copies for members of the choir, or the making of a slide or transparency. The "Guidelines for Educational Uses of Music," adopted by a group of music publishers and educators (and approved by the House of Representatives in its report on the Copyright Act of 1976), permit "emergency photocopying to replace purchased copies which for any reason are not available for an imminent performance provided purchased replacement copies shall be substituted in due course." This provision only applies to musical works, including sheet music.

[See sections 5.1(A), 5.2, and 6.1.]

SLIDES [see Transparencies]

SOFTWARE

Most churches own several software programs. Common examples are word processing, spreadsheet, database, financial, and audiovisual "presentation" software. It is common for many of these programs to be pre-installed on new computers, while other programs are purchased and installed after a computer is acquired. The Copyright Act allows software programs to be protected by copyright. This means that the copyright owner of a software program has the same exclusive rights as any copyright owner, including the exclusive rights to copy and publicly distribute the program. As a result, it is a violation of copyright law for anyone who owns or possesses a software program to copy it, with the following exceptions: (1) owners of a lawfully acquired software program can make an "intangible copy" in their computer's random access memory (RAM) in order to operate the program; (2) owners of a lawfully acquired software program can make a single backup copy for archival purposes; (3) copying software with the express permission of the copyright owner (usually through a license agreement that comes with the software); (4) copying software that is in the public domain.

[See section 8.1.]

SOLOS

Solo performances (vocal or instrumental) of copyrighted religious music in the course of worship services at a church or other place of religious assembly are exempted from infringement upon the copyright owner's exclusive right of public performance. However, note that this exemption does not apply to recordings or broadcasts of the solo performance (see "Broadcasts," "Compulsory Licenses," and "Tape Recordings"), or to copies made of the copyrighted work for an accompanist.

[See sections 5.1(A), 5.1(D), 5.2, 6.7, and 6.10.]

SONGBOOKS [see Chorus Booklets]

SONG LYRICS [see Lyrics]

STATEMENTS OF ACCOUNT [see Compulsory Licenses]

SUNDAY SCHOOL [see Classroom Teaching Activities—Making Copies, Classroom Teaching Activities—Performances and Displays, Copies, Libraries, Research, Transparencies]

TAPE RECORDINGS

Churches often record their services, both on audio and video tape. While the performance of copyrighted musical works in the course of a church service ordinarily creates no copyright problems, the recording of a service does since the act of recording constitutes the making of an unauthorized copy of any copyrighted works performed in the course of the service. In the case of musical works, this problem can be avoided in a variety of ways, including the acquisition of a compulsory license (see "Compulsory Licenses"), a blanket license (see "Blanket Licenses"), or some other form of authorization from the copyright owner. Other solutions are discussed in the text. Note, however, that the compulsory license is available only for "phonorecords" (including records or audio tapes), and not videotapes.

[See sections 5.1(A), 5.1(D), 5.2, 6.1, 6.7, 6.10, and 6.12.]

TEACHING ACTIVITIES [see Classroom Teaching Activities—Making Copies, and Classroom Teaching Activities—Performances and Displays]

TELEVISION [see Broadcasting]

TRANSFERS

Any or all of the exclusive rights, or any subdivision of those rights, of the copyright owner may be transferred, but the transfer is not valid unless it is in writing and signed by the owner of the rights conveyed. To illustrate, authors and composers who do not expressly transfer the copyright (or some specific exclusive right) in their works to a publisher by means of a signed writing have not transferred the copyright in their work. Much unnecessary confusion exists on this point. Authors and composers must be certain that their publishing contracts specify clearly what exclusive rights, if any, they are transferring. Also note that a copyright may be transferred "by operation of law," such as in a will.

[See sections 4.1 and 4.2.]

TRANSPARENCIES

Many churches use transparencies of songs in the course of congregational or choral singing. If the song is in the public domain, then a church is free to make and use its own transparency. Before making a transparency, a church must be certain that the lyrics (and music, if applicable) are no longer subject to copyright protection. If the song is still protected by copyright, then the act of making a transparency of the song ordinarily will constitute copyright infringement. It is no excuse to say that "only the lyrics were copied," since the lyrics comprise a substantial enough portion of the work (both in terms of quantity and quality) to negate a "fair use" defense in nearly every case. Fair use is ordinarily very difficult to establish. It will not be available if the amount of a copyrighted work that is copied is significant either in terms of quantity or quality, the copies serve the same function as the copyrighted work, and the copying is made in lieu of purchasing lawful copies of the work. This is so even if the copy is made from a purchased copy of the work. A number of courts (as noted in the text) have concluded that the act of copying lyrics constitutes copyright infringement. Churches are free to display lawfully acquired copies of any copyrighted work under certain conditions. This "display right" does not entitle a church to display copies fabricated by the church without authorization. Of course, a church is free to purchase a transparency and display it, since this will be the display of a lawfully acquired copy. And, a church is free to obtain authorization from the copyright owner to make a transparency. Many music publishers give churches the right to make a transparency for a nominal fee. Also, churches that obtain a blanket license from a publisher or an agent of one or more publishers often have the right to make transparencies of any song on a master list.

[See sections 5.1(A), 5.1(E), 5.2, 6.1, 6.7, 7.1, and 7.2.]

UNPUBLISHED MANUSCRIPTS

An unpublished manuscript is entitled to copyright protection so long as the work is original. This "initial" copyright protection continues up until the time the work is published. Copies of the work distributed following publication must contain a valid copyright notice to ensure that copyright protection will continue. To avoid inadvertent publication of the work without a valid notice, some authors and composers affix a notice to any copy of their work that leaves their control. Such a notice often takes the following form: "Unpublished work—Copyright 1989 John Doe." If the work is submitted to publishers or other individuals for review purposes, the following additional statement could be affixed below the notice: "Unpublished manuscript submitted for review purposes only; publication or reproduction is prohibited without the author's written consent."

[See sections 1.3, 3.1, 3.2, and 4.2.]

VIDEOTAPES

Videotapes raise a couple of important copyright questions. First, the videotaping of a church service in which copyrighted musical (or other) works are performed constitutes a reproduction of those works. Unless such taping is authorized by the copyright owners, it constitutes an infringement upon their exclusive right to reproduce copies of their works. Since the compulsory license procedure is not available for videotape recordings, the remaining forms of authorization include blanket licenses or specific authorizations from the copyright owner. Churches are free to record services that do not contain performances of any copyrighted works, and they can record services that do contain performances of copyrighted works if the videocamera is switched off during such performances. In some cases, a church may be entitled to make a videotape for archival purposes (see "Archival Copies"). The second issue pertains to the use of videotapes in the course of church activities. For example, a youth group rents movies from a local video rental center for display during activities. Assuming that the person renting the video acquires a license to use it only for private "in-home" viewing, the showing of the video to the youth group would constitute copyright infringement.

Motion Picture Licensing Corporation, 5455 Centinela Avenue, Los Angeles, CA 90066-6970 (telephone 1-800-462-8855, web site mplc.com) is an independent copyright licensing service exclusively authorized by major motion picture studios and independent producers to grant "umbrella licenses" to nonprofit groups, including churches, to publicly display videos licenses for private, in-home use. The license allows unlimited use of all MPLC authorized motion picture titles within licensed facilities. The license period is generally one year and there is a low annual fee.

[See sections 5.1(A), 5.1(D), 5.1(E), 5.2, 6.1, 6.5, 6.7, and 6.12.]

WEB SITES [see Internet]

WORKS MADE FOR HIRE

A "work made for hire" is a work that is either (1) prepared by an employee within the scope of his or her employment, or (2) a work specially commissioned for use as a contribution to a collective work, audiovisual work, translation, supplementary work, or instructional work. The employer and not the employee is considered to be the author of a work made for hire, unless the parties stipulate otherwise in a signed writing.

[See section 1.4(A).]

WORLD WIDE WEB [see Internet]

WORSHIP SERVICES [see Religious Services]

APPENDIX 1

Selected Provisions of the Copyright Act of 1976

Chapter 1:
Subject Matter and Scope of Copyright

§ 101. Definitions

Except as otherwise provided in this title, as used in this title, the following terms and their variant forms mean the following:

An "anonymous work" is a work on the copies or phonorecords of which no natural person is identified as author.

"Audiovisual works" are works that consist of a series of related images which are intrinsically intended to be shown by the use of machines or devices such as projectors, viewers, or electronic equipment, together with accompanying sounds, if any, regardless of the nature of the material objects, such as films or tapes, in which the works are embodied.

The "Berne Convention" is the Convention for the Protection of Literary and Artistic Works, signed at Berne, Switzerland, on September 9, 1886, and all acts, protocols, and revisions thereto.

The "best edition" of a work is the edition, published in the United States at any time before the date of deposit, that the Library of Congress determines to be most suitable for its purposes.

A "collective work" is a work, such as a periodical issue, anthology, or encyclopedia, in which a number of contributions, constituting separate and independent works in themselves, are assembled into a collective whole.

A "compilation" is a work formed by the collection and assembling of preexisting materials or of data that are selected, coordinated, or arranged in such a way that the resulting work as a whole constitutes an original work of authorship. The term "compilation" includes collective works.

"Copies" are material objects, other than phonorecords, in which a work is fixed by any method now known or later developed, and from which the work can be perceived, reproduced, or otherwise communicated, either directly or with the aid of a machine or device. The term "copies" includes the material object, other than a phonorecord, in which the work is first fixed.

"Copyright owner", with respect to any one of the exclusive rights comprised in a copyright, refers to the owner of that particular right.

A work is "created" when it is fixed in a copy or phonorecord for the first time; where a work is prepared over a period of time, the portion of it that has been fixed at any particular time constitutes the work as of that time, and where the work has been prepared in different versions, each version constitutes a separate work.

A "derivative work" is a work based upon one or more preexisting works, such as a translation, musical arrangement, dramatization, fictionalization, motion picture version, sound recording, art reproduction, abridgment, condensation, or any other form in which a work may be recast, transformed, or adapted. A work consisting of editorial revisions, annotations, elaborations, or other modifications, which, as a whole, represent an original work of authorship, is a "derivative work".

A "device", "machine", or "process" is one now known or later developed.

A "digital transmission" is a transmission in whole or in part in a digital or other non-analog format.

To "display" a work means to show a copy of it, either directly or by means of a film, slide, television image, or any other device or process or, in the case of a motion picture or other audiovisual work, to show individual images nonsequentially.

An "establishment" is a store, shop, or any similar place of business open to the general public for the primary purpose of selling goods or services in which the majority of the gross square feet of space that is nonresidential is used for that purpose, and in which nondramatic musical works are performed publicly.

A work is "fixed" in a tangible medium of expression when its embodiment in a copy or phonorecord, by or under the authority of the author, is sufficiently permanent or stable to permit it to be perceived, reproduced, or otherwise communicated for a period of more than transitory duration. A work consisting of sounds, images, or both, that are being transmitted, is "fixed" for purposes of this title if a fixation of the work is being made simultaneously with its transmission.

A "joint work" is a work prepared by two or more authors with the intention that their contributions be merged into inseparable or interdependent parts of a unitary whole.

"Literary works" are works, other than audiovisual works, expressed in words, numbers, or other verbal or numerical symbols or indicia, regardless of the nature of the material objects, such as books, periodicals, manuscripts, phonorecords, film, tapes, disks, or cards, in which they are embodied.

"Motion pictures" are audiovisual works consisting of a series of related images which, when shown in succession, impart an impression of motion, together with accompanying sounds, if any.

To "perform" a work means to recite, render, play, dance, or act it, either directly or by means of any device or process or, in the case of a motion picture or other audiovisual work, to

show its images in any sequence or to make the sounds accompanying it audible.

A "performing rights society" is an association, corporation, or other entity that licenses the public performance of nondramatic musical works on behalf of copyright owners of such works, such as the American Society of Composers, Authors and Publishers (ASCAP), Broadcast Music, Inc. (BMI), and SESAC, Inc.

"Phonorecords" are material objects in which sounds, other than those accompanying a motion picture or other audiovisual work, are fixed by any method now known or later developed, and from which the sounds can be perceived, reproduced, or otherwise communicated, either directly or with the aid of a machine or device. The term "phonorecords" includes the material object in which the sounds are first fixed.

"Pictorial, graphic, and sculptural works" include two-dimensional and three-dimensional works of fine, graphic, and applied art, photographs, prints and art reproductions, maps, globes, charts, diagrams, models, and technical drawings, including architectural plans. Such works shall include works of artistic craftsmanship insofar as their form but not their mechanical or utilitarian aspects are concerned; the design of a useful article, as defined in this section, shall be considered a pictorial, graphic, or sculptural work only if, and only to the extent that, such design incorporates pictorial, graphic, or sculptural features that can be identified separately from, and are capable of existing independently of, the utilitarian aspects of the article.

A "pseudonymous work" is a work on the copies or phonorecords of which the author is identified under a fictitious name.

"Publication" is the distribution of copies or phonorecords of a work to the public by sale or other transfer of ownership, or by rental, lease, or lending. The offering to distribute copies or phonorecords to a group of persons for purposes of further distribution, public performance, or public display, constitutes publication. A public performance or display of a work does not of itself constitute publication.

To perform or display a work "publicly" means-

(1) to perform or display it at a place open to the public or at any place where a substantial number of persons outside of a normal circle of a family and its social acquaintances is gathered; or

(2) to transmit or otherwise communicate a performance or display of the work to a place specified by clause (1) or to the public, by means of any device or process, whether the members of the public capable of receiving the performance or display receive it in the same place or in separate places and at the same time or at different times.

"Sound recordings" are works that result from the fixation of a series of musical, spoken, or other sounds, but not including the sounds accompanying a motion picture or other audiovisual work, regardless of the nature of the material objects, such as disks, tapes, or other phonorecords, in which they are embodied.

A "transfer of copyright ownership" is an assignment, mortgage, exclusive license, or any other conveyance, alienation, or hypothecation of a copyright or of any of the exclusive rights comprised in a copyright, whether or not it is limited in time or place of effect, but not including a nonexclusive license.

A "transmission program" is a body of material that, as an aggregate, has been produced for the sole purpose of transmission to the public in sequence and as a unit.

To "transmit" a performance or display is to communicate it by any device or process whereby images or sounds are received beyond the place from which they are sent.

A "work of visual art" is-

(1) a painting, drawing, print or sculpture, existing in a single copy, in a limited edition of 200 copies or fewer that are signed and consecutively numbered by the author, or, in the case of a sculpture, in multiple cast, carved, or fabricated sculptures of 200 or fewer that are consecutively numbered by the author and bear the signature or other identifying mark of the author; or

(2) a still photographic image produced for exhibition purposes only, existing in a single copy that is signed by the author, or in a limited edition of 200 copies or fewer that are signed and consecutively numbered by the author.

A work of visual art does not include-

(A)(i) any poster, map, globe, chart, technical drawing, diagram, model, applied art, motion picture or other audiovisual work, book, magazine, newspaper, periodical, data base, electronic information service, electronic publication, or similar publication;

(ii) any merchandising item or advertising, promotional, descriptive, covering, or packaging material or container;

(iii) any portion or part of any item described in clause (i) or (ii);

(B) any work made for hire; or

(C) any work not subject to copyright protection under this title.

A "work made for hire" is-

(1) a work prepared by an employee within the scope of his or her employment; or

(2) a work specially ordered or commissioned for use as a contribution to a collective work, as a part of a motion picture or other audiovisual work as a sound recording, as a translation, as a supplementary work, as a compilation, as an instructional text, as a test, as answer material for a test, or as an atlas, if the parties expressly agree in a written instrument signed by them that the work shall be considered a work made for hire. For the purpose of the foregoing sentence, a "supplementary work" is a work prepared for publication as a secondary adjunct to a work by another author for the purpose of introducing, concluding, illustrating, explaining, revising, commenting upon, or assisting in the use of the other work, such as forewords, afterwords, pictorial illustrations, maps, charts, tables, editorial notes, musical arrangements, answer material for tests, bibliographies, appendixes, and indexes, and an "instructional text" is a literary, pictorial, or graphic work prepared for publication and with the purpose of use in systematic instructional activities.

A "computer program" is a set of statements or instructions to be used directly or indirectly in a computer in order to bring about a certain result.

§ 102. Subject matter of copyright: In general

(a) Copyright protection subsists, in accordance with this title, in original works of authorship fixed in any tangible medium of expression, now known or later developed, from which they can be perceived, reproduced, or otherwise communicated, either directly or with the aid of a machine or device. Works of authorship include the following categories:

(1) literary works;

(2) musical works, including any accompanying words;

(3) dramatic works, including any accompanying music;

(4) pantomimes and choreographic works;

(5) pictorial, graphic, and sculptural works;

(6) motion pictures and other audiovisual works;

(7) sound recordings; and

(8) architectural works.

(b) In no case does copyright protection for an original work of authorship extend to any idea, procedure, process, system, method of operation, concept, principle, or discovery, regardless of the form in which it is described, explained, illustrated, or embodied in such work.

§ 103. Subject matter of copyright: Compilations and derivative works

(a) The subject matter of copyright as specified by section 102 includes compilations and derivative works, but protection for a work employing preexisting material in which copyright subsists does not extend to any part of the work in which such material has been used unlawfully.

(b) The copyright in a compilation or derivative work extends only to the material contributed by the author of such work, as distinguished from the preexisting material employed in the work, and does not imply any exclusive right in the preexisting material. The copyright in such work is independent of, and does not affect or enlarge the scope, duration, ownership, or subsistence of, any copyright protection in the preexisting material.

§ 106. Exclusive rights in copyrighted works

Subject to sections 107 through 121, the owner of copyright under this title has the exclusive rights to do and to authorize any of the following:

(1) to reproduce the copyrighted work in copies or phonorecords;

(2) to prepare derivative works based upon the copyrighted work;

(3) to distribute copies or phonorecords of the copyrighted work to the public by sale or other transfer of ownership, or by rental, lease, or lending;

(4) in the case of literary, musical, dramatic, and choreographic works, pantomimes, and motion pictures and other audiovisual works, to perform the copyrighted work publicly;

(5) in the case of literary, musical, dramatic, and choreographic works, pantomimes, and pictorial, graphic, or sculptural works, including the individual images of a motion picture or other audiovisual work, to display the copyrighted work publicly; and

(6) in the case of sound recordings, to perform the copyrighted work publicly by means of a digital audio transmission.

§ 107. Limitations on exclusive rights: Fair use

Notwithstanding the provisions of sections 106 and 106A, the fair use of a copyrighted work, including such use by reproduction in copies or phonorecords or by any other means specified by that section, for purposes such as criticism, comment, news reporting, teaching (including multiple copies for classroom use), scholarship, or research, is not an infringement of copyright. In determining whether the use made of a work in any particular case is a fair use the factors to be considered shall include-

(1) the purpose and character of the use, including whether such use is of a commercial nature or is for nonprofit educational purposes;

(2) the nature of the copyrighted work;

(3) the amount and substantiality of the portion used in relation to the copyrighted work as a whole; and

(4) the effect of the use upon the potential market for or value of the copyrighted work.

The fact that a work is unpublished shall not itself bar a finding of fair use if such finding is made upon consideration of all the above factors.

§ 108. Limitations on exclusive rights: Reproduction by libraries and archives

(a) Except as otherwise provided in this title and notwithstanding the provisions of section 106, it is not an infringement of copyright for a library or archives, or any of its employees acting within the scope of their employment, to reproduce no more than one copy or phonorecord of a work, except as provided in subsections (b) and (c), or to distribute such copy or phonorecord, under the conditions specified by this section, if-

(1) the reproduction or distribution is made without any purpose of direct or indirect commercial advantage;

(2) the collections of the library or archives are (i) open to the public, or (ii) available not only to researchers affiliated with the library or archives or with the institution of which it is a part, but also to other persons doing research in a specialized field; and

(3) the reproduction or distribution of the work includes a notice of copyright that appears on the copy or phonorecord that is reproduced under the provisions of this section, or includes a legend stating that the work may be protected by copy-right if no such notice can be found on the copy or phonorecord that is reproduced under the provisions of this section.

(b) The rights of reproduction and distribution under this section apply to three copies or phonorecords of an unpublished work duplicated solely for purposes of preservation and security or for deposit for research use in another library or archives of the type described by clause (2) of subsection (a), if-

(1) the copy or phonorecord reproduced is currently in the collections of the library or archives; and

(2) any such copy or phonorecord that is reproduced in digital format is not otherwise distributed in that format and is not made available to the public in that format outside the premises of the library or archives.

(c) The right of reproduction under this section applies to three copies or phonorecords of a published work duplicated solely for the purpose of replacement of a copy or phonorecord that is damaged, deteriorating, lost, or stolen, or if the existing format in which the work is stored has become obsolete, if-

(1) the library or archives has, after a reasonable effort, determined that an unused replacement cannot be obtained at a fair price; and

(2) any such copy or phonorecord that is reproduced in digital format is not made available to the public in that format outside the premises of the library or archives in lawful possession of such copy.

For purposes of this subsection, a format shall be considered obsolete if the machine or device necessary to render perceptible a work stored in that format is no longer manufactured or is no longer reasonably available in the commercial marketplace.

(d) The rights of reproduction and distribution under this section apply to a copy, made from the collection of a library or archives where the user makes his or her request or from that of another library or archives, of no more than one article or other contribution to a copyrighted collection or periodical issue, or to a copy or phonorecord of a small part of any other copyrighted work, if -

(1) the copy or phonorecord becomes the property of the user, and the library or archives has had no notice that the copy or phonorecord would be used for any purpose other than private study, scholarship, or research; and

(2) the library or archives displays prominently, at the place where orders are accepted, and includes on its order form, a warning of copyright in accordance with requirements that the Register of Copyrights shall prescribe by regulation.

(e) The rights of reproduction and distribution under this section apply to the entire work, or to a substantial part of it, made from the collection of a library or archives where the user makes his or her request or from that of another library or archives, if the library or archives has first determined, on the basis of a reasonable investigation, that a copy or phonorecord of the copyrighted work cannot be obtained at a fair price, if-

(1) the copy or phonorecord becomes the property of the user, and the library or archives has had no notice that the copy or phonorecord would be used for any purpose other than private study, scholarship, or research; and

(2) the library or archives displays prominently, at the place where orders are accepted, and includes on its order form, a warning of copyright in accordance with requirements that the Register of Copyrights shall prescribe by regulation.

(f) Nothing in this section-

(1) shall be construed to impose liability for copyright infringement upon a library or archives or its employees for the unsupervised use of reproducing equipment located on its premises: Provided, That such equipment displays a notice that the making of a copy may be subject to the copyright law;

(2) excuses a person who uses such reproducing equipment or who requests a copy or phonorecord under subsection (d) from liability for copyright infringement for any such act, or for any later use of such copy or phonorecord, if it exceeds fair use as provided by section 107;

(3) shall be construed to limit the reproduction and distribution by lending of a limited number of copies and excerpts by a library or archives of an audiovisual news program, subject to clauses (1), (2), and (3) of subsection (a); or

(4) in any way affects the right of fair use as provided by section 107, or any contractual obligations assumed at any time by the library or archives when it obtained a copy or phonorecord of a work in its collections.

(g) The rights of reproduction and distribution under this section extend to the isolated and unrelated reproduction or distribution of a single copy or phonorecord of the same material on separate occasions, but do not extend to cases where the library or archives, or its employee-

(1) is aware or has substantial reason to believe that it is engaging in the related or concerted reproduction or distribution of multiple copies or phonorecords of the same material, whether made on one occasion or over a period of time, and whether intended for aggregate use by one or more individuals or for separate use by the individual members of a group; or

(2) engages in the systematic reproduction or distribution of single or multiple copies or phonorecords of material described in subsection (d): Provided, That nothing in this clause prevents a library or archives from participating in interlibrary arrangements that do not have, as their purpose or effect, that the library or archives receiving such copies or phonorecords for distribution does so in such aggregate quantities as to substitute for a subscription to or purchase of such work.

(h)(1) For purposes of this section, during the last 20 years of any term of copyright of a published work, a library or archives, including a nonprofit educational institution that functions as such, may reproduce, distribute, display, or perform in facsimile or digital form a copy or phonorecord of such work, or portions thereof, for purposes of preservation, scholarship, or research, if such library or archives has first determined, on the basis of a reasonable investigation, that none of the conditions set forth in subparagraphs (A), (B), and (C) of paragraph (2) apply.

(2) No reproduction, distribution, display, or performance is authorized under this subsection if-

(A) the work is subject to normal commercial exploitation;

(B) a copy or phonorecord of the work can be obtained at a reasonable price; or

(C) the copyright owner or its agent provides notice pursuant to regulations promulgated by the Register of Copyrights that either of the conditions set forth in subparagraphs (A) and (B) applies.

(3) The exemption provided in this subsection does not apply to any subsequent uses by users other than such library or archives.

(i) The rights of reproduction and distribution under this section do not apply to a musical work, a pictorial, graphic or sculptural work, or a motion picture or other audiovisual work other than an audiovisual work dealing with news, except that no such limitation shall apply with respect to rights granted by subsections (b) and (c), or with respect to pictorial or graphic works published as illustrations, diagrams, or similar adjuncts to works of which copies are reproduced or distributed in accordance with subsections (d) and (e).

§ 109. Limitations on exclusive rights: Effect of transfer of particular copy or phonorecord

(a) Notwithstanding the provisions of section 106(3), the owner of a particular copy or phonorecord lawfully made under this title, or any person authorized by such owner, is entitled, without the authority of the copyright owner, to sell or otherwise dispose of the possession of that copy or phonorecord. Notwithstanding the preceding sentence, copies or phonorecords of works subject to restored copyright under section 104A that are manufactured before the date of restoration of copyright or, with respect to reliance parties, before publication or service of notice under section 104A(e), may be sold or otherwise disposed of without the authorization of the owner of the restored copyright for purposes of direct or indirect commercial advantage only during the 12-month period beginning on-

(1) the date of the publication in the Federal Register of the notice of intent filed with the Copyright Office under section 104A(d)(2)(A), or

(2) the date of the receipt of actual notice served under section 104A(d)(2)(B), whichever occurs first.

(b)(1)(A) Notwithstanding the provisions of subsection (a), unless authorized by the owners of copyright in the sound recording or the owner of copyright in a computer program (including any tape, disk, or other medium embodying such program), and in the case of a sound recording in the musical works embodied therein, neither the owner of a particular phonorecord nor any person in possession of a particular copy of a computer program (including any tape, disk, or other medium embodying such program), may, for the purposes of direct or indirect commercial advantage, dispose of, or authorize the disposal of, the possession of that phonorecord or computer program (including any tape, disk, or other medium embodying such program) by rental, lease, or lending, or by any other act or practice in the nature of rental, lease, or lending. Nothing in the preceding sentence shall apply to the rental, lease, or lending of a phonorecord for nonprofit purposes by a nonprofit library or nonprofit educational institution. The transfer of possession of a lawfully made copy of a computer program by a nonprofit educational institution to another nonprofit educational institution or to faculty, staff, and students does not constitute rental, lease, or lending for direct or indirect commercial purposes under this subsection.

(B) This subsection does not apply to-

(i) a computer program which is embodied in a machine or product and which cannot be copied during the ordinary operation or use of the machine or product; or

(ii) a computer program embodied in or used in conjunction with a limited purpose computer that is designed for playing video games and may be designed for other purposes.
(C) Nothing in this subsection affects any provision of chapter 9 of this title.

(2)(A) Nothing in this subsection shall apply to the lending of a computer program for nonprofit purposes by a nonprofit library, if each copy of a computer program which is lent by such library has affixed to the packaging containing the program a warning of copyright in accordance with requirements that the Register of Copyrights shall prescribe by regulation.

(B) Not later than three years after the date of the enactment of the Computer Software Rental Amendments Act of 1990, and at such times thereafter as the Register of Copyrights considers appropriate, the Register of Copyrights, after consultation with representatives of copyright owners and librarians, shall submit to the Congress a report stating whether this paragraph has achieved its intended purpose of maintaining the integrity of the copyright system while providing nonprofit libraries the capability to fulfill their function. Such report shall advise the Congress as to any information or recommendations that the Register of Copyrights considers necessary to carry out the purposes of this subsection.

(3) Nothing in this subsection shall affect any provision of the antitrust laws. For purposes of the preceding sentence, "antitrust laws" has the meaning given that term in the first section of the Clayton Act and includes section 5 of the Federal Trade Commission Act to the extent that section relates to unfair methods of competition.

(4) Any person who distributes a phonorecord or a copy of a computer program (including any tape, disk, or other medium embodying such program) in violation of paragraph (1) is an infringer of copyright under section 501 of this title and is subject to the remedies set forth in sections 502, 503, 504, 505, and 509. Such violation shall not be a criminal offense under section 506 or cause such person to be subject to the criminal penalties set forth in section 2319 of title 18.

(c) Notwithstanding the provisions of section 106(5), the owner of a particular copy lawfully made under this title, or any person authorized by such owner, is entitled, without the authority of the copyright owner, to display that copy publicly, either directly or by the projection of no more than one image at a time, to viewers present at the place where the copy is located.

(d) The privileges prescribed by subsections (a) and (c) do not, unless authorized by the copyright owner, extend to any person who has acquired possession of the copy or phonorecord from the copyright owner, by rental, lease, loan, or otherwise, without acquiring ownership of it.

(e) Notwithstanding the provisions of sections 106(4) and 106(5), in the case of an electronic audiovisual game intended for use in coin-operated equipment, the owner of a particular copy of such a game lawfully made under this title, is entitled, without the authority of the copyright owner of the game, to publicly perform or display that game in coin-operated equipment, except that this subsection shall not apply to any work of authorship embodied in the audiovisual game if the copyright owner of the electronic audiovisual game is not also the copyright owner of the work of authorship.

§ 110. Limitations on exclusive rights: Exemption of certain performances and displays

Notwithstanding the provisions of section 106, the following are not infringements of copyright:

(1) performance or display of a work by instructors or pupils in the course of face-to-face teaching activities of a nonprofit educational institution, in a classroom or similar place devoted to instruction, unless, in the case of a motion picture or other audiovisual work, the performance, or the display of individual images, is given by means of a copy that was not lawfully made under this title, and that the person responsible for the performance knew or had reason to believe was not lawfully made;

(2) performance of a nondramatic literary or musical work or display of a work, by or in the course of a transmission, if—

(A) the performance or display is a regular part of the systematic instructional activities of a governmental body or a nonprofit educational institution; and

(B) the performance or display is directly related and of material assistance to the teaching content of the transmission; and

(C) the transmission is made primarily for—

(i) reception in classrooms or similar places normally devoted to instruction, or

(ii) reception by persons to whom the transmission is directed because their disabilities or other special circumstances prevent their attendance in classrooms or similar places normally devoted to instruction, or
(iii) reception by officers or employees of governmental bodies as a part of their official duties or employment;

(3) performance of a nondramatic literary or musical work or of a dramatico-musical work of a religious nature, or display of a work, in the course of services at a place of worship or other religious assembly;

(4) performance of a nondramatic literary or musical work otherwise than in a transmission to the public, without any purpose of direct or indirect commercial advantage and without payment of any fee or other compensation for the performance to any of its performers, promoters, or organizers, if—

(A) there is no direct or indirect admission charge; or

(B) the proceeds, after deducting the reasonable costs of producing the performance, are used exclusively for educational, religious, or charitable purposes and not for private financial gain, except where the copyright owner has served notice of objection to the performance under the following conditions;

(i) the notice shall be in writing and signed by the copyright owner or such owner's duly authorized agent; and

(ii) the notice shall be served on the person responsible for the performance at least seven days before the date of the performance, and shall state the reasons for the objection; and

(iii) the notice shall comply, in form, content, and manner of service, with requirements that the Register of Copyrights shall prescribe by regulation;

(5)(A) except as provided in subparagraph (B), communication of a transmission embodying a performance or display of a work by the public reception of the transmission on a single receiving apparatus of a kind commonly used in private homes, unless —

(i) a direct charge is made to see or hear the transmission; or

(ii) the transmission thus received is further transmitted to the public;

(B) communication by an establishment of a transmission or retransmission embodying a performance or display of a nondramatic musical work intended to be received by the general public, originated by a radio or television broadcast station licensed as such by the Federal Communications Commission, or, if an audiovisual transmission, by a cable system or satellite carrier, if—

(i) in the case of an establishment other than a food service or drinking establishment, either the establishment in which the communication occurs has less than 2,000 gross square feet of space (excluding space used for customer parking and for no other purpose), or the establishment in which the communication occurs has 2,000 or more gross square feet of space (excluding space used for customer parking and for no other purpose) and-

(I) if the performance is by audio means only, the performance is communicated by means of a total of not more than 6 loudspeakers, of which not more than 4 loudspeakers are located in any 1 room or adjoining outdoor space; or

(II) if the performance or display is by audiovisual means, any visual portion of the performance or display is communicated by means of a total of not more than 4 audiovisual devices, of which not more than 1 audiovisual device is located in any 1 room, and no such audiovisual device has a diagonal screen size greater than 55 inches, and any audio portion of the performance or display is communicated by means of a total of not more than 6 loudspeakers, of which not more than 4 loudspeakers are located in any 1 room or adjoining outdoor space . . .

(iii) no direct charge is made to see or hear the transmission or retransmission;

(iv) the transmission or retransmission is not further transmitted beyond the establishment where it is received; and

(v) the transmission or retransmission is licensed by the copyright owner of the work so publicly performed or displayed . . .

The exemptions provided under paragraph (5) shall not be taken into account in any administrative, judicial, or other governmental proceeding to set or adjust the royalties payable to copyright owners for the public performance or display of their works. Royalties payable to copyright owners for any public performance or display of their works other than such performances or displays as are exempted under paragraph (5) shall not be diminished in any respect as a result of such exemption.

§ 112. Limitations on exclusive rights: Ephemeral recordings

(a)(1) Notwithstanding the provisions of section 106, and except in the case of a motion picture or other audiovisual work, it is not an infringement of copyright for a transmitting organization entitled to transmit to the public a performance or display of a work, under a license, including a statutory license under section 114(f), or transfer of the copyright or under the limitations on exclusive rights in sound recordings specified by section 114 (a) or for a transmitting organization that is a broadcast radio or television station licensed as such by the Federal Communications Commission and that makes a broadcast transmission of a performance of a sound recording in a digital format on a nonsubscription basis, to make no more than one copy or phonorecord of a particular transmission program embodying the performance or display, if-

(A) the copy or phonorecord is retained and used solely by the transmitting organization that made it, and no further copies or phonorecords are reproduced from it; and

(B) the copy or phonorecord is used solely for the transmitting organization's own transmissions within its local service area, or for purposes of archival preservation or security; and

(C) unless preserved exclusively for archival purposes, the copy or phonorecord is destroyed within six months from the date the transmission program was first transmitted to the public.

(2) In a case in which a transmitting organization entitled to make a copy or phonorecord under paragraph (1) in connection with the transmission to the public of a performance or display of a work is prevented from making such copy or phonorecord by reason of the application by the copyright owner of technical measures that prevent the reproduction of the work, the copyright owner shall make available to the transmitting organization the necessary means for permitting the making of such copy or phonorecord as permitted under that paragraph, if it is technologically feasible and economically reasonable for the copyright owner to do so. If the copyright owner fails to do so in a timely manner in light of the transmitting organization's reasonable business requirements, the transmitting organization shall not be liable for a violation of section 1201(a)(1) of this title for engaging in such activities as are necessary to make such copies or phonorecords as permitted under paragraph (1) of this subsection.

(b) Notwithstanding the provisions of section 106, it is not an infringement of copyright for a governmental body or other nonprofit organization entitled to transmit a performance or display of a work, under section 110(2) or under the limitations on exclusive rights in sound recordings specified by section 114(a), to make no more than thirty copies or phonorecords of a particular transmission program embodying the performance or display, if-

(1) no further copies or phonorecords are reproduced from the copies or phonorecords made under this clause; and

(2) except for one copy or phonorecord that may be preserved exclusively for archival purposes, the copies or phonorecords are destroyed within seven years from the date the transmission program was first transmitted to the public.

(c) Notwithstanding the provisions of section 106, it is not an infringement of copyright for a governmental body or other nonprofit organization to make for distribution no more than one copy or phonorecord, for each transmitting organization specified in clause (2) of this subsection, of a particular transmission program embodying a performance of a nondramatic musical work of a religious nature, or of a sound recording of such a musical work, if-

(1) there is no direct or indirect charge for making or distributing any such copies or phonorecords; and

(2) none of such copies or phonorecords is used for any performance other than a single transmission to the public by a transmitting organization entitled to transmit to the public a performance of the work under a license or transfer of the copyright; and

(3) except for one copy or phonorecord that may be preserved exclusively for archival purposes, the copies or phonorecords are all destroyed within one year from the date the transmission program was first transmitted to the public.

§ 114. Scope of exclusive rights in sound recordings

(a) The exclusive rights of the owner of copyright in a sound recording are limited to the rights specified by clauses (1), (2), (3) and (6) of section 106, and do not include any right of performance under section 106(4).

(b) The exclusive right of the owner of copyright in a sound recording under clause (1) of section 106 is limited to the right to duplicate the sound recording in the form of phonorecords or copies that directly or indirectly recapture the actual sounds fixed in the recording. The exclusive right of the owner of copyright in a sound recording under clause (2) of section 106 is limited to the right to prepare a derivative work in which the actual sounds fixed in the sound recording are rearranged, remixed, or otherwise altered in sequence or quality. The exclusive rights of the owner of copyright in a sound recording under clauses (1) and (2) of section 106 do not extend to the making or duplication of another sound recording that consists entirely of an independent fixation of other sounds, even though such sounds imitate or simulate those in the copyrighted sound recording. The exclusive rights of the owner of copyright in a sound recording under clauses (1), (2), and (3) of section 106 do not apply to sound recordings included in educational television and radio programs (as defined in section 397 of title 47) distributed or transmitted by or through public broadcasting entities

(as defined by section 118(g)): Provided, That copies or phonorecords of said programs are not commercially distributed by or through public broadcasting entities to the general public.

(c) This section does not limit or impair the exclusive right to perform publicly, by means of a phonorecord, any of the works specified by section 106(4). . . .

§ 115. Scope of exclusive rights in nondramatic musical works: Compulsory license for making and distributing phonorecords

In the case of nondramatic musical works, the exclusive rights provided by clauses (1) and (3) of section 106, to make and to distribute phonorecords of such works, are subject to compulsory licensing under the conditions specified by this section.

(a) Availability and Scope of Compulsory License.-

(1) When phonorecords of a nondramatic musical work have been distributed to the public in the United States under the authority of the copyright owner, any other person, including those who make phonorecords or digital phonorecord deliveries, may, by complying with the provisions of this section, obtain a compulsory license to make and distribute phonorecords of the work. A person may obtain a compulsory license only if his or her primary purpose in making phonorecords is to distribute them to the public for private use, including by means of a digital phonorecord delivery. A person may not obtain a compulsory license for use of the work in the making of phonorecords duplicating a sound recording fixed by another, unless:

(i) such sound recording was fixed lawfully; and

(ii) the making of the phonorecords was authorized by the owner of copyright in the sound recording or, if the sound recording was fixed before February 15, 1972, by any person who fixed the sound recording pursuant to an express license from the owner of the copyright in the musical work or pursuant to a valid compulsory license for use of such work in a sound recording.

(2) A compulsory license includes the privilege of making a musical arrangement of the work to the extent necessary to conform it to the style or manner of interpretation of the performance involved, but the arrangement shall not change the basic melody or fundamental character of the work, and

shall not be subject to protection as a derivative work under this title, except with the express consent of the copyright owner.

(b) Notice of Intention To Obtain Compulsory License.-

(1) Any person who wishes to obtain a compulsory license under this section shall, before or within thirty days after making, and before distributing any phonorecords of the work, serve notice of intention to do so on the copyright owner. If the registration or other public records of the Copyright Office do not identify the copyright owner and include an address at which notice can be served, it shall be sufficient to file the notice of intention in the Copyright Office. The notice shall comply, in form, content, and manner of service, with requirements that the Register of Copyrights shall prescribe by regulation.

(2) Failure to serve or file the notice required by clause (1) forecloses the possibility of a compulsory license and, in the absence of a negotiated license, renders the making and distribution of phonorecords actionable as acts of infringement under section 501 and fully subject to the remedies provided by sections 502 through 506 and 509.

(c) Royalty Payable Under Compulsory License.

(1) To be entitled to receive royalties under a compulsory license, the copyright owner must be identified in the registration or other public records of the Copyright Office. The owner is entitled to royalties for phonorecords made and distributed after being so identified, but is not entitled to recover for any phonorecords previously made and distributed.

(2) Except as provided by clause (1), the royalty under a compulsory license shall be payable for every phonorecord made and distributed in accordance with the license. For this purpose, and other than as provided in paragraph (3), a phonorecord is considered "distributed" if the person exercising the compulsory license has voluntarily and permanently parted with its possession. With respect to each work embodied in the phonorecord, the royalty shall be either two and three-fourths cents, or one-half of one cent per minute of playing time or fraction thereof, whichever amount is larger.

(3)(A) A compulsory license under this section includes the right of the compulsory licensee to distribute or authorize the distribution of a phonorecord of a nondramatic musical work by means of a digital transmission which constitutes a digital phonorecord delivery, regardless of whether the digital transmission is also a public performance of the sound recording under section 106(6) of this title or of any nondramatic musical work embodied therein under section 106(4) of this title. For every digital phonorecord delivery by or under the authority of the compulsory licensee-

(i) on or before December 31, 1997, the royalty payable by the compulsory licensee shall be the royalty prescribed under paragraph (2) and chapter 8 of this title; and

(ii) on or after January 1, 1998, the royalty payable by the compulsory licensee shall be the royalty prescribed under subparagraphs (B) through (F) and chapter 8 of this title.

(B) Notwithstanding any provision of the antitrust laws, any copyright owners of nondramatic musical works and any persons entitled to obtain a compulsory license under subsection (a)(1) may negotiate and agree upon the terms and rates of royalty payments under this paragraph and the proportionate division of fees paid among copyright owners, and may designate common agents to negotiate, agree to, pay or receive such royalty payments. Such authority to negotiate the terms and rates of royalty payments includes, but is not limited to, the authority to negotiate the year during which the royalty rates prescribed under subparagraphs (B) through (F) and chapter 8 of this title shall next be determined. . . .

(4) A compulsory license under this section includes the right of the maker of a phonorecord of a nondramatic musical work under subsection (a)(1) to distribute or authorize distribution of such phonorecord by rental, lease, or lending (or by acts or practices in the nature of rental, lease, or lending). In addition to any royalty payable under clause (2) and chapter 8 of this title, a royalty shall be payable by the compulsory licensee for every act of distribution of a phonorecord by or in the nature of rental, lease, or lending, by or under the authority of the compulsory licensee. With respect to each nondramatic musical work embodied in the phonorecord, the royalty shall be a proportion of the revenue received by the compulsory licensee from every such act of distribution of the phonorecord under this clause equal to the proportion of the revenue received by the compulsory licensee from distribution of the phonorecord under clause (2) that is payable by a compulsory licensee under that clause and under chapter 8. The Register of Copyrights shall issue regulations to carry out the purpose of this clause.

(5) Royalty payments shall be made on or before the twentieth day of each month and shall include all royalties for

the month next preceding. Each monthly payment shall be made under oath and shall comply with requirements that the Register of Copyrights shall prescribe by regulation. The Register shall also prescribe regulations under which detailed cumulative annual statements of account, certified by a certified public accountant, shall be filed for every compulsory license under this section. The regulations covering both the monthly and the annual statements of account shall prescribe the form, content, and manner of certification with respect to the number of records made and the number of records distributed.

(6) If the copyright owner does not receive the monthly payment and the monthly and annual statements of account when due, the owner may give written notice to the licensee that, unless the default is remedied within thirty days from the date of the notice, the compulsory license will be automatically terminated. Such termination renders either the making or the distribution, or both, of all phonorecords for which the royalty has not been paid, actionable as acts of infringement under section 501 and fully subject to the remedies provided by sections 502 through 506 and 509. . . .

§ 117. Limitations on exclusive rights: Computer programs

(a) Making of Additional Copy or Adaptation by Owner of Copy. Notwithstanding the provisions of section 106, it is not an infringement for the owner of a copy of a computer program to make or authorize the making of another copy or adaptation of that computer program provided:

(1) that such a new copy or adaptation is created as an essential step in the utilization of the computer program in conjunction with a machine and that it is used in no other manner, or

(2) that such new copy or adaptation is for archival purposes only and that all archival copies are destroyed in the event that continued possession of the computer program should cease to be rightful.

(b) Lease, Sale, or Other Transfer of Additional Copy or Adaptation. Any exact copies prepared in accordance with the provisions of this section may be leased, sold, or otherwise transferred, along with the copy from which such copies were prepared, only as part of the lease, sale, or other transfer of all rights in the program. Adaptations so prepared may be transferred only with the authorization of the copyright owner.

(c) Machine Maintenance or Repair. Notwithstanding the provisions of section 106, it is not an infringement for the owner or lessee of a machine to make or authorize the making of a copy of a computer program if such copy is made solely by virtue of the activation of a machine that lawfully contains an authorized copy of the computer program, for purposes only of maintenance or repair of that machine, if-

(1) such new copy is used in no other manner and is destroyed immediately after the maintenance or repair is completed; and

(2) with respect to any computer program or part thereof that is not necessary for that machine to be activated, such program or part thereof is not accessed or used other than to make such new copy by virtue of the activation of the machine.

(d) Definitions. For purposes of this section—

(1) the "maintenance" of a machine is the servicing of the machine in order to make it work in accordance with its original specifications and any changes to those specifications authorized for that machine; and

(2) the "repair" of a machine is the restoring of the machine to the state of working in accordance with its original specifications and any changes to those specifications authorized for that machine.

Chapter 2:
Copyright Ownership and Transfer

§ 201. Ownership of copyright

(a) Initial Ownership. Copyright in a work protected under this title vests initially in the author or authors of the work. The authors of a joint work are co-owner of copyright in the work.

(b) Works Made for Hire. In the case of a work made for hire, the employer or other person for whom the work was prepared is considered the author for purposes of this title, and, unless the parties have expressly agreed otherwise in a written instrument signed by them, owns all of the rights comprised in the copyright.

(c) Contributions to Collective Works. Copyright in each separate contribution to a collective work is distinct from copyright in the collective work as a whole, and vests initially in the author of the contribution. In the absence of an express transfer of the copyright or of any rights under it, the owner of copyright in the collective work is presumed to have acquired only the privilege of reproducing and distributing the contribution as part of that particular collective work, any revision of that collective work, and any later collective work in the same series.

(d) Transfer of Ownership.

(1) The ownership of a copyright may be transferred in whole or in part by any means of conveyance or by operation of law, and may be bequeathed by will or pass as personal property by the applicable laws of intestate succession.

(2) Any of the exclusive rights comprised in a copyright, including any subdivision of any of the rights specified by section 106, may be transferred as provided by clause (1) and owned separately. The owner of any particular exclusive right is entitled, to the extent of that right, to all of the protection and remedies accorded to the copyright owner by this title.

(e) Involuntary Transfer. When an individual author's ownership of a copyright, or of any of the exclusive rights under a copyright, has not previously been transferred voluntarily by that individual author, no action by any governmental body or other official or organization purporting to seize, expropriate, transfer, or exercise rights of ownership with respect to the copyright, or any of the exclusive rights under a copyright, shall be given effect under this title, except as provided under title 11.

§ 202. Ownership of copyright as distinct from ownership of material object

Ownership of a copyright, or of any of the exclusive rights under a copyright, is distinct from ownership of any material object in which the work is embodied. Transfer of ownership of any material object, including the copy or phonorecord in which the work is first fixed, does not of itself convey any rights in the copyrighted work embodied in the object; nor, in the absence of an agreement, does transfer of ownership of a copyright or of any exclusive rights under a copyright convey property rights in any material object.

§ 203. Termination of transfers and licenses granted by the author

(a) Conditions for Termination. In the case of any work other than a work made for hire, the exclusive or nonexclusive grant of a transfer or license of copyright or of any right under a copyright, executed by the author on or after January 1, 1978, otherwise than by will, is subject to termination under the following conditions:

(1) In the case of a grant executed by one author, termination of the grant may be effected by that author or, if the author is dead, by the person or persons who, under clause (2) of this subsection, own and are entitled to exercise a total of more than one-half of that author's termination interest. In the case of a grant executed by two or more authors of a joint work, termination of the grant may be effected by a majority of the authors who executed it; if any of such authors is dead, the termination interest of any such author may be exercised as a unit by the person or persons who, under clause (2) of this subsection, own and are entitled to exercise a total of more than one-half of that author's interest.

(2) Where an author is dead, his or her termination interest is owned, and may be exercised, as follows:

(A) the widow or widower owns the author's entire termination interest unless there are any surviving children or grandchildren of the author, in which case the widow or widower owns one-half of the author's interest;

(B) the author's surviving children, and the surviving children of any dead child of the author, own the author's entire termination interest unless there is a widow or widower, in which case the ownership of one-half of the author's interest is divided among them;

(C) the rights of the author's children and grandchildren are in all cases divided among them and exercised on a per stirpes basis according to the number of such author's children represented; the share of the children of a dead child in a termination interest can be exercised only by the action of a majority of them.

(D) In the event that the author's widow or widower, children, and grandchildren are not living, the author's executor, administrator, personal representative, or trustee shall own the author's entire termination interest.

(3) Termination of the grant may be effected at any time during a period of five years beginning at the end of thirty-five years from the date of execution of the grant; or, if the grant covers the right of publication of the work, the period begins at the end of thirty-five years from the date of

publication of the work under the grant or at the end of forty years from the date of execution of the grant, whichever term ends earlier.

(4) The termination shall be effected by serving an advance notice in writing, signed by the number and proportion of owners of termination interests required under clauses (1) and (2) of this subsection, or by their duly authorized agents, upon the grantee or the grantee's successor in title.

(A) The notice shall state the effective date of the termination, which shall fall within the five-year period specified by clause (3) of this subsection, and the notice shall be served not less than two or more than ten years before that date. A copy of the notice shall be recorded in the Copyright Office before the effective date of termination, as a condition to its taking effect.

(B) The notice shall comply, in form, content, and manner of service, with requirements that the Register of Copyrights shall prescribe by regulation.

(5) Termination of the grant may be effected notwithstanding any agreement to the contrary, including an agreement to make a will or to make any future grant.

(b) Effect of Termination.-Upon the effective date of termination, all rights under this title that were covered by the terminated grants revert to the author, authors, and other persons owning termination interests under clauses (1) and (2) of subsection (a), including those owners who did not join in signing the notice of termination under clause (4) of subsection (a), but with the following limitations:

(1) A derivative work prepared under authority of the grant before its termination may continue to be utilized under the terms of the grant after its termination, but this privilege does not extend to the preparation after the termination of other derivative works based upon the copyrighted work covered by the terminated grant.

(2) The future rights that will revert upon termination of the grant become vested on the date the notice of termination has been served as provided by clause (4) of subsection (a). The rights vest in the author, authors, and other persons named in, and in the proportionate shares provided by, clauses (1) and (2) of subsection (a).

(3) Subject to the provisions of clause (4) of this subsection, a further grant, or agreement to make a further grant, of any right covered by a terminated grant is valid only if it is signed by the same number and proportion of the owners, in whom the right has vested under clause (2) of this subsection, as are required to terminate the grant under clauses (1) and (2) of subsection (a). Such further grant or agreement is effective with respect to all of the persons in whom the right it covers has vested under clause (2) of this subsection, including those who did not join in signing it. If any person dies after rights under a terminated grant have vested in him or her, that person's legal representatives, legatees, or heirs at law represent him or her for purposes of this clause.

(4) A further grant, or agreement to make a further grant, of any right covered by a terminated grant is valid only if it is made after the effective date of the termination. As an exception, however, an agreement for such a further grant may be made between the persons provided by clause (3) of this subsection and the original grantee or such grantee's successor in title, after the notice of termination has been served as provided by clause (4) of subsection (a).

(5) Termination of a grant under this section affects only those rights covered by the grants that arise under this title, and in no way affects rights arising under any other Federal, State, or foreign laws.

(6) Unless and until termination is effected under this section, the grant, if it does not provide otherwise, continues in effect for the term of copyright provided by this title.

§ 204. Execution of transfers of copyright ownership

(a) A transfer of copyright ownership, other than by operation of law, is not valid unless an instrument of conveyance, or a note or memorandum of the transfer, is in writing and signed by the owner of the rights conveyed or such owner's duly authorized agent.

(b) A certificate of acknowledgment is not required for the validity of a transfer, but is prima facie evidence of the execution of the transfer if-

(1) in the case of a transfer executed in the United States, the certificate is issued by a person authorized to administer oaths within the United States; or

(2) in the case of a transfer executed in a foreign country, the certificate is issued by a diplomatic or consular officer of the

United States, or by a person authorized to administer oaths whose authority is proved by a certificate of such an officer.

§ 205. Recordation of transfers and other documents

(a) Conditions for Recordation. Any transfer of copyright ownership or other document pertaining to a copyright may be recorded in the Copyright Office if the document filed for recordation bears the actual signature of the person who executed it, or if it is accompanied by a sworn or official certification that it is a true copy of the original, signed document.

(b) Certificate of Recordation. The Register of Copyrights shall, upon receipt of a document as provided by subsection (a) and of the fee provided by section 708, record the document and return it with a certificate of recordation.

(c) Recordation as Constructive Notice. Recordation of a document in the Copyright Office gives all persons constructive notice of the facts stated in the recorded document, but only if-

(1) the document, or material attached to it, specifically identifies the work to which it pertains so that, after the document is indexed by the Register of Copyrights, it would be revealed by a reasonable search under the title or registration number of the work; and

(2) registration has been made for the work.

(d) Priority Between Conflicting Transfers. As between two conflicting transfers, the one executed first prevails if it is recorded, in the manner required to give constructive notice under subsection (c), within one month after its execution in the United States or within two months after its execution outside the United States, or at any time before recordation in such manner of the later transfer. Otherwise the later transfer prevails if recorded first in such manner, and if taken in good faith, for valuable consideration or on the basis of a binding promise to pay royalties, and without notice of the earlier transfer.

(e) Priority Between Conflicting Transfer of Ownership and Nonexclusive License. A nonexclusive license, whether recorded or not, prevails over a conflicting transfer of copyright ownership if the license is evidenced by a written instrument signed by the owner of the rights licensed or such owner's duly authorized agent, and if

(1) the license was taken before execution of the transfer; or

(2) the license was taken in good faith before recordation of the transfer and without notice of it.

Chapter 3: Duration of Copyright

§ 302. Duration of copyright: Works created on or after January 1, 1978

(a) In General. Copyright in a work created on or after January 1, 1978, subsists from its creation and, except as provided by the following subsections, endures for a term consisting of the life of the author and 70 years after the author's death.

(b) Joint Works. In the case of a joint work prepared by two or more authors who did not work for hire, the copyright endures for a term consisting of the life of the last surviving author and 70 years after such last surviving author's death.

(c) Anonymous Works, Pseudonymous Works, and Works Made for Hire. In the case of an anonymous work, a pseudonymous work, or a work made for hire, the copyright endures for a term of 95 years from the year of its first publication, or a term of 120 years from the year of its creation, whichever expires first. If, before the end of such term, the identity of one or more of the authors of an anonymous or pseudonymous work is revealed in the records of a registration made for that work under subsections (a) or (d) of section 408, or in the records provided by this subsection, the copyright in the work endures for the term specified by subsection (a) or (b), based on the life of the author or authors whose identity has been revealed. Any person having an interest in the copyright in an anonymous or pseudonymous work may at any time record, in records to be maintained by the Copyright Office for that purpose, a statement identifying one or more authors of the work; the statement shall also identify the person filing it, the nature of that person's interest, the source of the information recorded, and the particular work affected, and shall comply in form and content with requirements that the Register of Copyrights shall prescribe by regulation.

(d) Records Relating to Death of Authors. Any person having an interest in a copyright may at any time record in the Copyright Office a statement of the date of death of the author of the copyrighted work, or a statement that the author is still living on a particular date. The statement shall identify the person filing it, the nature of that person's interest, and the source of the information recorded, and shall comply in form and content with requirements that the Register of Copyrights shall prescribe by regulation. The Register shall maintain current records of information relating to the death of authors of copyrighted works, based on such recorded statements and, to the extent the Register considers practicable, on data contained in any of the records of the Copyright Office or in other reference sources.

(e) Presumption as to Author's Death. After a period of 95 years from the year of first publication of a work, or a period of 120 years from the year of its creation, whichever expires first, any person who obtains from the Copyright Office a certified report that the records provided by subsection (d) disclose nothing to indicate that the author of the work is living, or died less than 70 years before, is entitled to the benefit of a presumption that the author has been dead for at least 70 years. Reliance in good faith upon this presumption shall be a complete defense to any action for infringement under this title.

§ 303. Duration of copyright: Works created but not published or copyrighted before January 1, 1978

(a) Copyright in a work created before January 1, 1978, but not theretofore in the public domain or copyrighted, subsists from January 1, 1978, and endures for the term provided by section 302. In no case, however, shall the term of copyright in such a work expire before December 31, 2002; and, if the work is published on or before December 31, 2002, the term of copyright shall not expire before December 31, 2047.

(b) The distribution before January 1, 1978, of a phonorecord shall not for any purpose constitute a publication of the musical work embodied therein.

§ 304. Duration of copyright: Subsisting copyrights

(a) Copyrights in Their First Term on January 1, 1978.

(1)(A) Any copyright, in the first term of which is subsisting on January 1, 1978, shall endure for 28 years from the date it was originally secured.

(B) In the case of–

(i) any posthumous work or of any periodical, cyclopedic, or other composite work upon which the copyright was originally secured by the proprietor thereof, or

(ii) any work copyrighted by a corporate body (otherwise than as assignee or licensee of the individual author) or by an employer for whom such work is made for hire,

the proprietor of such copyright shall be entitled to a renewal and extension of the copyright in such work for the further term of 67 years.

(C) In the case of any other copyrighted work, including a contribution by an individual author to a periodical or to a cyclopedic or other composite work-

(i) the author of such work, if the author is still living,

(ii) the widow, widower, or children of the author, if the author is not living,

(iii) the author's executors, if such author, widow, widower, or children are not living, or

(iv) the author's next of kin, in the absence of a will of the author, shall be entitled to a renewal and extension of the copyright in such work for a further term of 67 years.

(2)(A) At the expiration of the original term of copyright in a work specified in paragraph (1)(B) of this subsection, the copyright shall endure for a renewed and extended further term of 67 years, which-

(i) if an application to register a claim to such further term has been made to the Copyright Office within 1 year before the expiration of the original term of copyright, and the claim is registered, shall vest, upon the beginning of such further term, in the proprietor of the copyright who is entitled to claim the renewal of copyright at the time the application is made; or

(ii) if no such application is made or the claim pursuant to such application is not registered, shall vest, upon the beginning of such further term, in the person or entity that was the proprietor of the copyright as of the last day of the original term of copyright.

(B) At the expiration of the original term of copyright in a work specified in paragraph (1)(C) of this subsection, the copyright shall endure for a renewed and extended further term of 67 years, which-

(i) if an application to register a claim to such further term has been made to the Copyright Office within 1 year before the expiration of the original term of copyright, and the claim is registered, shall vest, upon the beginning of such further term, in any person who is entitled under paragraph (1)(C) to the renewal and extension of the copyright at the time the application is made; or

(ii) if no such application is made or the claim pursuant to such application is not registered, shall vest, upon the beginning of such further term, in any person entitled under paragraph (1)(C), as of the last day of the original term of copyright, to the renewal and extension of the copyright.

(3)(A) An application to register a claim to the renewed and extended term of copyright in a work may be made to the Copyright Office–

(i) within 1 year before the expiration of the original term of copyright by any person entitled under paragraph (1)(B) or (C) to such further term of 67 years; and

(ii) at any time during the renewed and extended term by any person in whom such further term vested, under paragraph (2)(A) or (B), or by any successor or assign of such person, if the application is made in the name of such person.

(B) Such an application is not a condition of the renewal and extension of the copyright in a work for a further term of 67 years.

(4)(A) If an application to register a claim to the renewed and extended term of copyright in a work is not made within 1 year before the expiration of the original term of copyright in a work, or if the claim pursuant to such application is not registered, then a derivative work prepared under authority of a grant of a transfer or license of the copyright that is made before the expiration of the original term of copyright may continue to be used under the terms of the grant during the renewed and extended term of copyright without infringing the copyright, except that such use does not extend to the preparation during such renewed and extended term of other derivative works based upon the copyrighted work covered by such grant.

(B) If an application to register a claim to the renewed and extended term of copyright in a work is made within 1 year before its expiration, and the claim is registered, the certificate of such registration shall constitute prima facie evidence as to the validity of the copyright during its renewed and extended term and of the facts stated in the certificate. The evidentiary weight to be accorded the certificates of a registration of a renewed and extended term of copyright made after the end of that 1-year period shall be within the discretion of the court.

(b) Copyrights in Their Renewal Term at the Time of the Effective Date of the Sonny Bono Copyright Term Extension Act. Any copyright still in its renewal term at the time that the Sonny Bono Copyright Term Extension Act becomes effective shall have a copyright term of 95 years from the date copyright was originally secured.

(c) Termination of Transfers and Licenses Covering Extended Renewal Term. -In the case of any copyright subsisting in either its first or renewal term on January 1, 1978, other than a copyright in a work made for hire, the exclusive or nonexclusive grant of a transfer or license of the renewal copyright or any right under it, executed before January 1, 1978, by any of the persons designated by subsection (a)(1)(C) of this section, otherwise than by will, is subject to termination under the following conditions:

(1) In the case of a grant executed by a person or persons other than the author, termination of the grant may be effected by the surviving person or persons who executed it. In the case of a grant executed by one or more of the authors of the work, termination of the grant may be effected, to the extent of a particular author's share in the ownership of the renewal copyright, by the author who executed it or, if such author is dead, by the person or persons who, under clause (2) of this subsection, own and are entitled to exercise a total of more than one-half of that author's termination interest.

(2) Where an author is dead, his or her termination interest is owned, and may be exercised, as follows:

(A) the widow or widower owns the author's entire termination interest unless there are any surviving children or grandchildren of the author, in which case the widow or widower owns one-half of the author's interest;

(B) the author's surviving children, and the surviving children of any dead child of the author, own the author's entire termination interest unless there is a widow or widower, in which case the ownership of one-half of the author's interest is divided among them;

(C) the rights of the author's children and grandchildren are in all cases divided among them and exercised on a per stirpes basis according to the number of such author's children represented; the share of the children of a dead child in a termination interest can be exercised only by the action of a majority of them.

(D) In the event that the author's widow or widower, children, and grandchildren are not living, the author's executor, administrator, personal representative, or trustee shall own the author's entire termination interest.

(3) Termination of the grant may be effected at any time during a period of five years beginning at the end of fifty-six years from the date copyright was originally secured, or beginning on January 1, 1978, whichever is later.

(4) The termination shall be effected by serving an advance notice in writing upon the grantee or the grantee's successor in title. In the case of a grant executed by a person or persons other than the author, the notice shall be signed by all of those entitled to terminate the grant under clause (1) of this subsection, or by their duly authorized agents. In the case of a grant executed by one or more of the authors of the work, the notice as to any one author's share shall be signed by that author or his or her duly authorized agent or, if that author is dead, by the number and proportion of the owners of his or her termination interest required under clauses (1) and (2) of this subsection, or by their duly authorized agents.

(A) The notice shall state the effective date of the termination, which shall fall within the five-year period specified by clause (3) of this subsection, or, in the case of a termination under subsection (d), within the five-year period specified by subsection (d)(2), and the notice shall be served not less than two or more than ten years before that date. A copy of the notice shall be recorded in the Copyright Office before the effective date of termination, as a condition to its taking effect.

(B) The notice shall comply, in form, content, and manner of service, with requirements that the Register of Copyrights shall prescribe by regulation.

(5) Termination of the grant may be effected notwithstanding any agreement to the contrary, including an agreement to make a will or to make any future grant.

(6) In the case of a grant executed by a person or persons other than the author, all rights under this title that were covered by the terminated grant revert, upon the effective date of termination, to all of those entitled to terminate the grant under clause (1) of this subsection. In the case of a grant executed by one or more of the authors of the work, all of a particular author's rights under this title that were covered by the terminated grant revert, upon the effective date of termination, to that author or, if that author is dead, to the persons owning his or her termination interest under clause (2) of this subsection, including those owners who did not join in signing the notice of termination under clause

(4) of this subsection. In all cases the reversion of rights is subject to the following limitations:

(A) A derivative work prepared under authority of the grant before its termination may continue to be utilized under the terms of the grant after its termination, but this privilege does not extend to the preparation after the termination of other derivative works based upon the copyrighted work covered by the terminated grant.

(B) The future rights that will revert upon termination of the grant become vested on the date the notice of termination has been served as provided by clause (4) of this subsection.

(C) Where the author's rights revert to two or more persons under clause (2) of this subsection, they shall vest in those persons in the proportionate shares provided by that clause. In such a case, and subject to the provisions of subclause (D) of this clause, a further grant, or agreement to make a further grant, of a particular author's share with respect to any right covered by a terminated grant is valid only if it is signed by the same number and proportion of the owners, in whom the right has vested under this clause, as are required to terminate the grant under clause (2) of this subsection. Such further grant or agreement is effective with respect to all of the persons in whom the right it covers has vested under this subclause, including those who did not join in signing it. If any person dies after rights under a terminated grant have vested in him or her, that person's legal representatives, legatees, or heirs at law represent him or her for purposes of this subclause.

(D) A further grant, or agreement to make a further grant, of any right covered by a terminated grant is valid only if it is made after the effective date of the termination. As an exception, however, an agreement for such a further grant may be made between the author or any of the persons provided by the first sentence of clause (6) of this subsection, or between the persons provided by subclause (C) of this clause, and the original grantee or such grantee's successor in title, after the notice of termination has been served as provided by clause (4) of this subsection.

(E) Termination of a grant under this subsection affects only those rights covered by the grant that arise under this title, and in no way affects rights arising under any other Federal, State, or foreign laws.

(F) Unless and until termination is effected under this subsection, the grant, if it does not provide otherwise, continues in effect for the remainder of the extended renewal term.

(d) Termination Rights Provided in Subsection (c) Which Have Expired on or Before the Effective Date of the Sonny Bono Copyright Term Extension Act.—In the case of any copyright other than a work made for hire, subsisting in its renewal term on the effective date of the Sonny Bono Copyright Term Extension Act[9] for which the termination right provided in subsection (c) has expired by such date, where the author or owner of the termination right has not previously exercised such termination right, the exclusive or nonexclusive grant of a transfer or license of the renewal copyright or any right under it, executed before January 1, 1978, by any of the persons designated in subsection (a)(1)(C) of this section, other than by will, is subject to termination under the following conditions:

(1) The conditions specified in subsections (c) (1), (2), (4), (5), and (6) of this section apply to terminations of the last 20 years of copyright term as provided by the amendments made by the Sonny Bono Copyright Term Extension Act.

(2) Termination of the grant may be effected at any time during a period of 5 years beginning at the end of 75 years from the date copyright was originally secured.

§ 305. Duration of copyright: Terminal date

All terms of copyright provided by sections 302 through 304 run to the end of the calendar year in which they would otherwise expire.

Chapter 4:
Copyright Notice, Deposit, and Registration

§ 401. Notice of copyright: Visually perceptible copies

(a) General Provisions. Whenever a work protected under this title is published in the United States or elsewhere by authority of the copyright owner, a notice of copyright as provided by this section may be placed on publicly distributed copies from which the work can be visually perceived, either directly or with the aid of a machine or device.

(b) Form of Notice. If a notice appears on the copies, it shall consist of the following three elements:

(1) the symbol © (the letter C in a circle), or the word "Copyright", or the abbreviation "Copr."; and

(2) the year of first publication of the work; in the case of compilations or derivative works incorporating previously published material, the year date of first publication of the compilation or derivative work is sufficient. The year date may be omitted where a pictorial, graphic, or sculptural work, with accompanying text matter, if any, is reproduced in or on greeting cards, postcards, stationery, jewelry, dolls, toys, or any useful articles; and

(3) the name of the owner of copyright in the work, or an abbreviation by which the name can be recognized, or a generally known alternative designation of the owner.

(c) Position of Notice. The notice shall be affixed to the copies in such manner and location as to give reasonable notice of the claim of copyright. The Register of Copyrights shall prescribe by regulation, as examples, specific methods of affixation and positions of the notice on various types of works that will satisfy this requirement, but these specifications shall not be considered exhaustive.

(d) Evidentiary Weight of Notice. If a notice of copyright in the form and position specified by this section appears on the published copy or copies to which a defendant in a copyright infringement suit had access, then no weight shall be given to such a defendant's interposition of a defense based on innocent infringement in mitigation of actual or statutory damages, except as provided in the last sentence of section 504(c)(2).

§ 402. Notice of copyright: Phonorecords of sound recordings

(a) General Provisions. Whenever a sound recording protected under this title is published in the United States or elsewhere by authority of the copyright owner, a notice of copyright as provided by this section may be placed on publicly distributed phonorecords of the sound recording.

(b) Form of Notice. If a notice appears on the phonorecords, it shall consist of the following three elements:

(1) the symbol ℗ (the letter P in a circle); and

(2) the year of first publication of the sound recording; and

(3) the name of the owner of copyright in the sound recording, or an abbreviation by which the name can be recognized, or a generally known alternative designation of the owner; if the producer of the sound recording is named on the phonorecord labels or containers, and if no other name appears in conjunction with the notice, the producer's name shall be considered a part of the notice.

(c) Position of Notice. The notice shall be placed on the surface of the phonorecord, or on the phonorecord label or container, in such manner and location as to give reasonable notice of the claim of copyright.

(d) Evidentiary Weight of Notice. If a notice of copyright in the form and position specified by this section appears on the published phonorecord or phonorecords to which a defendant in a copyright infringement suit had access, then no weight shall be given to such a defendant's interposition of a defense based on innocent infringement in mitigation of actual or statutory damages, except as provided in the last sentence of section 504(c)(2).

§ 403. Notice of copyright: Publications incorporating United States Government works

Sections 401(d) and 402(d) shall not apply to a work published in copies or phonorecords consisting predominantly of one or more works of the United States Government unless the notice of copyright appearing on the published copies or phonorecords to which a defendant in the copyright infringement suit had access includes a statement identifying, either affirmatively or negatively, those portions of the copies or phonorecords embodying any work or works protected under this title.

§ 404. Notice of copyright: Contributions to collective works

(a) A separate contribution to a collective work may bear its own notice of copyright, as provided by sections 401 through 403. However, a single notice applicable to the collective work as a whole is sufficient to invoke the provisions of section 401(d) or 402(d), as applicable with respect to the separate contributions it contains (not including advertisements inserted on behalf of persons other than the owner of copyright in the collective work), regardless of the ownership of copyright in the contributions and whether or not they have been previously published.

(b) With respect to copies and phonorecords publicly distributed by authority of the copyright owner before the effective date of the Berne Convention Implementation Act of 1988, where the person named in a single notice applicable to a collective work as a whole is not the owner of copyright in a separate contribution that does not bear its own notice, the case is governed by the provisions of section 406(a).

§ 405. Notice of copyright: Omission of notice on certain copies and phonorecords

(a) Effect of Omission on Copyright. With respect to copies and phonorecords publicly distributed by authority of the copyright owner before the effective date of the Berne Convention Implementation Act of 1988, the omission of the copyright notice described in sections 401 through 403 from copies or phonorecords publicly distributed by authority of the copyright owner does not invalidate the copyright in a work if –

(1) the notice has been omitted from no more than a relatively small number of copies or phonorecords distributed to the public; or

(2) registration for the work has been made before or is made within five years after the publication without notice, and a reasonable effort is made to add notice to all copies or phonorecords that are distributed to the public in the United States after the omission has been discovered; or

(3) the notice has been omitted in violation of an express requirement in writing that, as a condition of the copyright owner's authorization of the public distribution of copies or phonorecords, they bear the prescribed notice.

(b) Effect of Omission on Innocent Infringers. Any person who innocently infringes a copyright, in reliance upon an authorized copy or phonorecord from which the copyright notice has been omitted and which was publicly distributed by authority of the copyright owner before the effective date of the Berne Convention Implementation Act of 1988, incurs no liability for actual or statutory damages under section 504 for any infringing acts committed before receiving actual notice that registration for the work has been made under section 408, if such person proves that he or she was misled by the omission of notice. In a suit for infringement in such a case the court may allow or disallow recovery of any of the infringer's profits attributable to the infringement, and may enjoin the continuation of the infringing undertaking or may require, as a condition for permitting the continuation of the infringing undertaking, that the infringer pay the copyright owner a reasonable license fee in an amount and on terms fixed by the court.

(c) Removal of Notice. Protection under this title is not affected by the removal, destruction, or obliteration of the notice, without the authorization of the copyright owner, from any publicly distributed copies or phonorecords.

§ 406. Notice of copyright: Error in name or date on certain copies and phonorecords

(a) Error in Name. With respect to copies and phonorecords publicly distributed by authority of the copyright owner before the effective date of the Berne Convention Implementation Act of 1988, where the person named in the copyright notice on copies or phonorecords publicly distributed by authority of the copyright owner is not the owner of copyright, the validity and ownership of the copyright are not affected. In such a case, however, any person who innocently begins an undertaking that infringes the copyright has a complete defense to any action for such infringement if such person proves that he or she was misled by the notice and began the undertaking in good faith under a purported transfer or license from the person named therein, unless before the undertaking was begun-

(1) registration for the work had been made in the name of the owner of copyright; or

(2) a document executed by the person named in the notice and showing the ownership of the copyright had been recorded.

The person named in the notice is liable to account to the copyright owner for all receipts from transfers or licenses purportedly made under the copyright by the person named in the notice.

(b) Error in Date. When the year date in the notice on copies or phonorecords distributed before the effective date of the Berne Convention Implementation Act of 1988 by authority of the copyright owner is earlier than the year in which publication first occurred, any period computed from the year of first publication under section 302 is to be computed from the year in the notice. Where the year date is more than one year later than the year in which publication first occurred, the work is considered to have been published without any notice and is governed by the provisions of section 405.

(c) Omission of Name or Date. Where copies or phonorecords publicly distributed before the effective date of the Berne Convention Implementation Act of 1988 by authority of the copyright owner contain no name or no date that could reasonably be considered a part of the notice, the work is considered to have been published without any notice and is governed by the provisions of section 405 as in effect on the day before the effective date of the Berne Convention Implementation Act of 1988.

§ 407. Deposit of copies or phonorecords for Library of Congress

(a) Except as provided by subsection (c), and subject to the provisions of subsection (e), the owner of copyright or of the exclusive right of publication in a work published in the United States shall deposit, within three months after the date of such publication –

(1) two complete copies of the best edition; or

(2) if the work is a sound recording, two complete phonorecords of the best edition, together with any printed or other visually perceptible material published with such phonorecords.

Neither the deposit requirements of this subsection nor the acquisition provisions of subsection (e) are conditions of copyright protection.

(b) The required copies or phonorecords shall be deposited in the Copyright Office for the use or disposition of the Library of Congress. The Register of Copyrights shall, when requested by the depositor and upon payment of the fee prescribed by section 708, issue a receipt for the deposit.

(c) The Register of Copyrights may by regulation exempt any categories of material from the deposit requirements of this section, or require deposit of only one copy or phonorecord with respect to any categories. Such regulations shall provide either for complete exemption from the deposit requirements of this section, or for alternative forms of deposit aimed at providing a satisfactory archival record of a work without imposing practical or financial hardships on the depositor, where the individual author is the owner of copyright in a pictorial, graphic, or sculptural work and

(i) less than five copies of the work have been published, or

(ii) the work has been published in a limited edition consisting of numbered copies, the monetary value of which would make the mandatory deposit of two copies of the best edition of the work burdensome, unfair, or unreasonable.

(d) At any time after publication of a work as provided by subsection(a), the Register of Copyrights may make written demand for the required deposit on any of the persons obligated to make the deposit under subsection (a). Unless deposit is made within three months after the demand is received, the person or persons on whom the demand was made are liable-

(1) to a fine of not more than $250 for each work; and

(2) to pay into a specially designated fund in the Library of Congress the total retail price of the copies or phonorecords demanded, or, if no retail price has been fixed, the reasonable cost to the Library of Congress of acquiring them; and

(3) to pay a fine of $2,500, in addition to any fine or liability imposed under clauses (1) and (2), if such person willfully or repeatedly fails or refuses to comply with such a demand.

(e) With respect to transmission programs that have been fixed and transmitted to the public in the United States but have not been published, the Register of Copyrights shall, after consulting with the Librarian of Congress and other interested organizations and officials, establish regulations governing the acquisition, through deposit or otherwise, of copies or phonorecords of such programs for the collections of the Library of Congress.

(1) The Librarian of Congress shall be permitted, under the standards and conditions set forth in such regulations, to make a fixation of a transmission program directly from a transmission to the public, and to reproduce one copy or phonorecord from such fixation for archival purposes.

(2) Such regulations shall also provide standards and procedures by which the Register of Copyrights may make written demand, upon the owner of the right of transmission in the United States, for the deposit of a copy or phonorecord of a specific transmission program. Such deposit may, at the option of the owner of the right of transmission in the United States, be accomplished by gift, by loan for purposes of reproduction, or by sale at a price not to exceed the cost of reproducing and supplying the copy or phonorecord. The regulations established under this clause shall provide reasonable periods of not less than three months for compliance with a demand, and shall allow for extensions of such periods and adjustments in the scope of the demand or the methods for fulfilling it, as reasonably

warranted by the circumstances. Willful failure or refusal to comply with the conditions prescribed by such regulations shall subject the owner of the right of transmission in the United States to liability for an amount, not to exceed the cost of reproducing and supplying the copy or phonorecord in question, to be paid into a specially designated fund in the Library of Congress.

(3) Nothing in this subsection shall be construed to require the making or retention, for purposes of deposit, of any copy or phonorecord of an unpublished transmission program, the transmission of which occurs before the receipt of a specific written demand as provided by clause (2).

(4) No activity undertaken in compliance with regulations prescribed under clauses (1) and (2) of this subsection shall result in liability if intended solely to assist in the acquisition of copies or phonorecords under this subsection.

§ 408. Copyright registration in general

(a) Registration Permissive. At any time during the subsistence of the first term of copyright in any published or unpublished work in which the copyright was secured before January 1, 1978, and during the subsistence of any copyright secured on or after that date, the owner of copyright or of any exclusive right in the work may obtain registration of the copyright claim by delivering to the Copyright Office the deposit specified by this section, together with the application and fee specified by sections 409 and 708. Such registration is not a condition of copyright protection.

(b) Deposit for Copyright Registration. Except as provided by subsection (c), the material deposited for registration shall include –

(1) in the case of an unpublished work, one complete copy or phonorecord;

(2) in the case of a published work, two complete copies or phonorecords of the best edition;

(3) in the case of a work first published outside the United States, one complete copy or phonorecord as so published;

(4) in the case of a contribution to a collective work, one complete copy or phonorecord of the best edition of the collective work.

Copies or phonorecords deposited for the Library of Congress under section 407 may be used to satisfy the deposit provisions of this section, if they are accompanied by the prescribed application and fee, and by any additional identifying material that the Register may, by regulation, require. The Register shall also prescribe regulations establishing requirements under which copies or phonorecords acquired for the Library of Congress under subsection (e) of section 407, otherwise than by deposit, may be used to satisfy the deposit provisions of this section.

(c) Administrative Classification and Optional Deposit.

(1) The Register of Copyrights is authorized to specify by regulation the administrative classes into which works are to be placed for purposes of deposit and registration, and the nature of the copies or phonorecords to be deposited in the various classes specified. The regulations may require or permit, for particular classes, the deposit of identifying material instead of copies or phonorecords, the deposit of only one copy or phonorecord where two would normally be required, or a single registration for a group of related works. This administrative classification of works has no significance with respect to the subject matter of copyright or the exclusive rights provided by this title.

(2) Without prejudice to the general authority provided under clause (1), the Register of Copyrights shall establish regulations specifically permitting a single registration for a group of works by the same individual author, all first published as contributions to periodicals, including newspapers, within a twelve-month period, on the basis of a single deposit, application, and registration fee, under the following conditions –

(A) if the deposit consists of one copy of the entire issue of the periodical, or of the entire section in the case of a newspaper, in which each contribution was first published; and

(B) if the application identifies each work separately, including the periodical containing it and its date of first publication.

(3) As an alternative to separate renewal registrations under subsection (a) of section 304, a single renewal registration may be made for a group of works by the same individual author, all first published as contributions to periodicals, including newspapers, upon the filing of a single application and fee, under all of the following conditions:

(A) the renewal claimant or claimants, and the basis of claim or claims under section 304(a), is the same for each of the works; and

(B) the works were all copyrighted upon their first publication, either through separate copyright notice and registration or by virtue of a general copyright notice in the periodical issue as a whole; and

(C) the renewal application and fee are received not more than twenty-eight or less than twenty-seven years after the thirty-first day of December of the calendar year in which all of the works were first published; and

(D) the renewal application identifies each work separately, including the periodical containing it and its date of first publication.

(d) Corrections and Amplifications. The Register may also establish, by regulation, formal procedures for the filing of an application for supplementary registration, to correct an error in a copyright registration or to amplify the information given in a registration. Such application shall be accompanied by the fee provided by section 708, and shall clearly identify the registration to be corrected or amplified. The information contained in a supplementary registration augments but does not supersede that contained in the earlier registration.

(e) Published Edition of Previously Registered Work. Registration for the first published edition of a work previously registered in unpublished form may be made even though the work as published is substantially the same as the unpublished version.

§ 409. Application for copyright registration

The application for copyright registration shall be made on a form prescribed by the Register of Copyrights and shall include –

(1) the name and address of the copyright claimant;

(2) in the case of a work other than an anonymous or pseudonymous work, the name and nationality or domicile of the author or authors, and, if one or more of the authors is dead, the dates of their deaths;

(3) if the work is anonymous or pseudonymous, the nationality or domicile of the author or authors;

(4) in the case of a work made for hire, a statement to this effect;

(5) if the copyright claimant is not the author, a brief statement of how the claimant obtained ownership of the copyright;

(6) the title of the work, together with any previous or alternative titles under which the work can be identified;

(7) the year in which creation of the work was completed;

(8) if the work has been published, the date and nation of its first publication;

(9) in the case of a compilation or derivative work, an identification of any preexisting work or works that it is based on or incorporates, and a brief, general statement of the additional material covered by the copyright claim being registered;

(10) in the case of a published work containing material of which copies are required by section 601 to be manufactured in the United States, the names of the persons or organizations who performed the processes specified by subsection (c) of section 601 with respect to that material, and the places where those processes were performed; and

(11) any other information regarded by the Register of Copyrights as bearing upon the preparation or identification of the work or the existence, ownership, or duration of the copyright.

If an application is submitted for the renewed and extended term provided for in section 304(a)(3)(A) and an original term registration has not been made, the Register may request information with respect to the existence, ownership, or duration of the copyright for the original term.

§ 410. Registration of claim and issuance of certificate

(a) When, after examination, the Register of Copyrights determines that, in accordance with the provisions of this title, the material deposited constitutes copyrightable subject matter and that the other legal and formal requirements of this title have been met, the Register shall register the claim and issue to the applicant a certificate of registration under the seal of the Copyright Office. The certificate shall contain the information given in the application, together with the number and effective date of the registration.

(b) In any case in which the Register of Copyrights determines that, in accordance with the provisions of this title, the material deposited does not constitute copyrightable

subject matter or that the claim is invalid for any other reason, the Register shall refuse registration and shall notify the applicant in writing of the reasons for such refusal.

(c) In any judicial proceedings the certificate of a registration made before or within five years after first publication of the work shall constitute prima facie evidence of the validity of the copyright and of the facts stated in the certificate. The evidentiary weight to be accorded the certificate of a registration made thereafter shall be within the discretion of the court.

(d) The effective date of a copyright registration is the day on which an application, deposit, and fee, which are later determined by the Register of Copyrights or by a court of competent jurisdiction to be acceptable for registration, have all been received in the Copyright Office.

§ 411. Registration and infringement actions

(a) Except for an action brought for a violation of the rights of the author under section 106A(a), and subject to the provisions of subsection (b), no action for infringement of the copyright in any United States work shall be instituted until registration of the copyright claim has been made in accordance with this title. In any case, however, where the deposit, application, and fee required for registration have been delivered to the Copyright Office in proper form and registration has been refused, the applicant is entitled to institute an action for infringement if notice thereof, with a copy of the complaint, is served on the Register of Copyrights. The Register may, at his or her option, become a party to the action with respect to the issue of registrability of the copyright claim by entering an appearance within sixty days after such service, but the Register's failure to become a party shall not deprive the court of jurisdiction to determine that issue.

(b) In the case of a work consisting of sounds, images, or both, the first fixation of which is made simultaneously with its transmission, the copyright owner may, either before or after such fixation takes place, institute an action for infringement under section 501, fully subject to the remedies provided by sections 502 through 506 and sections 509 and 510, if, in accordance with requirements that the Register of Copyrights shall prescribe by regulation, the copyright owner—

(1) serves notice upon the infringer, not less than 48 hours before such fixation, identifying the work and the specific time and source of its first transmission, and declaring an intention to secure copyright in the work; and

(2) makes registration for the work, if required by subsection (a), within three months after its first transmission.

§ 412. Registration as prerequisite to certain remedies for infringement

In any action under this title, other than an action brought for a violation of the rights of the author under section 106A(a) or an action instituted under section 411(b), no award of statutory damages or of attorney's fees, as provided by sections 504 and 505, shall be made for-

(1) any infringement of copyright in an unpublished work commenced before the effective date of its registration; or

(2) any infringement of copyright commenced after first publication of the work and before the effective date of its registration, unless such registration is made within three months after the first publication of the work.

Chapter 5: Copyright Infringement and Remedies

501. Infringement of copyright
504. Remedies for infringement: Damages and profits
505. Remedies for infringement: Costs and attorney's fees
506. Criminal offenses

§ 501. Infringement of copyright

(a) Anyone who violates any of the exclusive rights of the copyright owner as provided by sections 106 through 121 or of the author as provided in section 106A(a), or who imports copies or phonorecords into the United States in violation of section 602, is an infringer of the copyright or right of the author, as the case may be. For purposes of this chapter (other than section 506), any reference to copyright shall be deemed to include the rights conferred by section 106A(a). As used in this subsection, the term "anyone" includes any State, any instrumentality of a State, and any officer or employee of a State or instrumentality of a State acting in his or her official capacity. Any State, and any such instrumentality, officer, or employee, shall be subject to the provisions of this title in the same manner and to the same extent as any nongovernmental entity.

(b) The legal or beneficial owner of an exclusive right under a copyright is entitled, subject to the requirements of section 411, to institute an action for any infringement of that particular right committed while he or she is the owner of it. The court may require such owner to serve written notice of the action with a copy of the complaint upon any person shown, by the records of the Copyright Office or otherwise, to have or claim an interest in the copyright, and shall require that such notice be served upon any person whose interest is likely to be affected by a decision in the case. The court may require the joinder, and shall permit the intervention, of any person having or claiming an interest in the copyright.

(c) For any secondary transmission by a cable system that embodies a performance or a display of a work which is actionable as an act of infringement under subsection (c) of section 111, a television broadcast station holding a copyright or other license to transmit or perform the same version of that work shall, for purposes of subsection (b) of this section, be treated as a legal or beneficial owner if such secondary transmission occurs within the local service area of that television station.

(d) For any secondary transmission by a cable system that is actionable as an act of infringement pursuant to section 111(c)(3), the following shall also have standing to sue: (i) the primary transmitter whose transmission has been altered by the cable system; and (ii) any broadcast station within whose local service area the secondary transmission occurs.

(e) With respect to any secondary transmission that is made by a satellite carrier of a performance or display of a work embodied in a primary transmission and is actionable as an act of infringement under section 119(a)(5), a network station holding a copyright or other license to transmit or perform the same version of that work shall, for purposes of subsection (b) of this section, be treated as a legal or beneficial owner if such secondary transmission occurs within the local service area of that station.

(f)(1) With respect to any secondary transmission that is made by a satellite carrier of a performance or display of a work embodied in a primary transmission and is actionable as an act of infringement under section 122, a television broadcast station holding a copyright or other license to transmit or perform the same version of that work shall, for purposes of subsection (b) of this section, be treated as a legal or beneficial owner if such secondary transmission occurs within the local market of that station.

(2) A television broadcast station may file a civil action against any satellite carrier that has refused to carry television broadcast signals, as required under section 122(a)(2), to enforce that television broadcast station's rights under section 338(a) of the Communications Act of 1934.

§ 504. Remedies for infringement: Damages and profits

(a) In General. Except as otherwise provided by this title, an infringer of copyright is liable for either-

(1) the copyright owner's actual damages and any additional profits of the infringer, as provided by subsection (b); or

(2) statutory damages, as provided by subsection (c).

(b) Actual Damages and Profits. The copyright owner is entitled to recover the actual damages suffered by him or her as a result of the infringement, and any profits of the infringer that are attributable to the infringement and are not taken into account in computing the actual damages. In establishing the infringer's profits, the copyright owner is required to present proof only of the infringer's gross revenue, and the infringer is required to prove his or her deductible expenses and the elements of profit attributable to factors other than the copyrighted work.

(c) Statutory Damages.

(1) Except as provided by clause (2) of this subsection, the copyright owner may elect, at any time before final judgment is rendered, to recover, instead of actual damages and profits, an award of statutory damages for all infringements involved in the action, with respect to any one work, for which any one infringer is liable individually, or for which any two or more infringers are liable jointly and severally, in a sum of not less than $750 or more than $30,000 as the court considers just. For the purposes of this subsection, all the parts of a compilation or derivative work constitute one work.

(2) In a case where the copyright owner sustains the burden of proving, and the court finds, that infringement was committed willfully, the court in its discretion may increase the award of statutory damages to a sum of not more than $150,000. In a case where the infringer sustains the burden of proving, and the court finds, that such infringer was not aware and had no reason to believe that his or her acts constituted an infringement of copyright, the court in its discretion may reduce the award of statutory damages to a sum of not less than $200. The court shall remit statutory damages in any case where an infringer believed and had reasonable grounds for believing that his or her use of the copyrighted work was a fair use under section 107, if the infringer was: (i) an employee or agent of a nonprofit educational institution, library, or archives acting within the scope of his or her employment who, or such institution, library, or archives itself, which infringed by reproducing the work in copies or phonorecords; or (ii) a public broadcasting entity which or a person who, as a regular part of the nonprofit activities of a public broadcasting entity (as defined in subsection (g) of section 118) infringed by performing a published nondramatic literary work or by reproducing a transmission program embodying a performance of such a work.

(d) Additional Damages in Certain Cases. In any case in which the court finds that a defendant proprietor of an establishment who claims as a defense that its activities were exempt under section 110(5) did not have reasonable grounds to believe that its use of a copyrighted work was exempt under such section, the plaintiff shall be entitled to, in addition to any award of damages under this section, an additional award of two times the amount of the license fee that the proprietor of the establishment concerned should have paid the plaintiff for such use during the preceding period of up to 3 years.

§ 505. Remedies for infringement: Costs and attorney's fees

In any civil action under this title, the court in its discretion may allow the recovery of full costs by or against any party other than the United States or an officer thereof. Except as otherwise provided by this title, the court may also award a reasonable attorney's fee to the prevailing party as part of the costs.

§ 506. Criminal offenses

(a) Criminal Infringement. Any person who infringes a copyright willfully either –

(1) for purposes of commercial advantage or private financial gain, or

(2) by the reproduction or distribution, including by electronic means, during any 180-day period, or 1 or more copies or phonorecords of 1 or more copyrighted works, which have a total retail value of more than $1,000, shall be punished as provided under section 2319 of title 18, United States Code. For purposes of this subsection, evidence of reproduction or distribution of a copyrighted work, by itself, shall not be sufficient to establish willful infringement.

(b) Forfeiture and Destruction. When any person is convicted of any violation of subsection (a), the court in its judgment of conviction shall, in addition to the penalty therein prescribed, order the forfeiture and destruction or other disposition of all infringing copies or phonorecords and all implements, devices, or equipment used in the manufacture of such infringing copies or phonorecords.

(c) Fraudulent Copyright Notice. Any person who, with fraudulent intent, places on any article a notice of copyright or words of the same purport that such person knows to be false, or who, with fraudulent intent, publicly distributes or imports for public distribution any article bearing such notice or words that such person knows to be false, shall be fined not more than $2,500.

(d) Fraudulent Removal of Copyright Notice. Any person who, with fraudulent intent, removes or alters any notice of copyright appearing on a copy of a copyrighted work shall be fined not more than $2,500.

(e) False Representation. Any person who knowingly makes a false representation of a material fact in the application for copyright registration provided for by section 409, or in any written statement filed in connection with the application, shall be fined not more than $2,500.

(f) Rights of Attribution and Integrity. Nothing in this section applies to infringement of the rights conferred by section 106A(a).

APPENDIX 2: Selected Copyright Forms

⊘ Application Form PA ⊘

Detach and read these instructions before completing this form.
Make sure all applicable spaces have been filled in before you return this form.

BASIC INFORMATION

When to Use This Form: Use Form PA for registration of published or unpublished works of the performing arts. This class includes works prepared for the purpose of being "performed" directly before an audience or indirectly "by means of any device or process." Works of the performing arts include: (1) musical works, including any accompanying words; (2) dramatic works, including any accompanying music; (3) pantomimes and choreographic works; and (4) motion pictures and other audiovisual works.

Deposit to Accompany Application: An application for copyright registration must be accompanied by a deposit consisting of copies or phonorecords representing the entire work for which registration is made. The following are the general deposit requirements as set forth in the statute:

Unpublished Work: Deposit one complete copy (or phonorecord).

Published Work: Deposit two complete copies (or one phonorecord) of the best edition.

Work First Published Outside the United States: Deposit one complete copy (or phonorecord) of the first foreign edition.

Contribution to a Collective Work: Deposit one complete copy (or phonorecord) of the best edition of the collective work.

Motion Pictures: Deposit *both* of the following: (1) a separate written description of the contents of the motion picture; and (2) for a published work, one complete copy of the best edition of the motion picture; or, for an unpublished work, one complete copy of the motion picture or identifying material. Identifying material may be either an audiorecording of the entire soundtrack or one frame enlargement or similar visual print from each 10-minute segment.

LINE-BY-LINE INSTRUCTIONS

Please type or print using black ink. The form is used to produce the certificate.

1 SPACE 1: Title

Title of This Work: Every work submitted for copyright registration must be given a title to identify that particular work. If the copies or phonorecords of the work bear a title (or an identifying phrase that could serve as a title), transcribe that wording *completely* and *exactly* on the application. Indexing of the registration and future identification of the work will depend on the information you give here. If the work you are registering is an entire "collective work" (such as a collection of plays or songs), give the overall title of the collection. If you are registering one or more individual contributions to a collective work, give the title of each contribution, followed by the title of the collection. For an unpublished collection, you may give the titles of the individual works after the collection title.

Previous or Alternative Titles: Complete this space if there are any additional titles for the work under which someone searching for the registration might be likely to look, or under which a document pertaining to the work might be recorded.

Nature of This Work: Briefly describe the general nature or character of the work being registered for copyright. Examples: "Music"; "Song Lyrics"; "Words and Music"; "Drama"; "Musical Play"; "Choreography"; "Pantomime"; "Motion Picture"; "Audiovisual Work."

2 SPACE 2: Author(s)

General Instructions: After reading these instructions, decide who are the "authors" of this work for copyright purposes. Then, unless the work is a "collective work," give the requested information about every "author" who contributed any appreciable amount of copyrightable matter to this version of the work. If you need more space, request additional Continuation Sheets. In the case of a collective work such as a songbook or a collection of plays, give information about the author of the collective work as a whole.

Name of Author: The fullest form of the author's name should be given. Unless the work was "made for hire," the individual who actually created the work is its "author." In the case of a work made for hire, the statute provides that "the employer or other person for whom the work was prepared is considered the author."

What is a "Work Made for Hire"? A "work made for hire" is defined as: (1) "a work prepared by an employee within the scope of his or her employment"; or (2) "a work specially ordered or commissioned for use as a contribution to a collective work, as a part of a motion picture or other audiovisual work, as a translation, as a

supplementary work, as a compilation, as an instructional text, as a test, as answer material for a test, or as an atlas, if the parties expressly agree in a written instrument signed by them that the work shall be considered a work made for hire." If you have checked "Yes" to indicate that the work was "made for hire," you must give the full legal name of the employer (or other person for whom the work was prepared). You may also include the name of the employee along with the name of the employer (for example: "Elster Music Co., employer for hire of John Ferguson").

"Anonymous" or "Pseudonymous" Work: An author's contribution to a work is "anonymous" if that author is not identified on the copies or phonorecords of the work. An author's contribution to a work is "pseudonymous" if that author is identified on the copies or phonorecords under a fictitious name. If the work is "anonymous" you may: (1) leave the line blank; or (2) state "anonymous" on the line; or (3) reveal the author's identity. If the work is "pseudonymous" you may: (1) leave the line blank; or (2) give the pseudonym and identify it as such (example: "Huntley Haversock, pseudonym"); or (3) reveal the author's name, making clear which is the real name and which is the pseudonym (for example: "Judith Barton, whose pseudonym is Madeline Elster"). However, the citizenship or domicile of the author **must** be given in all cases.

Dates of Birth and Death: If the author is dead, the statute requires that the year of death be included in the application unless the work is anonymous or pseudonymous. The author's birth date is optional, but is useful as a form of identification. Leave this space blank if the author's contribution was a "work made for hire."

Author's Nationality or Domicile: Give the country of which the author is a citizen, or the country in which the author is domiciled. Nationality or domicile **must** be given in all cases.

Nature of Authorship: Give a brief general statement of the nature of this particular author's contribution to the work. Examples: "Words"; "Coauthor of Music"; "Words and Music"; "Arrangement"; "Coauthor of Book and Lyrics"; "Dramatization"; "Screen Play"; "Compilation and English Translation"; "Editorial Revisions."

3 SPACE 3: Creation and Publication

General Instructions: Do not confuse "creation" with "publication." Every application for copyright registration must state "the year in which creation of the work was completed." Give the date and nation of first publication only if the work has been published.

Creation: Under the statute, a work is "created" when it is fixed in a copy or phonorecord for the first time. Where a work has been prepared over a period of time, the part of the work existing in fixed form on a particular date constitutes the created work on that date. The date you give here should be the year in which the author completed the particular version for which registration is now being sought, even if other versions exist or if further changes or additions are planned.

Publication: The statute defines "publication" as "the distribution of copies or phonorecords of a work to the public by sale or other transfer of ownership, or by rental, lease, or lending"; a work is also "published" if there has been an "offering to distribute copies or phonorecords to a group of persons for purposes of further distribution, public performance, or public display." Give the full date (month, day, year) when, and the country where, publication first occurred. If first publication took place simultaneously in the United States and other countries, it is sufficient to state "U.S.A."

4 SPACE 4: Claimant(s)

Name(s) and Address(es) of Copyright Claimant(s): Give the name(s) and address(es) of the copyright claimant(s) in this work even if the claimant is the same as the author. Copyright in a work belongs initially to the author(s) of the work (including, in the case of a work made for hire, the employer or other person for whom the work was prepared). The copyright claimant is either the author or a person or organization to whom the copyright initially belonging to the author has been transferred.

Transfer: The statute provides that, if the copyright claimant is not the author, the application for registration must contain "a brief statement of how the claimant obtained ownership of the copyright." If any copyright claimant named in space 4 is not an author named in space 2, give a brief statement explaining how the claimant obtained ownership of the copyright. Examples: "By written contract"; "Transfer of all rights by author"; "Assignment"; "By will." Do not attach transfer documents or other attachments or riders.

5 SPACE 5: Previous Registration

General Instructions: The questions in space 5 are intended to show whether an earlier registration has been made for this work and, if so, whether there is any basis for a new registration. As a general rule, only one basic copyright registration can be made for the same version of a particular work.

Same Version: If this version is substantially the same as the work covered by a previous registration, a second registration is not generally possible unless: (1) the work has been registered in unpublished form and a second registration is now being sought to cover this first published edition; or (2) someone other than the author is identified as copyright claimant in the earlier registration, and the author is now seeking registration in his or her own name. If either of these two exceptions applies, check the appropriate box and give the earlier registration number and date. Otherwise, do not submit Form PA; instead, write the Copyright Office for information.

How to Register a Recorded Work: If the musical or dramatic work that you are registering has been recorded (as a tape, disk, or cassette), you may choose either copyright application Form PA (Performing Arts) or Form SR (Sound Recordings), depending on the purpose of the registration.

Form PA should be used to register the underlying musical composition or dramatic work. Form SR has been developed specifically to register a "sound recording" as defined by the Copyright Act—a work resulting from the "fixation of a series of sounds," separate and distinct from the underlying musical or dramatic work. Form SR should be used when the copyright claim is limited to the sound recording itself. (In one instance, Form SR may also be used to file for a copyright registration for both kinds of works—see (4) below.) Therefore:

(1) **File Form PA** if you are seeking to register the musical or dramatic work, not the "sound recording," even though what you deposit for copyright purposes may be in the form of a phonorecord.

(2) **File Form PA** if you are seeking to register the audio portion of an audiovisual work, such as a motion picture soundtrack; these are considered integral parts of the audiovisual work.

6 SPACE 6: Derivative Work or Compilation

General Instructions: Complete space 6 if this work is a "changed version," "compilation," or "derivative work," and if it incorporates one or more earlier works that have already been published or registered for copyright or that have fallen into the public domain. A "compilation" is defined as "a work formed by the collection and assembling of preexisting materials or of data that are selected, coordinated, or arranged in such a way that the resulting work as a whole constitutes an original work of authorship." A "derivative work" is "a work based on one or more preexisting works." Examples of derivative works include musical arrangements, dramatizations, translations, abridgments, condensations, motion picture versions, or "any other form in which a work may be recast, transformed, or adapted." Derivative works also include works "consisting of editorial revisions, annotations, or other modifications" if these changes, as a whole, represent an original work of authorship.

Preexisting Material (space 6a): Complete this space **and** space 6b for derivative works. In this space identify the preexisting work that has been recast, transformed, or adapted. For example, the preexisting material might be: "French version of Hugo's 'Le Roi s'amuse.'" Do not complete this space for compilations.

Material Added to This Work (space 6b): Give a brief, general statement of the additional new material covered by the copyright claim for which registration is sought. In the case of a derivative work, identify this new material. Examples: "Arrangement for piano and orchestra"; "Dramatization for television"; "New film version"; "Revisions throughout; Act III completely new." If the work is a compilation, give a brief, general statement describing both the material that has been compiled and the compilation itself. Example: "Compilation of 19th Century Military Songs."

Previous Registration Number and Date: If more than one previous registration has been made for the work, give the number and date of the latest registration.

7,8,9 SPACE 7, 8, 9: Fee, Correspondence, Certification, Return Address

Deposit Account: If you maintain a Deposit Account in the Copyright Office, identify it in space 7a. Otherwise, leave the space blank and send the fee of $30 (effective through June 30, 2002) with your application and deposit.

Correspondence (space 7b): This space should contain the name, address, area code, telephone number, fax number, and email address (if available) of the person to be consulted if correspondence about this application becomes necessary.

Certification (space 8): The application cannot be accepted unless it bears the date and the handwritten signature of the author or other copyright claimant, or of the owner of exclusive right(s), or of the duly authorized agent of the author, claimant, or owner of exclusive right(s).

Address for Return of Certificate (space 9): The address box must be completed legibly since the certificate will be returned in a window envelope.

MORE INFORMATION

tion about supplementary registration or recordation of transfers of copyright ownership.

Changed Version: If the work has been changed and you are now seeking registration to cover the additions or revisions, check the last box in space 5, give the earlier registration number and date, and complete both parts of space 6 in accordance with the instructions below.

The Copyright Notice: Before March 1, 1989, the use of copyright notice was mandatory on all published works, and any work first published before that date should have carried a notice. For works first published on and after March 1, 1989, use of the copyright notice is optional. For more information about copyright notice, see Circular 3, "Copyright Notice."

For Further Information: To speak to an information specialist, call (202) 707-3000 (TTY: (202) 707-6737). Recorded information is available 24 hours a day. Order forms and other publications from the address in space 9 or call the Forms and Publications Hotline at (202) 707-9100. Most circulars (but not forms) are available via fax. Call (202) 707-2600 from a touchtone phone. Access and download circulars, forms, and other information from the Copyright Office Website at www.loc.gov/copyright.

FORM PA
For a Work of the Performing Arts
UNITED STATES COPYRIGHT OFFICE

REGISTRATION NUMBER

_____ PA _____ PAU

EFFECTIVE DATE OF REGISTRATION

Month _____ Day _____ Year _____

DO NOT WRITE ABOVE THIS LINE. IF YOU NEED MORE SPACE, USE A SEPARATE CONTINUATION SHEET.

1 **TITLE OF THIS WORK ▼**

PREVIOUS OR ALTERNATIVE TITLES ▼

NATURE OF THIS WORK ▼ See instructions

2 **NAME OF AUTHOR ▼**
a
Was this contribution to the work a "work made for hire"?
☐ Yes
☐ No

AUTHOR'S NATIONALITY OR DOMICILE
Name of Country
OR { Citizen of ▶ _____
Domiciled in ▶ _____

DATES OF BIRTH AND DEATH
Year Born ▼ Year Died ▼

WAS THIS AUTHOR'S CONTRIBUTION TO THE WORK
Anonymous? ☐ Yes ☐ No
Pseudonymous? ☐ Yes ☐ No
If the answer to either of these questions is "Yes," see detailed instructions.

NATURE OF AUTHORSHIP Briefly describe nature of material created by this author in which copyright is claimed. ▼

NOTE
Under the law, the "author" of a "work made for hire" is generally the employer, not the employee (see instructions). For any part of this work that was "made for hire" check "Yes" in the space provided, give the employer (or other person for whom the work was prepared) as "Author" of that part, and leave the space for dates of birth and death blank.

b
NAME OF AUTHOR ▼
Was this contribution to the work a "work made for hire"?
☐ Yes
☐ No

AUTHOR'S NATIONALITY OR DOMICILE
Name of Country
OR { Citizen of ▶ _____
Domiciled in ▶ _____

DATES OF BIRTH AND DEATH
Year Born ▼ Year Died ▼

WAS THIS AUTHOR'S CONTRIBUTION TO THE WORK
Anonymous? ☐ Yes ☐ No
Pseudonymous? ☐ Yes ☐ No
If the answer to either of these questions is "Yes," see detailed instructions.

NATURE OF AUTHORSHIP Briefly describe nature of material created by this author in which copyright is claimed. ▼

c
NAME OF AUTHOR ▼
Was this contribution to the work a "work made for hire"?
☐ Yes
☐ No

AUTHOR'S NATIONALITY OR DOMICILE
Name of Country
OR { Citizen of ▶ _____
Domiciled in ▶ _____

DATES OF BIRTH AND DEATH
Year Born ▼ Year Died ▼

WAS THIS AUTHOR'S CONTRIBUTION TO THE WORK
Anonymous? ☐ Yes ☐ No
Pseudonymous? ☐ Yes ☐ No
If the answer to either of these questions is "Yes," see detailed instructions.

NATURE OF AUTHORSHIP Briefly describe nature of material created by this author in which copyright is claimed. ▼

3 **a** YEAR IN WHICH CREATION OF THIS WORK WAS COMPLETED This information must be given in all cases.
◀ Year ▼

b DATE AND NATION OF FIRST PUBLICATION OF THIS PARTICULAR WORK
Complete this information ONLY if this work has been published.
Month ▶ _____ Day ▶ _____ Year ▶ _____ ◀ Nation

4 **COPYRIGHT CLAIMANT(S)** Name and address must be given even if the claimant is the same as the author given in space 2. ▼

TRANSFER If the claimant(s) named here in space 4 is (are) different from the author(s) named in space 2, give a brief statement of how the claimant(s) obtained ownership of the copyright. ▼

See instructions before completing this space.

MORE ON BACK ▶ • Complete all applicable spaces (numbers 5-9) on the reverse side of this page.
• See detailed instructions. • Sign the form at line 8.

OFFICE USE ONLY
APPLICATION RECEIVED
ONE DEPOSIT RECEIVED
TWO DEPOSITS RECEIVED
FUNDS RECEIVED

FEE CHANGES
Fees are effective through June 30, 2002. After that date, check the Copyright Office Website at www.loc.gov/copyright or call (202) 707-3000 for current fee information.

FORM PA

EXAMINED BY _____
CHECKED BY _____
☐ CORRESPONDENCE
Yes

FOR COPYRIGHT OFFICE USE ONLY

DO NOT WRITE ABOVE THIS LINE. IF YOU NEED MORE SPACE, USE A SEPARATE CONTINUATION SHEET.

5 **PREVIOUS REGISTRATION** Has registration for this work, or for an earlier version of this work, already been made in the Copyright Office?
☐ Yes ☐ No If your answer is "Yes," why is another registration being sought? (Check appropriate box.) ▼ If your answer is "no," go to space 7.
a. ☐ This is the first published edition of a work previously registered in unpublished form.
b. ☐ This is the first application submitted by this author as copyright claimant.
c. ☐ This is a changed version of the work, as shown by space 6 on this application.
If your answer is "Yes," give: Previous Registration Number ▼ Year of Registration ▼

6 **DERIVATIVE WORK OR COMPILATION** Complete both space 6a and 6b for a derivative work; complete only 6b for a compilation.
a Preexisting Material Identify any preexisting work or works that this work is based on or incorporates. ▼

See instructions before completing this space.

b Material Added to This Work Give a brief, general statement of the material that has been added to this work and in which copyright is claimed. ▼

7 **a** DEPOSIT ACCOUNT If the registration fee is to be charged to a Deposit Account established in the Copyright Office, give name and number of Account.
Name ▼ Account Number ▼

b CORRESPONDENCE Give name and address to which correspondence about this application should be sent. Name/Address/Apt/City/State/ZIP ▼

Area code and daytime telephone number ▶ ( ) Fax number ▶ ( )
Email ▶

8 **CERTIFICATION*** I, the undersigned, hereby certify that I am the
Check only one ▶
☐ author
☐ other copyright claimant
☐ owner of exclusive right(s)
☐ authorized agent of _____
of the work identified in this application and that the statements made by me in this application are correct to the best of my knowledge.

Name of author or other copyright claimant, or owner of exclusive right(s) ▲

Typed or printed name and date ▼ If this application gives a date of publication in space 3, do not sign and submit it before that date.
_____ Date ▶ _____

Handwritten signature (X) ▼
X _____

9 Certificate will be mailed in window envelope to this address:
Name ▼
Number/Street/Apt ▼
City/State/ZIP ▼

*17 U.S.C. § 506(e): Any person who knowingly makes a false representation of a material fact in the application for copyright registration provided for by section 409, or in any written statement filed in connection with the application, shall be fined not more than $2,500.

June 1999—200,000 WEB REV: June 1999
Aa of July 1, 1999, the filing fee for Form PA is $30.

☆U.S. GOVERNMENT PRINTING OFFICE: 1999-454-879/98
♻ PRINTED ON RECYCLED PAPER

⊘ Application Form SR ⊘

Detach and read these instructions before completing this form.
Make sure all applicable spaces have been filled in before you return this form.

BASIC INFORMATION

When to Use This Form: Use Form SR for registration of published or unpublished sound recordings. It should be used when the copyright claim is limited to the sound recording itself, and it may also be used where the same copyright claimant is seeking simultaneous registration of the underlying musical, dramatic, or literary work embodied in the phonorecord.

With one exception, "sound recordings" are works that result from the fixation of a series of musical, spoken, or other sounds. The exception is for the audio portions of audiovisual works, such as a motion picture soundtrack or an audio cassette accompanying a filmstrip. These are considered a part of the audiovisual work as a whole.

Deposit to Accompany Application: An application for copyright registration must be accompanied by a deposit consisting of phonorecords representing the entire work for which registration is to be made.

Unpublished Work: Deposit one complete phonorecord.

Published Work: Deposit two complete phonorecords of the best edition, together with "any printed or other visually perceptible material" published with the phonorecords.

Work First Published Outside the United States: Deposit one complete phonorecord of the first foreign edition.

Contribution to a Collective Work: Deposit one complete phonorecord of the best edition of the collective work.

LINE-BY-LINE INSTRUCTIONS

Please type or print neatly using black ink. The form is used to produce the certificate.

1 SPACE 1: Title

Title of This Work: Every work submitted for copyright registration must be given a title to identify that particular work. If the phonorecords or any accompanying printed material bears a title (or an identifying phrase that could serve as a title), transcribe that wording completely and exactly on the application. Indexing of the registration and future identification of the work may depend on the information you give here.

Previous, Alternative, or Contents Titles: Complete this space if there are any previous or alternative titles for the work under which someone searching for the registration might be likely to look, or under which a document pertaining to the work might be recorded. You may also give the individual contents titles, if any, in this space or you may use a Continuation Sheet. Circle the term that describes each author's contribution.

2 SPACE 2: Author(s)

General Instructions: After reading these instructions, decide who are the "authors" of this work for copyright purposes. Then, unless the work is a "collective work," give information about every "author" who contributed any appreciable amount of copyrightable matter to this version of the work. If you need further space, request additional Continuation Sheets. In the case of a collective work such as a collection of previously published or registered sound recordings, give information about the author of the collective work as a whole. If you are submitting this Form SR to cover the recorded musical, dramatic, or literary work as well as the sound recording itself is to cover the material covered by this particular registration. If it is important for space 2 to include full information about the various authors of all of the material covered by the copyright claim, making clear the nature of each author's contribution.

Name of Author: The fullest form of the author's name should be given. Unless the work was "made for hire," the individual who actually created the work is its "author." In the case of a work made for hire, the statute provides that "the employer or other person for whom the work was prepared is considered the author."

What is a "Work Made for Hire"? A "work made for hire" is defined as: (1) "a work prepared by an employee within the scope of his or her employment"; or (2)

The Copyright Notice: Before March 1, 1989, the use of copyright notice was mandatory on all published works, and any work first published before that date should have carried a notice. For works first published on and after March 1, 1989, use of the copyright notice is optional. For information about copyright notice, see Circular 3, "Copyright Notices."

For Further Information: To speak to an information specialist, call (202) 707-3000 (TTY: (202) 707-6737). Recorded information is available 24 hours a day. Order forms and other publications from Library of Congress, Copyright Office, 101 Independence Avenue, S.E., Washington, D.C. 20559-6000 or call the Forms and Publications Hotline at (202) 707-9100. Most circulars (but not forms) are available via fax. Call (202) 707-2600 from a touchtone phone. Access and download circulars, forms, and other information from the Copyright Office Website at www.loc.gov/copyright.

3 SPACE 3: Creation and Publication

General Instructions: Do not confuse "creation" with "publication." Every application for copyright registration must state "the year in which creation of the work was completed." Give the date and nation of first publication only if the work has been published.

Creation: Under the statute, a work is "created" when it is fixed in a copy or phonorecord for the first time. Where a work has been prepared over a period of time, the part of the work existing in fixed form on a particular date constitutes the created work on that date. The date you give here should be the year in which the author completed the particular version for which registration is now being sought, even if other versions exist or if further changes or additions are planned.

Publication: The statute defines "publication" as "the distribution of copies or phonorecords of a work to the public by sale or other transfer of ownership, or by rental, lease, or lending"; a work is also "published" if there has been an "offering to distribute copies or phonorecords to a group of persons for purposes of further distribution, public performance, or public display." Give the full date (month, day, year) when, and the country where, publication first occurred. If first publication took place simultaneously in the United States and other countries, it is sufficient to state "U.S.A."

4 SPACE 4: Claimant(s)

Name(s) and Address(es) of Copyright Claimant(s): Give the name(s) and address(es) of the copyright claimant(s) in the work, even if the claimant is the same as the author. Copyright in a work belongs initially to the author of the work (including, in the case of a work made for hire, the employer or other person for whom the work was prepared). The copyright claimant is either the author of the work or a person or organization to whom the copyright initially belonging to the author has been transferred.

Transfer: The statute provides that, if the copyright claimant is not the author, the application for registration must contain "a brief statement of how the claimant obtained ownership of the copyright." If any copyright claimant named in space 4a is not an author named in space 2, give a brief statement explaining how the claimant(s) obtained ownership of the copyright. Examples: "By written contract"; "Transfer of all rights by author"; "Assignment"; "By will." Do not attach transfer documents or other attachments to the form.

5 SPACE 5: Previous Registration

General Instructions: The questions in space 5 are intended to show whether an earlier registration has been made for this work and, if so, whether there is any basis for a new registration. As a rule, only one basic copyright registration can be made for the same version of a particular work.

Same Version: If this version is substantially the same as the work covered by a previous registration, a second registration is not generally possible unless: (1) the work has been registered in unpublished form and a second registration is now being sought to cover this first published edition; or (2) someone other than the author is identified as copyright claimant in the earlier registration and the author is now seeking registration in his or her own name. If either of these two exceptions applies, check the appropriate box and give the earlier registration number and date. Otherwise, do not submit Form SR. Instead, write the Copyright Office for information about supplementary registration or recordation of transfers of copyright ownership.

"Works", "Works": not "copies" or "phonorecords." "'Works' are what copyright protects. The statute draws a sharp distinction between the "work" and "any material object in which the work is embodied."

"Copies" and "Phonorecords": These are the two types of material objects in which "works" are embodied. In general, "copies" are objects from which a work can be read or visually perceived, directly or with the aid of a machine or device, such as manuscripts, books, sheet music, film, and videotape. "Phonorecords" are objects embodying fixations of sounds, such as audio tapes and phonograph disks. For example, a song (the "work") can be reproduced in sheet music ("copies") or phonograph disks ("phonorecords"), or both.

"Sound Recordings": These are "works," not "copies" or "phonorecords." "Sound recordings" are "works that result from the fixation of a series of musical, spoken, or other sounds, but not including the sounds accompanying a motion picture or other audiovisual work." Example: When a record company issues a new release, the release will typically involve two distinct "works": the "musical work" that has been recorded, and the "sound recording" as a separate work in itself. The material objects that the record company sends out are "phonorecords": physical reproductions of both the "musical work" and the "sound recording."

Changed Version: If the work has been changed and you are now seeking registration to cover the additions or revisions, check the last box in space 5, give the earlier registration number and date, and complete both parts of space 6 in accordance with the instructions below.

Previous Registration Number and Date: If more than one previous registration has been made for the work, give the number and date of the latest registration.

6 SPACE 6: Derivative Work or Compilation

General Instructions: Complete space 6 if this work is a "changed version," "compilation," or "derivative work," and if it incorporates one or more earlier works that have already been published or registered for copyright, or that have fallen into the public domain, or sound recordings that were fixed before February 15, 1972. A "compilation" is defined as "a work formed by the collection and assembling of preexisting materials or of data that are selected, coordinated, or arranged in such a way that the resulting work as a whole constitutes an original work of authorship." A "derivative work" is "a work based on one or more preexisting works." Examples of derivative works include recordings reissued with substantial editorial revisions or abridgments of the recorded sounds, and recordings republished with new recorded material, or "any other form in which a work may be recast, transformed, or adapted." Derivative works also include works "consisting of editorial revisions, annotations, or other modifications" if these changes, as a whole, represent an original work of authorship.

Preexisting Material (space 6a): Complete this space and space 6b for derivative works. In this space identify the preexisting work that has been recast, transformed, or adapted. The preexisting work may be material that has been previously published, previously registered, or that is in the public domain. For example, the preexisting material might be: "1970 recording by Sperryville Symphony of Bach Double Concerto."

Material Added to This Work (space 6b): Give a brief, general statement of the additional new material covered by the copyright claim for which registration is sought. In the case of a derivative work, identify this new material. Examples: "Recorded performances on bands 1 and 3"; "Remixed sounds from original multitrack sound sources"; "New words, arrangement, and additional sounds." If the work is a compilation, give a brief, general statement describing both the material that has been compiled and the compilation itself. Example: "Compilation of 1938 Recordings by various swing bands."

7,8,9 SPACE 7,8,9: Fee, Correspondence, Certification, Return Address

Deposit Account: If you maintain a Deposit Account in the Copyright Office, identify it in space 7a. Otherwise, leave the space blank and send the filing fee of $30 (effective through June 30, 2002) with your application and deposit. (See space 8 on form.)

Correspondence (space 7b): This space should contain the name, address, area code, telephone number, fax number, and email address (if available) of the person to be consulted if correspondence about this application becomes necessary.

Certification (space 8): This application cannot be accepted unless it bears the date and the handwritten signature of the author or other copyright claimant, or of the owner of exclusive right(s), or of the duly authorized agent of the author, claimant, or owner of exclusive right(s).

Address for Return of Certificate (space 9): The address box must be completed legibly since the certificate will be returned in a window envelope.

MORE INFORMATION

Should You File More Than One Application? If your work consists of a recorded musical, dramatic, or literary work and if both that "work" and the sound recording as a separate "work" are eligible for registration, the application form you should file depends on the following:

File Only Form SR if: The copyright claimant is the same for both the musical, dramatic, or literary work and for the sound recording, and you are seeking a single registration in cover both of these "works."

File Only Form PA (or Form TX) if: You are seeking to register only the musical, dramatic, or literary work, not the sound recording. Form PA is appropriate for works of the performing arts; Form TX is for nondramatic literary works.

Separate Applications Should Be Filed on Form PA (or Form TX) and Form SR if: (1) The copyright claimant for the musical, dramatic, or literary work is different from the copyright claimant for the sound recording; or (2) You prefer to have separate registrations for the musical, dramatic, or literary work and for the sound recording.

FORM SR
For a Sound Recording
UNITED STATES COPYRIGHT OFFICE

Fees are effective through June 30, 2002.
After that date, check the Copyright Office
Website at www.loc.gov/copyright or call
(202) 707-3000 for current fee information.

REGISTRATION NUMBER

SR   SRU

EFFECTIVE DATE OF REGISTRATION

Month   Day   Year

DO NOT WRITE ABOVE THIS LINE. IF YOU NEED MORE SPACE, USE A SEPARATE CONTINUATION SHEET.

1   **TITLE OF THIS WORK** ▼

PREVIOUS, ALTERNATIVE, OR CONTENTS TITLES (CIRCLE ONE) ▼

2   **a**   **NAME OF AUTHOR** ▼

DATES OF BIRTH AND DEATH
Year Born ▼   Year Died ▼

Was this contribution to the work a "work made for hire"?
☐ Yes
☐ No

AUTHOR'S NATIONALITY OR DOMICILE
Name of Country
OR { Citizen of ▶
Domiciled in ▶

WAS THIS AUTHOR'S CONTRIBUTION TO THE WORK
Anonymous? ☐ Yes ☐ No
Pseudonymous? ☐ Yes ☐ No
If the answer to either of these questions is "Yes," see detailed instructions.

NATURE OF AUTHORSHIP Briefly describe nature of material created by this author in which copyright is claimed. ▼

NOTE
Under the law, the "author" of a "work made for hire" is generally the employer, not the employee (see instructions). For any part of this work that was "made for hire," check "Yes" in the space provided, give the employer (or other person for whom the work was prepared) as "Author" of that part, and leave the space for dates of birth and death blank.

b   **NAME OF AUTHOR** ▼

DATES OF BIRTH AND DEATH
Year Born ▼   Year Died ▼

Was this contribution to the work a "work made for hire"?
☐ Yes
☐ No

AUTHOR'S NATIONALITY OR DOMICILE
Name of Country
OR { Citizen of ▶
Domiciled in ▶

WAS THIS AUTHOR'S CONTRIBUTION TO THE WORK
Anonymous? ☐ Yes ☐ No
Pseudonymous? ☐ Yes ☐ No
If the answer to either of these questions is "Yes," see detailed instructions.

NATURE OF AUTHORSHIP Briefly describe nature of material created by this author in which copyright is claimed. ▼

c   **NAME OF AUTHOR** ▼

DATES OF BIRTH AND DEATH
Year Born ▼   Year Died ▼

Was this contribution to the work a "work made for hire"?
☐ Yes
☐ No

AUTHOR'S NATIONALITY OR DOMICILE
Name of Country
OR { Citizen of ▶
Domiciled in ▶

WAS THIS AUTHOR'S CONTRIBUTION TO THE WORK
Anonymous? ☐ Yes ☐ No
Pseudonymous? ☐ Yes ☐ No
If the answer to either of these questions is "Yes," see detailed instructions.

NATURE OF AUTHORSHIP Briefly describe nature of material created by this author in which copyright is claimed. ▼

3   **a**   YEAR IN WHICH CREATION OF THIS WORK WAS COMPLETED
This information must be given ◀ Year in all cases.

b   DATE AND NATION OF FIRST PUBLICATION OF THIS PARTICULAR WORK
Complete this information ONLY if this work has been published.
Month ▶   Day ▶   Year ▶   ◀ Nation

4   **a**   COPYRIGHT CLAIMANT(S) Name and address must be given even if the claimant is the same as the author given in space 2. ▼

APPLICATION RECEIVED
ONE DEPOSIT RECEIVED
TWO DEPOSITS RECEIVED
FUNDS RECEIVED
DO NOT WRITE HERE OFFICE USE ONLY

b   TRANSFER If the claimant(s) named here in space 4 is (are) different from the author(s) named in space 2, give a brief statement of how the claimant(s) obtained ownership of the copyright. ▼

See instructions before completing this space.

MORE ON BACK ▶ • Complete all applicable spaces (numbers 5-9) on the reverse side of this page.
• See detailed instructions. • Sign the form at line 8.

DO NOT WRITE HERE
Page 1 of ___ pages

EXAMINED BY

CHECKED BY

CORRESPONDENCE
☐ Yes

FOR COPYRIGHT OFFICE USE ONLY

FORM SR

DO NOT WRITE ABOVE THIS LINE. IF YOU NEED MORE SPACE, USE A SEPARATE CONTINUATION SHEET.

5   PREVIOUS REGISTRATION Has registration for this work, or for an earlier version of this work, already been made in the Copyright Office?
☐ Yes ☐ No If your answer is "Yes," why is another registration being sought? (Check appropriate box.) ▼
a. ☐ This is the first published edition of a work previously registered in unpublished form.
b. ☐ This is the first application submitted by this author as copyright claimant.
c. ☐ This is a changed version of the work, as shown by space 6 on this application.
If your answer is "Yes," give: Previous Registration Number ▼   Year of Registration ▼

6   DERIVATIVE WORK OR COMPILATION
a Preexisting Material Identify any preexisting work or works that this work is based on or incorporates. ▼

See instructions before completing this space.

b Material Added to This Work Give a brief, general statement of the material that has been added to this work and in which copyright is claimed. ▼

7   DEPOSIT ACCOUNT If the registration fee is to be charged to a Deposit Account established in the Copyright Office, give name and number of Account.
a Name ▼   Account Number ▼

b CORRESPONDENCE Give name and address to which correspondence about this application should be sent. Name/Address/Apt/City/State/ZIP ▼

Area code and daytime telephone number ▶   Fax number ▶
Email ▶

8   CERTIFICATION* I, the undersigned, hereby certify that I am the
Check only one ▼
☐ author
☐ other copyright claimant
☐ owner of exclusive right(s)
☐ authorized agent of ___ Name of author or other copyright claimant, or owner of exclusive right(s) ▲
of the work identified in this application and that the statements made by me in this application are correct to the best of my knowledge.

Typed or printed name and date ▼ If this application gives a date of publication in space 3, do not sign and submit it before that date.

Date ▶

Handwritten signature (x) ▼
X

9   Certificate will be mailed in window envelope to this address

Name ▼
Number/Street/Apt ▼
City/State/ZIP ▼

YOU MUST:
• Complete all necessary spaces
• Sign your application in space 8

SEND ALL ELEMENTS IN THE SAME PACKAGE:
1. Application form
2. Nonrefundable filing fee in check or money order payable to Register of Copyrights
3. Deposit material

MAIL TO:
Library of Congress
Copyright Office
101 Independence Avenue, S.E.
Washington, D.C. 20559-6000

As of July 1, 1999, the filing fee for Form SR is $30.

*17 U.S.C. § 506(e): Any person who knowingly makes a false representation of a material fact in the application for copyright registration provided for by section 409, or in any written statement filed in connection with the application, shall be fined not more than $2,500.

June 1999—50,000
WEB REV: June 1999

☼ PRINTED ON RECYCLED PAPER
✩U.S. GOVERNMENT PRINTING OFFICE: 1999-454-879/48

Application Form TX

Detach and read these instructions before completing this form.
Make sure all applicable spaces have been filled in before you return this form.

BASIC INFORMATION

When to Use This Form: Use Form TX for registration of published or unpublished nondramatic literary works, excluding periodicals or serial issues. This class includes a wide variety of works: fiction, nonfiction, poetry, textbooks, reference works, directories, catalogs, advertising copy, compilations of information, and computer programs. For periodicals and serials, use Form SE.

Deposit to Accompany Application: An application for copyright registration must be accompanied by a deposit consisting of copies or phonorecords representing the entire work for which registration is to be made. The following are the general deposit requirements as set forth in the statute:

Unpublished Work: Deposit one complete copy (or phonorecord)

Published Work: Deposit two complete copies (or one phonorecord) of the best edition.

Work First Published Outside the United States: Deposit one complete copy (or phonorecord) of the first foreign edition.

Contribution to a Collective Work: Deposit one complete copy (or phonorecord) of the best edition of the collective work.

The Copyright Notice: Before March 1, 1989, the use of copyright notice was mandatory on all published works, and any work first published before that date should have carried a notice. For works first published on and after March 1, 1989, use of the copyright notice is optional. For more information about copyright notice, see Circular 3, "Copyright Notices."

For Further Information: To speak to an information specialist, call (202) 707-3000 (TTY: (202) 707-6737). Recorded information is available 24 hours a day. Order forms and other publications from the address in space 9 or call the Forms and Publications Hotline at (202) 707-9100. Most circulars (but not forms) are available via fax. Call (202) 707-2600 from a touchtone phone. Access and download circulars, forms, and other information from the Copyright Office Website at www.loc.gov/copyright.

PRIVACY ACT ADVISORY STATEMENT Required by the Privacy Act of 1974 (P.L. 93-579)
The authority for requesting this information is title 17, U.S.C., secs. 409 and 410. Furnishing the requested information is voluntary. But if the information is not furnished, it may be necessary to delay or refuse registration and you may not be entitled to certain relief, remedies, and benefits provided in chapters 4 and 5 of title 17, U.S.C.
The principal uses of the requested information are the establishment and maintenance of a public record and the examination of the application for compliance with the registration requirements of the copyright code.
Other routine uses include public inspection and copying, preparation of public indexes, preparation of public catalogs of copyright registrations, and preparation of search reports upon request.
NOTE: No other advisory statement will be given in connection with this application. Please keep this statement and refer to it if we communicate with you regarding this application.

LINE-BY-LINE INSTRUCTIONS

Please type or print using black ink. The form is used to produce the certificate.

1 SPACE 1: Title

Title of This Work: Every work submitted for copyright registration must be given a title to identify that particular work. If the copies or phonorecords of the work bear a title or an identifying phrase that could serve as a title, transcribe that wording *completely* and *exactly* on the application. Indexing of the registration and future identification of the work will depend on the information you give here.

Previous or Alternative Titles: Complete this space if there are any additional titles for the work under which someone searching for the registration might be likely to look or under which a document pertaining to the work might be recorded.

Publication as a Contribution: If the work being registered is a contribution to a periodical, serial, or collection, give the title of the contribution in the "Title of This Work" space. Then, in the line headed "Publication as a Contribution," give information about the collective work in which the contribution appeared.

2 SPACE 2: Author(s)

General Instructions: After reading these instructions, decide who are the "authors" of this work for copyright purposes. Then, unless the work is a "collective work," give the requested information about every "author" who contributed any appreciable amount of copyrightable matter to this version of the work. If you need further space, request Continuation Sheets. In the case of a collective work, such as an anthology, collection of essays, or encyclopedia, give information about the author of the collective work as a whole.

Name of Author: The fullest form of the author's name should be given. Unless the work was "made for hire," the individual who actually created the work is its "author." In the case of a work made for hire, the statute provides that "the employer or other person for whom the work was prepared is considered the author."

What is a "Work Made for Hire"? A "work made for hire" is defined as (1) "a work prepared by an employee within the scope of his or her employment"; or (2) "a work specially ordered or commissioned for use as a contribution to a collective work, as a part of a motion picture or other audiovisual work, as a translation, as a supplementary work, as a compilation, as an instructional text, as a test, as answer material for a test, or as an atlas, if the parties expressly agree in a written instrument signed by them that the works shall be considered a work made for hire." If you have checked "Yes" to indicate that the work was "made for hire," you must give the full legal name of the employer (or other person for whom the work was prepared). You may also include the name of the employee along with the name of the employer (for example: "Elster Publishing Co., employer for hire of John Ferguson").

"Anonymous" or "Pseudonymous" Work: An author's contribution to a work is "anonymous" if that author is not identified on the copies or phonorecords of the work. An author's contribution to a work is "pseudonymous" if that author is identified on the copies or phonorecords under a fictitious name. If the work is "anonymous" you may: (1) leave the line blank; or (2) state "anonymous" on the line; or (3) reveal the author's identity. If the work is "pseudonymous" you may: (1) leave the line blank; or (2) give the pseudonym and identify it as such (for example: "Huntley Haverstock, pseudonym"); or (3) reveal the author's name, making clear which is the real name and which is the pseudonym (for example, "Judith Barton, whose pseudonym is Madeline Elster"). However, the citizenship or domicile of the author **must** be given in all cases.

Dates of Birth and Death: If the author is dead, the statute requires that the year of death be included in the application unless the work is anonymous or pseudonymous. The author's birth date is optional but is useful as a form of identification. Leave this space blank if the author's contribution was a "work made for hire."

Author's Nationality or Domicile: Give the country of which the author is a citizen or the country in which the author is domiciled. Nationality or domicile **must** be given in all cases.

Nature of Authorship: After the words "Nature of Authorship," give a brief general statement of the nature of this particular author's contribution to the work. Examples: "Entire text"; "Coauthor of entire text"; "Computer program"; "Editorial revisions"; "Compilation and English translation"; "New text."

3 SPACE 3: Creation and Publication

General Instructions: Do not confuse "creation" with "publication." Every application for copyright registration must state "the year in which creation of the work was completed." Give the date and nation of first publication only if the work has been published.

Creation: Under the statute, a work is "created" when it is fixed in a copy or phonorecord for the first time. Where a work has been prepared over a period of time, the part of the work existing in fixed form on a particular date constitutes the created work on that date. The date you give here should be the year in which the author completed the particular version for which registration is now being sought, even if other versions exist or if further changes or additions are planned.

Publication: The statute defines "publication" as "the distribution of copies or phonorecords of a work to the public by sale or other transfer of ownership, or by rental, lease, or lending." A work is also "published" if there has been an "offering to distribute copies or phonorecords to a group of persons for purposes of further distribution, public performance, or public display." Give the full date (month, day, year) when, and the country where, publication first occurred. If first publication took place simultaneously in the United States and other countries, it is sufficient to state "U.S.A."

4 SPACE 4: Claimant(s)

Name(s) and Address(es) of Copyright Claimant(s): Give the name(s) and address(es) of the copyright claimant(s) in this work even if the claimant is the same as the author. Copyright in a work belongs initially to the author of the work (including, in the case of a work made for hire, the employer or other person for whom the work was prepared). The copyright claimant is either the author of the work or a person or organization to whom the copyright initially belonging to the author has been transferred.

Transfer: The statute provides that, if the copyright claimant is not the author, the application for registration must contain "a brief statement of how the claimant obtained ownership of the copyright." If any copyright claimant named in space 4 is not an author named in space 2, give a brief statement explaining how the claimant(s) obtained ownership of the copyright. Examples: "By written contract"; "Transfer of all rights by author"; "Assignment"; "By will." Do not attach transfer documents or other attachments or riders.

5 SPACE 5: Previous Registration

General Instructions: The questions in space 5 are intended to show whether an earlier registration has been made for this work and, if so, whether there is any basis for a new registration. As a general rule, only one basic copyright registration can be made for the same version of a particular work.

Same Version: If this version is substantially the same as the work covered by a previous registration, a second registration is not generally possible unless: (1) the work has been registered in unpublished form and a second registration is now being sought to cover this first published edition; or (2) someone other than the author is identified as copyright claimant in the earlier registration, and the author is now seeking registration in his or her own name. If either of these two exceptions applies, check the appropriate box and give the earlier registration number and date. Otherwise, do not submit Form TX. Instead, write the Copyright Office for information about supplementary registration or recordation of transfers of copyright ownership.

Changed Version: If the work has been changed and you are now seeking registration to cover the additions or revisions, check the last box in space 5, give the earlier registration number and date, and complete both parts of space 6 in accordance with the instructions below.

Previous Registration Number and Date: If more than one previous registration has been made for the work, give the number and date of the latest registration.

6 SPACE 6: Derivative Work or Compilation

General Instructions: Complete space 6 if this work is a "changed version," "compilation," or "derivative work" and if it incorporates one or more earlier works that have already been published or registered for copyright or that have fallen into the public domain. A "compilation" is defined as "a work formed by the collection and assembling of preexisting materials or of data that are selected, coordinated, or arranged in such a way that the resulting work as a whole constitutes an original work of authorship." A "derivative work" is "a work based on one or more preexisting works." Examples of derivative works include translations, fictionalizations, abridgments, condensations, or "any other form in which a work may be recast, transformed, or adapted." Derivative works also include works "consisting of editorial revisions, annotations, or other modifications" if these changes, as a whole, represent an original work of authorship.

Preexisting Material (space 6a): For derivative works, complete this space **and** space 6b. In space 6a identify the preexisting work that has been recast, transformed, or adapted. The preexisting work may be material that has been previously published, previously registered, or that is in the public domain. An example of preexisting material might be: "Russian version of Goncharov's 'Oblomov.'"

Material Added to This Work (space 6b): Give a brief, general statement of the new material covered by the copyright claim for which registration is sought. **Derivative work** examples include: "Foreword, editing, critical annotations"; "Translation"; "Chapters 11-17." If the work is a **compilation**, describe both the compilation itself and the material that has been compiled. Example: "Compilation of certain 1917 Speeches by Woodrow Wilson." A work may be both a derivative work and compilation, in which case a sample statement might be: "Compilation and additional new material."

7,8,9 SPACE 7,8,9: Fee, Correspondence, Certification, Return Address

Deposit Account: If you maintain a Deposit Account in the Copyright Office, identify it in space 7a. Otherwise leave the space blank and send the fee of $30 (effective through June 30, 2002) with your application and deposit.

Correspondence (space 7b): This space should contain the name, address, area code, telephone number, fax number, and email address (if available) of the person to be consulted if correspondence about this application becomes necessary.

Certification (space 8): The application cannot be accepted unless it bears the date and the **handwritten signature** of the author or other copyright claimant, or of the owner of exclusive right(s), or of the duly authorized agent of author, claimant, or owner of exclusive right(s).

Address for Return of Certificate (space 9): The address box must be completed legibly since the certificate will be returned in a window envelope.

FORM TX
For a Nondramatic Literary Work
UNITED STATES COPYRIGHT OFFICE

REGISTRATION NUMBER

TX   TXU

EFFECTIVE DATE OF REGISTRATION

Month   Day   Year

DO NOT WRITE ABOVE THIS LINE. IF YOU NEED MORE SPACE, USE A SEPARATE CONTINUATION SHEET.

1

TITLE OF THIS WORK ▼

PREVIOUS OR ALTERNATIVE TITLES ▼

PUBLICATION AS A CONTRIBUTION If this work was published as a contribution to a periodical, serial, or collection, give information about the collective work in which the contribution appeared. **Title of Collective Work ▼**

If published in a periodical or serial give: **Volume ▼**   **Number ▼**   **Issue Date ▼**   **On Pages ▼**

2

a

NAME OF AUTHOR ▼

DATES OF BIRTH AND DEATH
Year Born ▼   **Year Died ▼**

Was this contribution to the work a "work made for hire"?
☐ Yes
☐ No

AUTHOR'S NATIONALITY OR DOMICILE
Name of Country
OR { Citizen of ▶
{ Domiciled in ▶

WAS THIS AUTHOR'S CONTRIBUTION TO THE WORK
Anonymous? ☐ Yes ☐ No
Pseudonymous? ☐ Yes ☐ No
If the answer to either of these questions is "Yes," see detailed instructions.

NATURE OF AUTHORSHIP Briefly describe nature of material created by this author in which copyright is claimed. ▼

NOTE

Under the law, the "author" of a "work made for hire" is generally the employer, not the employee (see instructions). For any part of this work that was "made for hire" check "Yes" in the space provided, give the employer (or other person for whom the work was prepared) as "Author" of that part, and leave the space for dates of birth and death blank.

b

NAME OF AUTHOR ▼

DATES OF BIRTH AND DEATH
Year Born ▼   **Year Died ▼**

Was this contribution to the work a "work made for hire"?
☐ Yes
☐ No

AUTHOR'S NATIONALITY OR DOMICILE
Name of Country
OR { Citizen of ▶
{ Domiciled in ▶

WAS THIS AUTHOR'S CONTRIBUTION TO THE WORK
Anonymous? ☐ Yes ☐ No
Pseudonymous? ☐ Yes ☐ No
If the answer to either of these questions is "Yes," see detailed instructions.

NATURE OF AUTHORSHIP Briefly describe nature of material created by this author in which copyright is claimed. ▼

c

NAME OF AUTHOR ▼

DATES OF BIRTH AND DEATH
Year Born ▼   **Year Died ▼**

Was this contribution to the work a "work made for hire"?
☐ Yes
☐ No

AUTHOR'S NATIONALITY OR DOMICILE
Name of Country
OR { Citizen of ▶
{ Domiciled in ▶

WAS THIS AUTHOR'S CONTRIBUTION TO THE WORK
Anonymous? ☐ Yes ☐ No
Pseudonymous? ☐ Yes ☐ No
If the answer to either of these questions is "Yes," see detailed instructions.

NATURE OF AUTHORSHIP Briefly describe nature of material created by this author in which copyright is claimed. ▼

3

a

YEAR IN WHICH CREATION OF THIS WORK WAS COMPLETED This information must be given ▼ Year in all cases.

b

DATE AND NATION OF FIRST PUBLICATION OF THIS PARTICULAR WORK
Complete this information Month ▶   Day ▶   Year ▶
ONLY if this work has been published.
◀ Nation

4

COPYRIGHT CLAIMANT(S) Name and address must be given even if the claimant is the same as the author given in space 2. ▼

APPLICATION RECEIVED

ONE DEPOSIT RECEIVED

TWO DEPOSITS RECEIVED

FUNDS RECEIVED

See instructions before completing this space.

TRANSFER If the claimant(s) named here in space 4 is (are) different from the author(s) named in space 2, give a brief statement of how the claimant(s) obtained ownership of the copyright. ▼

MORE ON BACK ▶   • Complete all applicable spaces (numbers 5-9) on the reverse side of this page.
• See detailed instructions.   • Sign the form at line 8.

DO NOT WRITE HERE
Page 1 of _____ pages

EXAMINED BY

CHECKED BY

☐ CORRESPONDENCE
☐ Yes

FOR COPYRIGHT OFFICE USE ONLY

5

DO NOT WRITE ABOVE THIS LINE. IF YOU NEED MORE SPACE, USE A SEPARATE CONTINUATION SHEET.

PREVIOUS REGISTRATION Has registration for this work, or for an earlier version of this work, already been made in the Copyright Office?
☐ Yes ☐ No   If your answer is "Yes," why is another registration being sought? (Check appropriate box.) ▼
a. ☐ This is the first published edition of a work previously registered in unpublished form.
b. ☐ This is the first application submitted by this author as copyright claimant.
c. ☐ This is a changed version of the work, as shown by space 6 on this application.
If your answer is "Yes," give: **Previous Registration Number ▶**   **Year of Registration ▶**

6

DERIVATIVE WORK OR COMPILATION
a Preexisting Material Identify any preexisting work or works that this work is based on or incorporates. ▼

See instructions before completing this space.

b Material Added to This Work Give a brief, general statement of the material that has been added to this work and in which copyright is claimed. ▼

7

a **DEPOSIT ACCOUNT** If the registration fee is to be charged to a Deposit Account established in the Copyright Office, give name and number of Account.
Name ▼   **Account Number ▼**

b **CORRESPONDENCE** Give name and address to which correspondence about this application should be sent.   Name/Address/Apt/City/State/ZIP ▼

Area code and daytime telephone number ▶   Fax number ▶
Email ▶

8

CERTIFICATION* I, the undersigned, hereby certify that I am the
Check only one ▶
☐ author
☐ other copyright claimant
☐ owner of exclusive right(s)
☐ authorized agent of _____
Name of author or other copyright claimant, or owner of exclusive right(s) ▲

of the work identified in this application and that the statements made by me in this application are correct to the best of my knowledge.

Typed or printed name and date ▼ If this application gives a date of publication in space 3, do not sign and submit it before that date.
_____   Date ▶

Handwritten signature (X) ▼
X _____

9

Certificate will be mailed in window envelope to this address:

Name ▼

Number/Street/Apt ▼

City/State/ZIP ▼

YOU MUST:
• Complete all necessary spaces
• Sign your application in space 8

SEND ALL 3 ELEMENTS IN THE SAME PACKAGE:
1. Application form
2. Nonrefundable filing fee in check or money order payable to Register of Copyrights
3. Deposit material

MAIL TO:
Library of Congress
Copyright Office
101 Independence Avenue, S.E.
Washington, D.C. 20559-6000

As of July 1, 1999, the filing fee for Form TX is $30.

*17 U.S.C. § 506(e): Any person who knowingly makes a false representation of a material fact in the application for copyright registration provided for by section 409, or in any written statement filed in connection with the application, shall be fined not more than $2,500.
June 1999—200,000   WEB REV: June 1999
☆U.S. GOVERNMENT PRINTING OFFICE: 1999-454-879/49

FEE CHANGES
Fees are effective through June 30, 2002. After that date, check the Copyright Office Website at www.loc.gov/copyright or call (202) 707-3000 for current fee information.

INDEX